Religious Controversies
of the Jacobean Age

Peter Milward

Religious Controversies of the Jacobean Age

A Survey of Printed Sources

London
The Scolar Press   1978

Published in Great Britain by The Scolar Press
39 Great Russell Street, London WC1B 3PH

Printed in Great Britain by The Scolar Press,
Ilkley, West Yorkshire

ISBN 0 85967 451 7

CONTENTS

Contents

Chapter 4
CATHOLIC v. ANGLICAN

Chapter 5
FRAGMENTS OF CONTROVERSIES   228

Preface

Turning from the Elizabethan to the Jacobean Age, one is naturally aware of a certain continuity in the religious controversies. The religious policy of James, as declared by him at the Hampton Court Conference, is substantially the same — at least in his intention and that of his advisers — as that of his great predecessor. Yet one is also aware, whatever the policy of the ruler, of a marked difference in these controversies, both in quality and in quantity.

The quantity, to be sure, is impressive. In the twenty-two years of James's reign we have over seven hundred published items of religious controversy recorded in these pages — even allowing for some duplications in the record and overlappings with the preceding or the following reign. On the other hand, in my previous volume of *Religious Controversies of the Elizabethan Age* there are considerably fewer than seven hundred items in a reign of forty-five years. Yet the religious issue was much more burning during that previous reign; and the controversies played a much more important part on the surface of events, whereas now they seem to withdraw from the stage of history — at least, as viewed from the twentieth century. Why is this?

During the reign of Queen Elizabeth, the art and science of printing made considerable progress; and by the Jacobean period the number of printing-houses has greatly increased. There are now more authors to provide copy for the printers — and controversial literature is still 'vendible copy', if only for a year or two. In the early decades of the reign the two universities were at a low ebb in learning, while the Catholic seminaries abroad were still in process of formation. But now, at the time of James's accession to the throne, the universities of Oxford and Cambridge are in a flourishing condition. The Catholic colleges and seminaries in the Low Countries, Spain and Rome are no less flourishing — sending not only priests but also books into England. As for the Puritans, after having been silenced during the last years of Elizabeth they again begin to make their voices heard at home, and to make their way across the seas to Holland, where they are free to practise their religion and to publish their books and pamphlets.

In quality, an increase in richness and mellowness may be noted in the writings of the established Church, though it is still intolerant of opposition, whether from Papists or from Puritans. It is no longer predominantly Calvinistic, though cold winds still blow occasionally from Geneva. With its development of patristic and even scholastic learning, it has become more willing to receive the ideas of human tradition and apostolic succession. It has in a sense come closer to the old Catholic position, which it claims rather for Canterbury than for post-Tridentine Rome. On the other hand, the Catholic position has found its great champion in Cardinal Bellarmine; and his influence has already been felt in England during the nineties of the past century. And there are increasing numbers of Jesuits in England to back up that influence.

As a result of the Hampton Court Conference, the Puritans are more and more driven into opposition on the question of ceremonies, faced as they are with the alternatives of subscription or loss of livings. Many of them take the latter course. They also turn, as in previous years, to criticize the bishops, who are now gradually coming – with the encouragement of the new Archbishop of Canterbury – to uphold the divine institution no less of bishops than of kings. These issues, moreover, under James as king of both realms, are increasingly extended northwards across the border; as it is the royal pleasure to establish the Scottish Church along lines similar to those of the Anglican Church. Those of Puritan sympathies who remain in their livings and accept subscription form a Calvinist wing in the Church, represented by such ecclesiastics as the Abbot brothers, John Prideaux and George Carleton. The more radical Puritans, however, are driven abroad and develop their separatist tendencies in the freedom of Holland, which now becomes a nursery for English non-conformism.

In this new reign the controversies no longer follow that regular rhythm, decade by decade, which is observable in the Elizabethan Age. Then the Queen and her advisers found it politic to direct their repressive measures now against the Catholics, now against the Puritans, but rarely against both at one and the same time. Such a policy may have been painful to the poor victims. But at least it had the effect of bringing a certain order – comparable to the movement of a pendulum – into the disorderly controversies of religion. Now, however, with the accession of James, the pendulum seems to stop moving; for with the settled strength of the Anglican Church, bequeathed by the Queen and her Archbishop, the policy of alternating toleration and persecution of Papists and Puritans is now no longer required. Instead, at least while Bancroft is Archbishop in succession to Whitgift (from 1604 to 1610) there is equal repression on both sides; and he is regarded both by Papists and by Puritans as their deadly foe. But under the less effective rule of George Abbot, from 1611 onwards, we find a gradual relaxing of tension and of persecution.

It is therefore difficult to divide this short reign into shorter periods, and to deal now with one side, now with the other. The controversies of Anglican and Puritan, to begin with, continue through the reign from beginning to end, as a single unit – divided only according to special issues, such as ceremonies, or episcopacy, or Christ's descent into hell, or the Sabbath. The same is true of those controversies which appear among the Puritans of the separation, still generally known as Brownists, in Holland. Only, one finds here a more vigorous growth, as in the absence of any pressure to conform one group divides from another and so occasions another series of books and pamphlets in protest and self-defence.

Then there are the controversies between Catholic and Anglican, which are by far the most numerous and voluminous of the new reign. The main division here, though it is a difficult one to make, is between those of a more political and those of a more doctrinal nature. Those of the former kind move from the accession of James (with petitions for toleration) through the Gunpowder Plot (with apologies against conspiracy and equivocation) to the formulation of the Oath of Allegiance and an immense controversy involving the King of England on one side and two Cardinals of the Roman Church on the other, with a host of lesser theologians on either side.

As for the doctrinal controversies, the reign opens with a series of combats between noteworthy protagonists. These gradually degenerate with the passing of time into skirmishes on either side, or else general works of controversy in which no one is attacked by name. Yet they somehow grow to a head in the final years of the reign, in a controversy presided over by the King himself. Here the crucial question is that of the identity of the true Church of Christ: whether she is to be found in Rome or in Canterbury – with Geneva forgotten for the moment.

Much of the material contained in these pages will be new, even to specialists in the Stuart period. The Oath of Allegiance and the main controversy it produced, at least that between King James (supported by Bishop Andrewes) and Cardinal Bellarmine, will naturally be familiar to them, but not, I imagine, all its twisted ramifications. The calling of the Hampton Court Conference and the troubles over subscription, with the consequent exodus of many Puritans to Holland, especially their sailing thence to New England on the *Mayflower* in 1620, will be no less familiar. But the controversial literature which largely entered into these events, and to which these events in turn gave rise, will be unfamiliar in most of its details and even in its general course – seeing that it mostly survives only in the form of rare books obtainable in a few libraries on either side of the Atlantic.

These books, however, are of interest not only to the historian of the early Stuart period, nor only to the ecclesiastical historian or the theologian. My own interest in them is partly historical and partly theological, but I approach them principally as a student of literature and its religious background. It should not be forgotten that this is the Age of Shakespeare from *Othello* onwards, even if the name of Shakespeare does not occur in these pages. It is also the age of the Metaphysical Poets, one of whom, John Donne, has made two prose contributions to these controversies, and another of whom, Richard Crashaw, appears in relation to his father William, who is one of the more frequent (and more eccentric) contributors. It is, moreover, the age of the young Milton, much of whose earlier reading lies buried in these musty books and pamphlets, and whose later writing brought them to life again.

It remains for me to express my deep feelings of gratitude to Dr. James Thorpe, Director of the Huntington Library in California, where I have done most of my research for this volume in the peaceful atmosphere of the Rare Books Room during four summers; and also to Monsignor James Hourihan, who has provided me with the warm hospitality of his Rectory at St Andrew's Church, Pasadena, for two of those summers. What even the Huntington Library has lacked – for no single library has more than three-quarters of the books I have needed – I have found in the Bodleian Library at Oxford, the University Library at Cambridge, the British Library and a host of smaller libraries scattered around England. I have finally to express my deep indebtedness to the compilers of the *STC* and also to my good friends David Rogers and Anthony Allison, who compiled the *Catalogue of Catholic Books*... and thereby laid the foundations for the *English Recusant Literature* series of facsimile reprints. At the same time, I should add a word of apology in advance for the defects that will assuredly be discovered in this work by subsequent researchers in the field. I cannot pretend to have said the last word – far from it. But I can at least claim (I think) to have said the first – so far as a general survey is concerned. And that perhaps is something.

Sophia University, Tokyo　　　　　　　　　　　　　　　　Peter Milward, S.J.
1 September 1976

ABBREVIATIONS

AR   *A Catalogue of Catholic Books in English Printed Abroad or Secretly in England, 1558–1640,*
by A. F. Allison and D. M. Rogers (Bognor Regis, 1956)

ERL *English Recusant Literature, 1558–1640,*
edited by D. M. Rogers: series of facsimile reprints
(The Scolar Press, London and Ilkley)

GS   *General Series* of Scolar Press facsimiles
(London and Ilkley)

STC *A Short-Title Catalogue of Books Printed in England, Scotland, & Ireland and of English Books Printed Abroad, 1475–1640,*
compiled by A. W. Pollard and G. R. Redgrave (London, 1926)

Wing *Short-Title Catalogue of Books Printed in England, Scotland, Ireland, Wales, and British America and of English Books Printed in Other Countries, 1641–1700,*
compiled by Donald Wing (3 vols.; New York, 1945)

NOTE *In the bibliographical entries
only the first editions are noticed,
except where special mention is made in the text
of other editions varying from the first.
Fuller bibliographical information
may be found in the* STC *and* AR.

CHAPTER 1

Anglican v. Puritan

a) *The Hampton Court Conference*

The accession of King James of Scotland to the English throne on 24 March 1603 brought a renewal of hope as well to the Catholics for toleration as to the Puritans for the reform they had long been striving for. On his way to London in April the Puritans presented him with a document later known as the Millenary Petition on account of its claim to represent upwards of a thousand ministers of the English Church — though it bore less than eight hundred signatures. It was entitled:

1. *The Humble Petition of the Ministers of the Church of England,
   desiring Reformation of certaine Ceremonies and abuses of the Church.*

Its first printed form appeared that year in the context of a rebuttal drawn up by the university of Oxford and endorsed by the university of Cambridge:

2. *The Answere of the Vicechancelour, the Doctors, both the Proctors,
   and other the Heads of Houses in the Universitie of Oxford: (Agreeable,
   undoubtedly, to the ioint and Uniforme opinion, of all the Deanes and
   Chapters, and all other the learned and obedient Cleargy, in the Church
   of England.) To the humble Petition of the Ministers of the Church of
   England, desiring Reformation of certaine Ceremonies and Abuses of
   the Church.* 1603   (STC 19010)

   (The edition of 1604 has the additional words on the title-page: 'And
   confirmed by the expresse consent of the Universitie of Cambridge.'
   Then follows 'To the humble Petition . . .'   (STC 19013))

Other Puritan books came out in the following year, supporting the Petition and urging reform on a larger scale than it had requested. In a book dedicated to the King himself, the semi-separatist Henry Jacob, from the safety of Middelburg in Zealand, sought to prove the necessity of reform according to the Word of God and to refute the *Answere* of the universities.

   3. *Reasons Taken out of Gods Word and the best Humane Testimonies Proving a Necessitie of Reforming Our Churches in England. Framed and applied to 4 Assertions wherein the foresaid purpose is contained. The 4 Assertions are set downe in the Page next following.* 1604 (STC 14338)

   (The four assertions were listed as follows:

   1. 'It is necessarie to reforme the Churches of England, their ministerie, and Ceremonies.'
   2. 'For the space of 200 yeares after Christ the Visible Churches using governement were not Diocesan Churches, but particular ordinary Congregations only.'
   3. 'The Scriptures of the New Testament do containe . . . an ordinary forme of Church-governement used then.'
   4. 'The ordinary forme of Church-governement set forth unto us in the New Testament . . . ought necessarily to be kept still by us.')

In another book, written many years before during the reign of Elizabeth and now refurbished for the present need, William Stoughton went further and urged the imposition of a presbyterian discipline on all churches:

   4. *An Assertion For true and Christian Church-Policie. Wherein certaine politike obiections made against the planting of Pastours and Elders in every Congregation, are sufficientlie aunswered. And wherein also sundrie proiectes are set downe, how the Discipline by Pastors & Elders may be planted, without any derogation to the Kings Royal prerogative, any indignitie to the three Estates in Parleament, or any greater alteration of the laudable Lawes, Statutes, or Customes of the Realme, then may well be made without damage to the people.* 1604 (STC 23318)

   A pacific attitude towards the religious problem was, moreover, advocated by Sir Francis Bacon in a well-considered memorandum which he drew up for the King at this time:

   5. *Certaine Considerations touching the better pacification and Edification of the Church of England: Dedicated to his most Excellent Maiestie.* 1604   (STC 1118)

This chimed in with the conciliatory mood of James on his arrival in England. A proclamation was issued on 24 October 1603, announcing a conference to be held between the opposing parties, Episcopal and Puritan, at Hampton Court early in the following year:

6. *By the King. As we have ever from our infancie had manifold proofes of Gods great goodnes towards us* . . . 1603 (STC 8336)

When this conference opened on 14 January 1604, the Episcopal party were led by Richard Bancroft, Bishop of London, in the absence of the ailing Archbishop of Canterbury, John Whitgift; while the four Puritan representatives were Laurence Chaderton, John Knewstub, Thomas Spark and their leader, John Reynolds. The proceedings of the conference, in which the King took a very active part, were compiled and published by the Dean of Chester, William Barlow, with a strong bias in favour of the Episcopal party:

7. *The Summe and Substance of the Conference, which, it pleased his Excellent Maiestie to have with the Lords, Bishops, and other of his Clergie, (at which the most of the Lordes of the Councell were present) in his Maiesties Privy-Chamber, at Hampton Court. Ianuary 14. 1603. Contracted by William Barlow, Doctor of Divinity, and Deane of Chester. Whereunto are added, some Copies, (scattered abroad,) unsavory, and untrue.* 1604 (STC 1456)

   (In these above-mentioned 'copies' the Puritans claimed a measure of victory for their side against the bishops; but they soon belied this claim by their anger against their representatives, whom they blamed for not having urged the cause of reform more effectively.)

After the conference the Episcopal party were encouraged to pass a series of canons for the province of Canterbury, which came to be regarded as binding on the whole English Church. They were formally ratified by the King in the same year, 1604, and published both in Latin and in English:

8. *Constitutiones sive Canones Ecclesiastici, Per Episcopum Londiniensem, Praesidem Synodi pro Cantuariensi Provincia, ac reliquos Episcopos, & Clerum eiusdem Provinciae ex Regia authoritate tractati, & conclusi In ipsorum Synodo inchoata Londini, Anno Salutis millesimo, sexcentesimo tertio, regnique Serenissimi Principis Clementissimi Domini nostri Iacobi Dei gratia Angliae Franciae & Hiberniae Regis primo, & Scotiae tricesimo septimo: Ab eadem Regia Maiestate deinceps approbati, ratihabiti, ac confirmati, eiusdemque auctoritate sub magno Sigillo Angliae promulgati, per utramque Provinciam tam Cantuariensem quam Eboracensem diligenter observandi.* 1604 (STC 10068)

9. *Constitutions and Canons Ecclesiasticall, Treated upon by the Bishop of London, President of the Convocation for the Province of Canterbury,*

and the rest of the Bishops and Clergie of the said Province: And agreed
upon with the Kings Maiesties Licence in their Synode begun at
London Anno Dom. 1603. And in the yeere of the raigne of our
Soveraigne Lord Iames by the grace of God King of England, France
and Ireland the first, and of Scotland the 37. And now published for
the due observation of them by his Maiesties authoritie, under the great
Seale of England. 1604   (STC 10069)

These canons were followed up by two royal proclamations, dated 5 March
and 16 July 1604, and requiring conformity to the Book of Common Prayer
(with all its ceremonies) throughout the realm. Subscription to the
ceremonies was also demanded of all ministers of the Church – as in 1566
under Archbishop Parker and in 1583 under Archbishop Whitgift – on pain
of ejection from their livings if they refused to subscribe.

10. *By the King. A Proclamation for Authorizing an Uniformitie of the*
    Booke of Common Prayer to be used throughout the Realme. 1604
    (STC 8344)

11. *By the King. The Care which Wee have had, and Paines which Wee have*
    taken to settle the Affaires 1604   (STC 8355)

The second of these proclamations was particularly urged upon 'the
bretheren of the newfangled faction' by one of the king's chaplains, William
Wilkes, in a treatise on *Obedience*, which he dedicated to the King and
published in 1605. He reissued his book in 1608 under the altered title of *A*
Second Memento for Magistrates.

12. *Obedience Or Ecclesiasticall Union. Treatised by William Wilkes Doctor*
    in Theologie, and one of his Maiesties Chaplaines in ordinarie. 1605
    (STC 25633)

13. *A Second Memento for Magistrates. Directing how to reduce all*
    offenders, and beeing reduced, how to preserve them in unitie and love
    both in Church and commonwealth. By W. W. Doctor of Divinity, and
    one of his Maiesties Chaplains in Ordinary. 1608   (STC 25634)

The same exhortation to unity and obedience was repeated in many sermons
of the time, some of which were also published. Thus we have Egeon
Askew's sermon on *Brotherly Reconcilement* in 1605, and Francis
Holyoke's *Sermon of Obedience* in 1610.

14. *Brotherly Reconcilement: Preached in Oxford for the union of some,*
    and now published with larger meditations for the unitie of all in this
    Church and Common-wealth: With An Apologie of the use of Fathers,

and Secular learning in Sermons. By Egeon Askew of Queenes Colledge.
1605   (STC 855)

15. *A Sermon of Obedience especially unto authoritie Ecclesiasticall*
    wherein the principall controversies of our church are handled, and
    many of their obiections which are refractorie to the government
    established, answered though briefly as time and place could permit;
    beeing preached at a Visitation of the Right Worsh: Mr. D. Hinton, in
    Coventree. By Fran: Holyoke. 1610   (STC 13622)

b) *Controversy over Subscription*

The outcome of the Hampton Court conference with its firm assertion of
Episcopal policy, reinforced as it was by the Canons and the royal
Proclamations of 1604, was by no means acceptable to the Puritan ministers.
Faced with the strict requirement of subscription, many of them refused to
conform and were therefore ejected from their livings. In particular, they
were required (as in 1583) to subscribe to three articles: of the royal
supremacy in ecclesiastical affairs, of the thirty-nine articles of faith, and of
the Book of Common Prayer with its prescribed ceremonies. It was to this
third article that they chiefly objected, particularly to the ceremonies of the
use of the surplice, the sign of the cross in baptism, and the custom of
kneeling to receive communion. This time the Puritan opposition was first
manifested in Lincoln, by a minister there, John Burges, who had formerly
subscribed to the Prayer-Book, interpreting his action in a general sense. But
now, in a sermon he preached before the King on 19 June 1604, he spoke
critically of the ceremonies in question. For his words he was imprisoned in
the Tower of London. When the Proclamation of 16 July was issued, he
refused to subscribe to the ceremonies and in a written apology he set forth
his reasons for refusing and submitted them to the King and Bishop
Bancroft. His lead was followed by other ministers of Lincoln, who
presented their further apology to the King on 1 December. The following
year, this apology was published in the form of *An Abridgment:*

16. *An Abridgment of that Booke which the Ministers of Lincoln Diocess*
    delivered to his Maiestie upon the first of December last. Being the First
    Part of an Apologye for themselves and their brethren that refuse the
    subscription, and conformitie which is required. Wherunto is annexed, a
    table of sondry poynts not handled in this Abridgment, which are other
    exceptions they take to the subscription requyred, and shalbe the
    Argument of the second part of their Apology. 1605   (STC 15646)

The Anglican answer to Burges and his friends was entrusted to William
Covell, who had recently defended Hooker against the authors of the

Christian Letter and criticized Josias Nichols for his *Plea of the Innocent*. He soon came out with *A Briefe Answer* to Burges' apology, which he printed in full after his opening Dedication 'To the Kings most excellent Maiestie':

17. *A Briefe Answer unto Certaine Reasons by way of an Apologie delivered to the Right Reverend Father in God, the L. Bishop of Lincolne, by Mr. Iohn Burges: wherin he laboureth to proove, that having heretofore subscribed foure times, and now refusing (as a thing unlawfull) that he hath notwithstanding done lawfully in both. Written by William Covell, Doctor in Divinitie.* 1606   (STC 5880)

A similar controversy broke out in the West Country, where some ministers of Devon and Cornwall had submitted their reasons for refusing subscription to the Bishop of Exeter. They were answered on the bishop's behalf by Thomas Hutton, of Oxford, in two parts of a book entitled *Reasons for Refusal* which came out successively in 1605 and 1606:

18. *Reasons for Refusal of Subscription to the booke of Common praier, under the hands of certaine Ministers of Devon, and Cornwall word for word as they were exhibited by them to the Right Reverend Father in God William Coton Doctor of Divinitie L. Bishop of Exceter. With an Answere at severall times returned them in publike conference and in diverse sermons upon occasion preached in the Cathedrall Church of Exceter, by Thomas Hutton, Bachiler of Divinitie & fellow of St. Iohns Coll. in Oxon. And now published at the very earnest intreatie of some especiall friends for a farther contentment of other the Kings Maiesties good and loyall Subiects.* 1605 (STC 14035 = 16449)

19. *The Second and Last Part of Reasons for Refusall of Subscription to the Booke of Common prayer, under the hands of certaine Ministers of Devon, and Cornwall, as they were exhibited by them to the right Reverend Father in God William Cotton Doctor of Divinitie, and Lord Bishop of Exceter. As also an Appendix, or Compendious Briefe of all other Exceptions taken by others against the Bookes of Communion, Homilies, and Ordination, word for word, as it came to the hands of an Honourable Personage. With an Answere to both at severall times returned them in publike conference, and in diverse Sermons upon occasion preached in the Cathedrall Church of Exceter by Thomas Hutton Bachiler of Divinitie, and Fellow of S. Iohns Colledge in Oxon.* 1606   (STC 14036 = 16449a)

To the first of these volumes the ministers concerned published their reply in 1606:

20. *The Remooval Of certaine Imputations laid upon the Ministers of*

Devon: and Cornwall by one M. T. H. and in them, upon all other
Ministers els-where, refusing to Subscribe. 1606   (STC 14037)

It was also from Devon that there appeared an anonymous *Dialogue* from
the pen of a Puritan minister, Samuel Hieron, with an appendix stating once
again the reasons for refusing subscription:

21. *A Short Dialogue proving that the Ceremonyes, and some other*
    corruptions now in question, are defended, by none other Arguments
    then such as the Papists have here tofore used; And our Protestant
    writers have long since answered. Whereunto are annexed, Certayne
    Considerations why the Ministers should not be removed for the
    Subscription and Ceremonies. 1605   (STC 6814)

    (The appendix bears the title:

    Certayne Reasons why it seemeth that the Preachers who refuse the
    subscription and ceremonies urged, should not for that their refusall be
    remooved from their charges or inhibitted to preach: humbly offered to
    consideration.)

The same anonymous author followed this up with *A Defence of the*
Ministers Reasons against the writings of both Hutton and Covell — as well as
against other writings that are yet to be mentioned, by Thomas Spark,
Francis Mason and Thomas Rogers. This *Defence* he published in three parts,
as further writings came up to be refuted, but they may be listed together
here for convenience:

22. *A Defence of the Ministers Reasons, for Refusall of Subscription to the*
    Booke of Common Prayer, and of Conformitie. Against the severall
    answers. of T. Hutton Bachiler of Divinity, in his two Bookes against
    the Minist: of Dev. and Cornwall. William Covel, D. in Divinitie, in his
    Booke against M. I. Burges. Tho: Spark, D. in Divinitie in his Brotherly
    perswasion to Unitie and Uniformitie. So farr as any thing is sayd by
    them concerning the holy Scriptures, and Apocrypha. Devided into two
    partes. The first parte, concerning the holy Scriptures. The second
    parte, concerning the holy Scriptures and Apocrypha. 1607
    (STC 13395)

23. *The Second Parte of the Defence of the Ministers Reasons For refusal*
    of Subscription & Conformitie to the book of Common prayer. Against
    the several answers of Th. Hutton Bachiler of Divinity, in his two
    bookes against the Minist. of Dev & Cornwel. William Covel D. in
    Divinitie, in his Book against M. Iohn Burges. Th. Spark, D. in Divinity,
    in his Brotherly perswasion to Unitie & Uniformitie. Fran. Mason
    Bachiler in Divinitie in his sermon upon I Cor.14.40. Concerning the
    holy Scriptures and Apocrypha. 1608   (STC 13395)

24. *A Dispute upon the Question of Kneeling, in the acte of receiving the sacramentall bread and wine, proving it to be unlawfull. Or a third parte of the Defence of the Ministers reasons for refusall of the Subscription and Conformitie requyred. Against the severall answers, of 1. D. Spark, in his brotherly perswasion to unitie &c: 2. D. Covel, in his booke against M. Iohn Burges, 3. Thomas Hutton, in his 2 booke against the Ministers of Devonshire and Cornwell. 4. Thomas Rogers in his two Dialogues, printed this yeare 1608. 1608* (STC 13395)

In the Midlands yet another group of ministers adopted a more legal line of defence, maintaining that the canons approved by the recent synod were only valid for the diocese of Canterbury, and were therefore inapplicable to other dioceses, such as that of Worcester:

25. *Certaine Considerations drawne from the Canons of the last Sinod, and other the Kings Ecclesiasticall and statute law, ad informandum animum Domini Episcopi Wigornensis, seu alterius cuiusvis iudicis ecclesiastici, ne temere & inconsulto prosiliant ad deprivationem Ministrorum Ecclesiae: for not subscription, for the not exact use of the order and forme of the booke of common prayer, within the Diocesse of Worcester, or for the not precise practise of the rites, ceremonies, & ornaments of the Church. 1605* (STC 4585)

At the same time other ministers presented *Certaine Demandes* to the Archbishop of Canterbury (now Richard Bancroft, in succession to John Whitgift, who had died in 1604), and the Bishops of London, Worcester, Exeter and Peterborough:

26. *Certaine Demandes with their grounds, drawne out of holy Writ, and propounded in foro conscientiae by some religious Gentl. unto the reverend Fathers, Richard Archbishop of Canterbury, Richard Bishop of London, Garvase Bishop of Worcester, William Bishop of Exeter, & Thomas Bishop of Peterborough, whereunto the said Gentl. require that it would please their Lordships to make a true, plaine, direct, honest and resolute aunswere. 1605* (STC entered twice without number: under Bancroft, R. – 'see Demands'; and under Demands – 'see Bancroft, R.')

Shortly afterwards, a group of twenty-two London preachers addressed a 'Petition to the Kings most Excellent Maiestie', protesting their inability to subscribe to the Book of Common Prayer. This they followed up, like the Lincoln ministers, with a detailed explanation of their grievances in *A Survey Of the Booke of Common Prayer*, with an appendix giving the text of their Petition:

27. *A Survey Of the Booke of Common Prayer, By way of 197. Queres grounded upon 58. places, ministring iust matter of question, with a View of London Ministers exceptions. All humbly propounded, That They may be syncerely answered: Or else Offences Religiously removed.* 1606   (STC 16450)

An appeal was also made to the Parliament of 1606 on behalf of 'the Ministers now silenced' and published in the form of *Certaine Arguments.* Unlike the preceding works this was immediately answered by Gabriel Powell, chaplain to Richard Vaughan, Bishop of London, in *A Consideration.*

28. *Certaine Arguments to perswade and provoke the most honorable and high Court of Parliament now assembled, and also all other in any high authority, or in any grace, and credite with them that are in high authority, to promote and advance the sincere Ministery of the Gospell: as also zealously to speake for the Ministers therof now degraded, deprived, silenced, or admonished, or afterward like to be called into question, for Subscription, Ceremonyes, strict observation of the booke of common prayer, or for other conformitie.* 1606   (STC 740)

29. *A Consideration of the Deprived and Silenced Ministers Arguments, for their Restitution to the use and libertie of their Ministerie; Exhibited in their late Supplication, unto the Honorable States assembled in this present Parliament. By Gabriel Powel.* 1606   (STC 20142)

Powell's answer was in turn answered by the Puritan William Bradshaw in *A Myld and Iust Defence* in 1606. But Powell again came out with *A Reioynder* in the following year.

30. *A Myld and Iust Defence of Certeyne Arguments, at the last session of Parliament directed to that most Honorable High Court, in behalfe of the Ministers suspended and deprived &c.: for not Subscribing and Conforming themselves etc. Against an intemperat and uniust Consideration of them by M. Gabril Powell. The chiefe and generall contents wherof are breefely layd downe immediatly after the Epistle.* 1606   (STC 3522)

31. *A Reioynder unto the Mild Defence, iustifying the consideration of the silenced Ministers Supplication unto the high Court of Parliament. Wherein is plainely discovered the vanitie of the Ministers Arguments for their Restitution; and they are irrefutably evinced to be properly Schismatiques, Unworthie to be restored againe to the use and libertie of their Ministerie; By Gabriel Powel.* 1607   (STC 20143)

c) *Bradshaw and his Opponents*

About this time one of the most vocal of the Puritan writers was William Bradshaw, then living in retirement at the house of a friend in Staffordshire. From Amsterdam he brought out a series of anonymous pamphlets to urge the requests of the Millenary Petition and its criticisms of the Book of Common Prayer, and to protest against the requirement of subscription:

32. *A Consideration of Certaine Positions Archiepiscopall.* 1604
    (STC 3509)

33. *A Treatise of Divine Worship, tending to prove that the Ceremonies imposed upon the Ministers of the Gospell in England, in present controversie, are in their use unlawfull.* 1604   (STC 3528)

34. *A Shorte Treatise, Of the crosse in Baptisme contracted into this syllogisme. No humane ordinance becomming an Idoll, may lawfully be used in the service of God. But the signe of the crosse being a humane ordinance is become an Idoll: ergo The signe of the crosse may not lawfully be used in the service of God.* 1604   (STC 3526)

35. *A Proposition concerning kneeling in the very act of receiving howsoever. Published to satisfie professours, yet humblie, Submitted to the iudgment of Prophets.* 1605   (STC 3524)

36. *Twelve generall arguments, proving that the ceremonies are unlawfull.* 1605   (STC 3531)

37. *A Treatise of the Nature and use of Things Indifferent. Tendinge to prove, that the Ceremonies in present controversie Amongst the ministers of the gospell in the Realme of England, are neither in nature or use Indifferent.* 1605   (STC 3530)

38. *A Protestacion of the Kings Supremacie. Made in the name of the afflicted Ministers, and opposed to the shamefull Calumniations of the Prelates.* 1605   (STC 3525)

This series culminated in Bradshaw's classic exposition of *English Puritanisme* in 1605. Later translated into Latin by the Puritan scholar William Ames in 1610, it was reprinted in its original English form in 1640 and mistakenly attributed to Ames.

39. *English Puritanisme Containening. The maine opinions of the rigidest sort of those that are called Puritanes In the Realme of England.* 1605
    (STC 3516)

40. *Puritanismus Anglicanus, sive Præcipua Dogmata eorum, qui inter vulgo dictos Puritanos in Anglia, rigidiores habentur. Quibus annectitur scholastica disceptatio de circulo pontificio & eorum omnium* ἀκαταληψία *qui in scripturis non acquiescunt.* 1610.

    (The Preface is signed Guilielmus Amesius.)

41. *English Puritanisme. Containing The maine Opinions of the rigidest sort of those that are called Puritanes in the Realme of England. Written by William Ames D. of Divinitie.* 1640   (STC 3517)

The last of these works, Bradshaw's defence of *English Puritanisme*, was immediately countered by Oliver Ormerod in his popular *Picture of a Puritane* – at least by implication. This was followed by a companion piece, *The Picture of a Papist*, in 1606 – to be considered in its proper place later on (529).

42. *The Picture of a Puritane: or, A Relation of the opinions, qualities, and practises of the Anabaptists in Germanie, and of the Puritanes in England. Wherein is firmely prooved, that the Puritanes doe resemble the Anabaptists, in above fourescore severall thinges. By Oliver Ormerod, of Emmanuel Colledge in Cambridge. Wherunto is annexed a short treatise, entituled, Puritano-papismus: or a discoverie of Puritan-Papisme.* 1605   (STC 18851)

In the same year, Bradshaw's treatise *Of the crosse in Baptisme* was answered by an Oxford scholar, Leonard Hutten, in *An Answere to a certaine Treatise*. This was followed in 1606 by *A Defence of Church Government*, the work of another Oxford scholar, John Dove, who dealt particularly with Bradshaw's treatise in his second part.

43. *An Answere to a certaine Treatise of the Crosse in Baptisme, Intituled A Short Treatise of the Crosse in Baptisme, contracted into this Syllogisme. No humane ordinance becomming an Idoll may lawfully be used in the service of God. But the signe of the Crosse, being an humane ordinance is become an Idoll. Ergo: The signe of the Crosse, may not lawfully bee used in the service of God. Wherein not only the weaknesse of the Syllogisme it selfe, but also the grounds and proofes thereof, are plainely discovered. By L. H. Doct. of Divinitie.* 1605 (STC 14023)

    (The Dedication is signed Leon. Hutten.)

44. *A Defence of Church Government. Dedicated to the high Court of Parliament. Wherein, the Church Government established in England, is directly proved to be consonant to the Word of God, and that subiects*

> ought of dutie to conforme themselves to the state Ecclesiasticall.
> Together with, A Defence of the Crosse in Baptisme; as it is used in our
> Church, being not repugnant to the word: and by a consequent, the
> brethren which are silenced, ought to subscribe unto it, rather then to
> burie their Talents in the ground. By Iohn Dove, Doctour of Divinity.
> 1606   (STC 7081)

On the other hand, Bradshaw's position was defended in 1607 by the Puritan
Robert Parker, who published his *Scholasticall Discourse* against 'the
sophistications of such, as have written for the Crosse in Baptisme'. The
author was, however, forced soon after to take refuge in Holland to avoid
prosecution by the court of high commission.

> 45. *A Scholasticall Discourse against Symbolizing with Antichrist in
>   Ceremonies: especially in the Signe of the Crosse.* 1607   (STC 19294)

Another opponent to Bradshaw was the above-mentioned Gabriel Powell.
Already before their clash over the *Certaine Arguments* presented to the
Parliament of 1606, they came into conflict with each other on the subject
of 'things indifferent', namely ceremonies. Powell now replied to Bradshaw's
Treatise on this point with a number of scholastic theses in Latin entitled *De
Adiaphoris*. This was soon after translated into English by Thomas Jackson,
and bound with Powell's *Reioynder* as though a sequel to the latter work.

> 46. *Gabrielis Poueli Ordovicis Britanni, De Adiaphoris Theses Theologicae
>   ac Scholasticae. Ubi etiam methodicè atque succinctè explicantur Loci
>   de Magistratu Civili & Ecclesiastico, de Legibus Humanis, de Libertate
>   Christiana, de Scandalo, de Cultu Die. Libellus Votivus, sopiendis (per
>   Dei gratiam) Dissidiis in Ecclesia Anglicana ortis, destinatus.* 1606
>   (STC 20145)

> 47. *De Adiaphoris. Theological and Scholastical Positions, concerning the
>   Nature and Use of Things Indifferent. Where also is methodically and
>   briefely handled, of Civill and Ecclesiasticall Magistrates, of Humane
>   Lawes, of Christian Libertie, of Scandall, and of the Worship of God. A
>   Vowed Worke, destinated (by the Grace of God) to appease the
>   Dissentions of the Church of England. Written in Latine by M. Gabriel
>   Powel, and translated into English by T. I.* 1607   (STC 20146)

The last of Bradshaw's little treatises to receive critical attention was that
concerning kneeling. This was dealt with by Thomas Rogers in the second of
his *Two Dialogues*, published in 1608. Here the author slightingly refers to 'a
certaine printed Libell, of not above two sheetes of paper (of which bulke,
or thereabouts, myselfe have seene divers treatises published by the
Sectaries, An.1605 . . .) published I wot not by whom, and printed I know

not where, but doubtlesse beyond the Sea.' The first dialogue is concerned with a manuscript on the same subject by one Seffray. Both *Dialogues* were answered in the same year by Samuel Hieron in the above-mentioned *Dispute upon the Question of kneeling*, as well as other works defending the Anglican position.

48. *Two Dialogues, or Conferences (about an old question lately renued, and by the Schismaticall company, both by printed Pamphlets, and otherwise to the disturbance of the Churches quiet, and of peaceable minds, very hotly pursued.) Concerning Kneeling in the very act of receiving the Sacramental bread and wine, in the Supper of the Lord. The former Betweene two Ministers of the word, the one refractarie, and deprived; the other not so. The latter Betweene an humorous Schismatike and a setled professor.* 1608 (STC 21241)

(The inner title of the second dialogue is as follows: *The Second Dialogue about Kneeling in the very act of receiving the holy Communion.*)

d) *Sporadic Contributions*

Various other books, of a more generally controversial nature, appeared on either side during these years, but without attacking any works in particular. First came two works on the Episcopal side, both significantly dedicated to the Archbishop of Canterbury, who was active in encouraging the publication of such books. In 1605 Samuel Gardiner published his *Dialogue* between 'an absolute formalist' (as those of the Episcopal party were often called) and one recently deprived of his living representing 'the disciplinarians of our days'. In 1606 the former seminary priest, Thomas Bell, turned in *The Regiment of the Church* from his customary attacks on the Papists to a criticism of 'the Presbyterie' for a change.

49. *A Dialogue or Conference between Irenaeus and Antimachus, about the rites and Ceremonies of the Church of England: By Samuel Gardiner, Doctor of Divinitie.* 1605 (STC 11575)

50. *The Regiment of the Church: as it is agreable with Scriptures, all Antiquities of the Fathers, and moderne Writers, from the Apostles themselves, unto this present age.* 1606 (STC 1827)

On the Puritan side, Henry Jacob again came forward in 1606 with *A Christian and Modest Offer* of another conference between the prelates and the ministers, while lamenting the recent controversy 'about the Prelacy, Ceremonies, & Subscription'. In this book he unwittingly provided the

Catholic controversialists of the age with useful ammunition, by pointing out that the Anglican bishops, upholding as they did the divine institution of episcopacy, had no right to secede from Rome.

51. *A Christian and Modest Offer of a most Indifferent Conference, or Disputation, about the maine and principall Controversies betwixt the Prelats, and the late silenced and deprived Ministers in England: Tendered by some of the said Ministers to the Archbishops, and Bishops, and all their adherents.* 1606   (STC 14329)

Two laymen also came to the defence of the Puritans about this time. In his *Discourse of the Abuses*, published in 1606, Thomas Whetenhall spoke out against 'the adversaries of the Churches reformation in England', and claimed the great champions of Elizabethan Protestantism, Fulke, Nowell and Jewel, for his side. The legal position of the Puritans was also defended by Nicholas Fuller in his *Argument* against the practices of the court of high commission and 'the uniust usurpation of the Prelates', in the following year.

52. *A Discourse of the Abuses now in Question in the Churches of Christ, of their creeping in, growing up, and flowrishing in the Babilonish Church of Rome, how they are spoken against not only by the scriptures, but also by the ancient Fathers as long as there remayned any face of a true Church maintained by publique authority. And likewise by the lights of the Gospell, and blessed Martyrs of late in the middest of the Antichristian darknes. By Thomas Whetenhall Esquier.* 1606   (STC 25332)

53. *The Argument of Master Nicholas Fuller, in the case of Thomas Lad, and Richard Maunsell, his Clients. Wherein it is plainely proved, that the Ecclesiasticall Commissioners have no power, by vertue of their Commission, to Imprison, to put to the Oath Ex Officio, or to fine any of his Maiesties Subiects.* 1607   (STC 11460)

That year, 1607, saw the publication of three major contributions to the Episcopal position. Thomas Rogers, who had defended the previous subscription in the time of Archbishop Whitgift with his *English Creede* (1585), now returned to the same subject with his more elaborate exposition of the thirty-nine Articles in *The Faith, Doctrine, and religion ... of England*. In his Dedicatory Preface to Archbishop Bancroft the author recalled the long history of subscription, with special reference to those Puritan ministers now refusing to subscribe.

54. *The Faith, Doctrine, and religion, professed, and protected in the Realme of England, and dominions of the same: Expressed in 39 Articles, concordablie agreed upon by the reverend Bishops, and*

Clergie of this Kingdome, at two severall meetings, or Convocations of theirs, in the yeares of our Lord, 1562, and 1604: The said Articles analised into Propositions, and the Propositions prooved to be agreeable both to the written word of God, and to the extant Confessions of all the neighbour Churches Christianlie reformed: The adversaries also of note, and name, which from the Apostles daies, and primitive Church hetherto, have crossed, or contradicted the said Articles in generall, or any particle, or proposition arising from anie of them in particular, heereby are discovered, laid open, and so confuted. Perused, and by the lawfull authoritie of the Church of England, allowed to be publique. 1607 (STC 21228)

(The Preface is signed Thomas Rogers.)

The edition of 1639 bore the altered title:

A Treatise upon Sundry Matters contained in the Thirty Nine Articles of Religion, which are professed in the Church of England. Long since written and published by Thomas Rogers. (STC 21233)

Another contributor was Thomas Spark, one of the four Puritan representatives at the Hampton Court conference, who had not only consented to subscription, but also undertook to write in defence of it. He now published his *Brotherly Perswasion*, both to encourage the Puritan ministers to follow his example and to justify himself against 'the hard censure of many for conforming myselfe as I have to the orders of our Church'.

55. *A Brotherly Perswasion to Unitie, and Uniformitie in Iudgment, and Practise touching the received, and present Ecclesiasticall government, and the authorised rites and ceremonies of the Church of England. Written by Thomas Sparke Doctor in Divinitie. And seene, allowed, and commended by publike authoritie to be Printed.* 1607 (STC 23020)

The third contributor was Francis Mason, who published a sermon on *The Authoritie of the Church*, with special reference to the ceremonies enjoined in the Book of Common Prayer.

56. *The Authoritie of the Church in making Canons and Constitutions concerning things indifferent, And the obedience thereto required: with particular application to the present estate of the Church of England. Delivered in a Sermon preached in the Greene yard at Norwich the third Sunday after Trinitie. 1605. By Fran. Mason, Bacheler of Divinitie, and sometime fellow of Merton College in Oxford. And now in sundrie points by him enlarged.* 1607 (STC 17595)

It was against these works that Samuel Hieron came out in the successive parts of his *Defence of the Ministers Reasons*, mentioned above: against

Spark in all three parts; against Mason in the second; and against Rogers' other book, the *Two Dialogues*, in the third.

The controversy may be said to have petered out by 1610, though it was renewed later on in the reign. On the Episcopal side, John Tichbourne upheld the resort to excommunication and subscription by the bishops in publishing *A Triple Antidote* in 1609. Then in 1612 there appeared a somewhat eccentric book entitled ΄ΕΙΡΗΝΟΚΟΙΝΩΝΙΑ (written in English), by the Scottish Dean of Salisbury, John Gordon. In this he proposed four theses defending the use of white garments for ceremonies and the practice of kneeling to receive the sacrament.

57. *A Triple Antidote, against certaine very common Scandals of this time, which, like infections and epidemicall diseases, have generally annoyed most sorts of people amongst us, poisoned also not a few, and divers waies plagued and afflicted the whole State. By Iohn Tichborne, Doctor of Divinity, and sometimes fellow of Trinity Colledge in Cambridge.* 1609 (STC 24064)

58. *΄ΕΙΡΗΝΟΚΟΙΝΩΝΙΑ. The Peace of the Communion of the Church of England. Or The Conformitie of the Ceremonies of the Communion of the Church of England, with the Ensamples and Doctrine of the holy Scriptures, and Primitive Church, established by the Apostles of Christ, and the holy Martyrs, and Bishops, their Successors. By Io: Gordon, Doctor of Divinitie, and Deane of Salisbury.* 1612 (STC 12056)

Finally, from the Puritan side Henry Jacob addressed *An humble Supplication for Toleration* to the King in 1609, on behalf of 'the silenced and disgraced Ministers of the Gospel' — with some reference to Bradshaw's earlier *Protestacion of the Kings Supremacie.*

59. *To the right High and mightie Prince, Iames by the grace of God, King of Great Britannie, France, and Irelande, Defender of the faith, &c. An humble Supplication for Toleration and libertie to enioy and observe the ordinances of Christ Iesus in th' administration of his Churches in lieu of humane constitutions.* 1609 (STC 14339)

e) *Controversy over Episcopacy*

In the controversy over subscription a more fundamental issue had been raised by Henry Jacob in his *Christian and Modest Offer* of 1606, when he complained of the Anglican bishops claiming an apostolic origin and a divine right for their episcopal institution. This claim is often traced back to Bancroft's *Sermon* of 1589 against Martin Marprelate; and he was followed shortly afterwards by Hadrian Saravia and Thomas Bilson. Now in the new reign of James their claim was reasserted by William Barlow, Bishop of Rochester, in a sermon *Concerning the Antiquitie and Superioritie of Bishops* before the King at Hampton Court on 21 September 1606. In it he openly declared that 'the author of this office' was no other than the Holy Spirit. In publishing his sermon, he stated that it had been printed at the King's commandment and according to the desire of some Scottish ministers in response to 'a Challenge offered in an Admonition Epistolar' to the Scottish Parliament held at Perth in that year, when the King was seeking to extend the Anglican episcopacy to Scotland.

60. *One of the foure Sermons Preached before the Kings Maiestie, at*
    Hampton Court in September last. This Concerning the Antiquitie and
    Superioritie of Bishops: Sept. 21. 1606. By the Reverend Father in God
    William Lord Bishop of Rochester. 1606   (STC 1451)

Two years later one of the King's chaplains, George Downame, proposed the same opinion, 'that the episcopall function is of apostolicall and divine institution', in another sermon on the occasion of the consecration of James Montagu as Bishop of Bath and Wells. Though he based his position on the doctrine of Bilson in *The Perpetual Governement of Christes Church*, which had appeared as long ago as 1593, he realized 'how unpleasing this Sermon will be to some, who are forestalled with preiudicate opinions'.

61. *Two Sermons, the one commending the Ministerie in generall: the other*
    defending the office of Bishops in particular: Both preached, and since
    enlarged by George Downame Doctor of Divinitie. 1608   (STC 7125)

    (The second of these sermons was published with a title-page of its
    own, and with fresh pagination, as follows:

    A Sermon defending the honourable function of Bishops,
    Preached, April 17. Anno D. 1608. at the Consecration of the right
    reverend Father in God, the L. Bishoppe of Bath and Wells: By
    George Downame, Doctor of Divinitie. 1608)

The Puritan opposition took the form, in the first place, of the publication of certain MS objections by the late John Reynolds, who had died in 1607, to Bancroft's controversial *Sermon* of 1589. To this was added other relevant material from Scotland, where it was a particularly important issue. In his preface 'to the Reader' the printer made particular reference to Dr. Downame's sermon at Lambeth, adding that 'many sound divines doe greive that so learned a man should discover such weakness'.

62. *Informations, or A Protestation, and A Treatise from Scotland.*
    Seconded with D. Reignoldes his Letter to Sir Francis Knollis. And Sir
    Francis Knollis his speach in Parliament. All suggesting the usurpation
    of Papal Bishops. 1608   (STC 14084)

(The several items had the following titles:

1. *A Protestation offered to the Parliament at S. Iohnstons 1 Iulii 1606.* (The 'Admonition Epistolar' mentioned by Barlow, as the occasion for the printing of his sermon.)
2. *A Treatise of Kirke Governement consisting of two partes, whereof this former conteineth a Demonstration of true Christian Discipline according to the word of God used in the Kirke of Scotland.*
3. *The second part of Kirke Governement, conteining a refutation of Episcopall Governement by Lord Bishopes.*
4. *Doctor Reignolds his Letter to Sir Frauncis Knollis, concerning Doctor Bancrofts Sermon at Paules crosse. 9 Feb: 1588. In the Parliament time.*
5. *Sir Francis Knollis his Speach in Parliament, related by himselfe to the late worthy Lo: Treasurer Sir William Cicil.*)

Downame's *Sermon* now gave rise to a controversy between himself and an anonymous Puritan 'answerer'. The latter maintained in his *Answere* that Downame's opinion – though he had professed to derive it from Bilson – was novel in the Church of England and contrary to her teachings. He appealed to 'all our worthy writers', not only Whitaker and Fulke, but such bishops as Jewel and Whitgift, who had seen the episcopal function as no more than 'iure humano'.

63. *An Answere to a Sermon Preached the 17 of April Anno D. 1608, by George Downame Doctour of Divinitie and intituled, A sermon defendinge the honorable function of Bishops; wherein, All his reasons, brought to prove the honorable function of our L. Bishops, to be of divine institution; are answered and refuted. 1609* (STC 20605 – where it is mistakenly attributed to John Reynolds, though he had died in 1607.)

To this Downame responded with *A Defence of the Sermon* in 1611, and dedicated his work to the King. But two years later he was again attacked by the same anonymous writer in *A Replye*.

64. *A Defence of the Sermon Preached at the Consecration of the Bishop of Bath and Welles, against a confutation thereof by a namelesse Author. Divided into 4 Bookes: The first, proving chiefly that the lay or onely-governing Elders have no warrant either in the Scriptures or other monuments of Antiquity.*
The second, shewing that the primitive Churches indued with power of Ecclesiasticall government, were not Parishes properly but Dioeceses, and consequently that the Angels of the Churches or ancient Bishops were not parishionall but Diocesan Bishops.

The third, defending the superioritie of Bishops above other Ministers,
and proving that Bishops alwayes had a prioritie not onely in order, but
also in degree, and a maioritie of power both for ordination and
iurisdiction.
The fourth, maintayning that the Episcopall function is of Apostolicall
and divine institution. By George Downame Doctor of Divinitie. 1611
(STC 7115)

65. *A Replye answering a defence of the Sermon, preached at the*
Consecration of the Bishop of Bathe and Welles, by George Downame,
Doctor of Divinitye. In defence of an Answere to the foresayd Sermon
Imprinted anno 1609. 1613   (STC 20620)

Finally, a somewhat belated attack on Downame appeared in 1621 from the
pen of Paul Baynes, under the auspices of the learned Puritan divine, William
Ames.

66. *The Diocesans Tryall, Wherein all the Sinnewes of Doctor Downhams*
Defence Are brought into three heads, and orderly dissolved. By M. Paul
Baynes. Published by Dr. William Amis. 1621   (STC 1640)

(The contents are given on the title-page as follows:

The questions discussed in this Diocesans tryall are these:
1. Whether Christ did institute, or the Apostles frame any Diocesan
forme of Churches, or parishionall onely.
2. Whether Christ ordained by himselfe, or by his Apostles, any
ordinary Pastours, as our Bishops, having both precedency of order, and
majority of power over others.
3. Whether Christ did immediately commit ordinary power Ecclesi-
asticall, and the exercise of it, to any one singular person, or to an
united multitude of Presbyters.)

In connection with this controversy, Henry Jacob brought out in 1610 a
sequel to his *Christian and Modest Offer* of 1606 with a work on *The Divine*
Beginning of the Church, but not of Bishops. Complaining that his offer of
disputation had been turned down by the bishops, he proceeded to criticize
two sorts of men: 'those who hold Christ instituted no certain form of
visible Church but left it to human discretion', and 'those who recognise
such a certain form of Church, yet admit a contrary practise', namely
subjection to bishops. He went on in the following year to clarify his position
in *A Declaration & plainer opening*, reassuring his readers that 'for my part
I never was, nor am separated' from the Church of England, though he was
then residing in Middelburg.

67. *The Divine Beginning and Institution of Christs true Visible or*

> *Ministeriall Church. also The Unchangeablenesse of the same by men;*
> *viz. in the forme and essentiall constitution thereof. Written by Henry*
> *Iacob.* 1610.   (STC 14336)

68. *A Declaration & plainer opening of certaine pointes, with a sounde*
    Confirmation of some other, contained in a treatise intituled, The
    Divine beginning and institution of Christes true visible and Ministeriall
    Church. Written in a letter by the Author of the said Treatise out of the
    low Countreys to a friend of his in England. 1612   (STC 14331)

In 1613 Jacob came out still more openly against the position of the bishops
in a book entitled *An Attestation*, with special reference to Bilson, his
opponent in another controversy on Christ's descent into hell (to be dealt
with in the next section), and Downame, over whom he laments that 'of a
friend he is not long since turned from us, and become our adversarie'.

69. *An Attestation of many Learned, Godly, and famous Divines, Lightes*
    of Religion, and pillars of the Gospell, iustifying this doctrine, viz. That
    the Church governement ought to bee alwayes with the peoples free
    consent. Also this; That a true Church under the Gospell contayneth no
    more ordinary Congregations but one. In the discourse whereof,
    specially Doctor Downames & also D. Bilsons chiefe matters in their
    writings against the same, are answered. 1613   (STC 14328)

(The name of Henry Iacob is signed to the Epistle Dedicatorie.)

For all his denial of separatism, however, it was in this direction that Jacob
was moving, as appeared a few years later when he returned to London and
founded the first Independent congregation in England. At the same time, in
1616, he published his *Confession and Protestation of the Faith* on behalf of
his followers, together with another *Petition* to the King for toleration. To
this he also added *A Collection of sundry matters*, which was bound with the
former but given distinct pagination.

70. *A Confession and Protestation of the Faith of Certaine Christians in*
    England, holding it necessary to observe, & keepe all Christes true
    substantiall Ordinances for his Church visible and Politicall (that is,
    indued with power of outward spirituall Government) under the
    Gospel; though the same doe differ from the common order of the
    Land. Published for the clearing of the said Christians from the slaunder
    of Schisme, and Noveltie, and also of Separation, & undutifullnes to the
    Magistrate, which their rash Adversaries doe falsely cast upon them.
    Also an humble Petition to the K. Maiestie for Toleration therein.
    1616   (STC 14330)

71. *A Collection of sundry matters; Tending to prove it necessary for all*

persons, actually to walke in the use and practise of the substancial
ordinances in the Gospell, appointed by God for his visible Church
spiritually politicall. Which Collection conteyneth. 1. Twentie Reasons
and Arguments. 2. Ten Conclusions. 3. Three Assertions. 1616
(STC 14330)

At the time of establishing his congregation, Jacob had conferred with a
number of leading Puritans in London, including Richard Maunsel. At first,
the latter had appeared to agree with him; but he later attacked him and
defended the use of the *Book of Common Prayer*. Jacob was, however,
supported by one of his followers, Sabine Staresmore, who published *The
Unlawfulnes of Reading in Prayer* in 1619.

72. *The Unlawfulnes of Reading in Prayer. Or, The Answer of Mr. Richard
Maunsel Preacher, unto Certain Arguments, or Reasons, drawne against
the using, or communicating, in, or with the Booke of Common Prayer
(imposed to be read for prayer to God) in the Parish Assemblies of
England. With A Defence of the same Reasons, by Sabine Staresmore.*
1619   (STC 23235)

f) *Controversy over Christ's Descent into Hell*

Parallel to the foregoing controversy over the episcopal institution was
another over the orthodox interpretation of the article on Christ's descent
into hell. This was also a continuation of a controversy from the preceding
reign, between Thomas Bilson, Bishop of Winchester, and Henry Jacob, with
the rather eccentric support of Hugh Broughton. After publishing his *Survey
of Christs Sufferings* in 1604, Bilson had let the matter lie, while Jacob had
turned his attention to the more pressing subject of Church government. But
in that very year, 1604, a new stage of the controversy was initiated with
two new champions: Richard Parkes on the Episcopal side, and Andrew
Willet on the Puritan side. Behind this controversy, as behind that on the
episcopal institution, there loomed the figure of Dr. John Reynolds, with an
unpublished MS maintaining the Calvinist interpretation — that Christ had
suffered the pains of hell in his death on the cross — in the form of
'Obiections and Reasons'. This now came to the attention of Parkes, who
published *A Briefe Answere* to Reynolds in 1604. At the same time, he
criticized other Puritan authors who had defended the same interpretation:
Alexander Hume in his *Reioynder to Doctor Hil* (1593), Henry Jacob in his
Treatise of the Sufferings and Victory of Christ (1598), and Andrew Willet in
his *Synopsis Papismi* (1592, with enlarged editions in 1594 and 1600).

73. *A Briefe Answere unto Certaine Obiections and Reasons against the
descension of Christ into hell, lately sent in writing unto a Gentleman
in the Countrey.* 1604   (STC 19296)

It was on account of Parkes' critical reference to Willet as 'our late generall Surveyor of Controversies' that the latter took up the controversy with his *Limbo-Mastix* in the same year.

74. *Limbo-Mastix: That is, A Canvise of Limbus Patrum, shewing by*
   evident places of Scripture, invincible reasons, and pregnant testimonies
   of some ancient writers, that Christ descended not in soule to Hell, to
   deliver the Fathers from thence. Containing also a briefe replie to so
   much of a Pamphlet lately published, intituled, An answere to certaine
   obiections against the descension &c. as lookes that way, and is
   personally directed against some writers of our Church. 1604
   (STC 25692)

In their writings the two champions had hitherto maintained a mask of anonymity. But now they both came into the open after a lapse of three years. In his *Apologie* of 1607, which he confidently dedicated to Archbishop Bancroft, Parkes dealt with the three passages of Scripture on which the article in question was based, interpreting them in much the same way as Bellarmine had done in his *Controversies*. He incorporated his previous *Answere* with some revisions, and added a refutation of Willet's book.

75. *An Apologie: of Three Testimonies of holy Scripture, concerning the*
   Article of our Creed, (He Descended Into Hell.) First impugned by
   certaine Obiections sent in writing by a Minister unto a Gentleman in
   the Countrie: and lately seconded by a Printed Pamphlet, masking
   under the name of Limbo-mastix. By Richard Parkes, Maister of Arts,
   of Brasen-nose Colledge in Oxford. 1607   (STC 19295)

   (This work is divided into two books, each with its own title-page as follows:

   The First Booke, conteining a briefe Answer to certaine Obiections,
   against Christs descension into Hell, sent in writing by a Minister unto a
   Gentleman in the Country: revised, enlarged and confirmed.

   The Second Booke containing, A Reioynder to a Reply made against
   the former Booke, lately published in a printed Pamphlet, intituled,
   Limbo-mastix.)

In reply, Willet brought out his *Loidoromastix* in the same year under his own name. He, too, dedicated his book to the Archbishop, complaining that he had been wrongfully charged with denial of an article of faith. He also recognized 'that godly learned man Dr. Reynolds' as 'the author of the obiections' in question.

76. *Loidoromastix: that is, A Scourge for a Rayler; containing a full and*
    sufficient answer unto the Unchristian raylings, slaunders, untruths, and
    other iniurious Imputations, vented of late by one Richard Parkes
    master of Arts, against the author of Limbomastix. Wherein three
    hundred raylings, errors, contradictions, falsifications of Fathers,
    corruptions of Scripture, with other grosse oversights, are observed out
    of the said uncharitable discourse, by Andrew Willet Professor of
    Divinitie. 1607   (STC 25693)

There the controversy rested for the time being. But two further books
were published on this subject in the following decade, one on either side.
The first of these was a Latin treatise by Hugh Sanford, completed after his
death by the Puritan Robert Parker, and published in Amsterdam in 1611.
Parker also went on to write a more general Latin treatise *De Politeia
Ecclesiastica Christi*, which was published at Frankfurt in 1616. In it he
mentioned his completion of Sanford's book; and so it may be inserted in
this place.

77. *De Descensu Domini Nostri Iesu Christi ad Inferos. Libri quatuor. Ab*
    auctore doctissimo, Hugone Sanfordo, Coomflorio, Anglo, Inchoati.
    Opera vero et studio Roberti Parkeri, ad umbilicum perducti, ac jam
    tandem In Lucem editi. 1611.

78. *De Politeia Ecclesiastica Christi et Hierarchica Opposita, Libri Tres. In*
    quibus tam verae disciplinae fundamenta: quam omnes ferè de eadem
    controversiae, summo cum judicio & doctrina methodicè|pertractantur.
    Authore Roberto Parkero Anglo, Theologo ad regnum Dei doctissimo.
    1616

From the Episcopal side came *A New Eight-fold Probation* by the Scotsman
James Maxwell, Antiquary of the newly founded Controversial College at
Chelsea, in 1617. Speaking in general against 'the Genevians', he began with a
defence of the Church's divine constitution – keeping in mind the controversy in his native country over the episcopal question. He then went on to
deal with the particular, but (as we have seen) associated question of Christ's
descent into hell. In his Dedication he refers to other books of his that have
not yet been printed, including one 'touching the seate of soules (and) our
Saviours descending into hell . . . a briefe of which part of that Booke, I have
here published in English'.

79. *A New Eight-fold Probation of the Church of Englands Divine*
    Constitution, prooved by many pregnant arguments, to be much more
    complete then any Genevian in the world, against the contrary assertion
    of the fifty three petitioner-preachers of Scotland in their petition
    presented in the late Parliament to the Kings most excellent Maiesty.

23

> *With a ten-folde probation of the same Churches doctrine touching one of the most important points of our Creede, which is of our Saviours descending into Hell. By Iames Maxwell Master of Artes &c.* 1617 (STC 17704)

g) *Renewal of the Controversy over Ceremonies*

After a lull of some eight or nine years the controversy over ceremonies again broke out in 1618, largely on account of events in the Scottish Church, where King James was seeking to impose the Anglican Liturgy. There he realized his aim at the Assembly of Perth in August 1618, when the Archbishop of Saint Andrews, John Spottiswoode, succeeded in persuading the Scottish clergy to accept five disputed articles — concerning kneeling at communion, private communion, private baptism, confirmation of children, and observance of feast-days. This decision was ratified by the Scottish Parliament three years later in 1621. But it did not pass without protest, as we shall see. Meanwhile, in England, too, the year 1618 was marked by an upsurge of controversy on much the same questions. No fewer than five books, three on the Episcopal and two on the Puritan side, came out in this year on the subject of ceremonies, particularly that of kneeling at communion.

The main controversy was carried on between Thomas Morton, Bishop of Chester (though he was soon translated to another see), and an anonymous Puritan in Holland, who has been variously identified as William Ames or the Scotsman David Calderwood. It was in his last year at Chester, where he had been much vexed over this question, that Morton brought out his *Defence* of the three ceremonies in dispute: the use of the surplice, the sign of the cross in baptism, and the practice of kneeling to receive holy communion. In his book he particularly criticized the arguments of 'the Assembly of the Lincolnshire Ministers, in their booke called the Abridgement, &c.' and of 'the Ministers in the Diocesse of Chester', who had submitted to him a manuscript of 'Reasons, of their Refusall of Subscription'. He therefore prefaced his criticism with 'An Epistle to the Non-conformists, to reduce them from their Superstitions, and Scandals against the Church'.

80. *A Defence of the Innocencie of the Three Ceremonies of the Church of England. viz. The Surplice, Crosse after Baptisme, and Kneeling at the receiving of the blessed Sacrament. Divided into two Parts: In the former whereof the Generall Arguments urged by the Non-conformists; and, in the second Part, their Particular Accusations, against those III Ceremonies severally, are answered, and refuted. Published by Authoritie.* 1618   (STC 18179)

(The Dedication is signed 'Tho: Cestren' — Thomas, Bishop of Chester.)

The arguments of Morton were answered several years later by his anonymous Puritan opponent, in two separate parts, dealing respectively with his *Generall Defence* in 1622, and his *Particular Defence* in 1623. The author clearly has the Scottish events in mind while presenting his case against Morton, since he refers in the Preface to 'this most unhappy deformation' in Scotland 'brought in by these late usurping Bishops'.

81. *A Reply to Dr. Mortons Generall Defence of Three Nocent Ceremonies. Viz. The Surplice, Crosse in Baptisme, and kneeling at the receiving of the sacramentall elements of Bread and Wine.* 1622   (STC 559)

82. *A Reply to Dr. Mortons Particular Defence of Three Nocent Ceremonies. Viz. The Surplice, Crosse in Baptisme, and kneeling at the receiving of the sacramentall elements of Bread and Wine.* 1623 (STC 560)

There the matter rested for the rest of the reign; but under the new King, Charles I, the former Lincoln minister John Burges, now pastor of Sutton Coldfield in Warwickshire and a conformist, came out in defence of Morton against his anonymous critic, with *An Answer Reioyned*. In the same year he added, by way of supplement, 'another little Treatise of like subject, first written in Answere of a Private Letter', entitled *The Lawfulnes of Kneeling*.

83. *An Answer Reioyned to that much applauded Pamphlet of a Namelesse Author, bearing this Title: viz. A Reply to Dr. Mortons Generall Defence of three Nocent Ceremonies, &c. The innocency and lawfulnesse whereof is againe in this Reioynder vindicated. By Dr. Iohn Burges, Pastor of Sutton Coldfield in Warwickshire. Published by his Maiesties speciall Command.* 1631   (STC 4113)

84. *The Lawfulnes of Kneeling in the act of receiving the Lords Supper. Wherein (by the way) also, somewhat of the Crosse in Baptisme. First written for satisfaction of a Friend, and now published for Common Benefit. By Dr. Iohn Burges, Pastor of Sutton Coldfield.* 1631 (STC 4114)

The second book on the Episcopal side in 1618 was by John Buckeridge, Bishop of Rochester, who had preached a sermon before the King the previous year on the subject of kneeling at the communion; and this he now published with an additional *Discourse* on the same subject. But it gave rise to no special controversy.

85. *A Sermon preached before His Maiestie At Whitehall, March 22. 1617. being Passion-Sunday, Touching Prostration, and Kneeling in the Worship of God. To which is added a Discourse concerning Kneeling at the Communion. By Iohn, Bishop of Rochester.* 1618   (STC 4005)

Of greater efficacy perhaps was the third contribution, by a former Non-conformist, the Puritan John Sprint, who had been persuaded of the practical necessity of conformity, when the alternative was deprivation. He was now encouraged to publish his reasons for changing his mind, in a book entitled *Cassander Anglicanus*. At the end of his book he appended an anonymous *Answere* to his discourse, with his further *Reply*. He was later criticized in 1622 by the anonymous opponent of Morton, who draws a contrast between 'D. Mortons way, who avoucheth the sayd ceremonies to be agreeable unto the rules of Gods word', and 'M. Sprints way, who confesseth the ceremonies to be imposed contrary unto the rules of Gods word, and yet contendeth that they are to be used in case of deprivation'.

> 86. *Cassander Anglicanus; Shewing the necessity of conformitie to the prescribed ceremonies of our Church, In case of Deprivation. By Iohn Sprint, Minister of Thornbury in Glocester-Shire, sometimes of Christ-Church in Oxon.* 1618 (STC 23108)
>
> (The two appendices bear the following titles:
>
> *A Briefe and plaine Answere to Master Sprints discourse concerning the necessity of conformity in case of Deprivation.*
>
> *A Reply to the Answere of my first Reason for Conformitie in case of Deprivation.*)

On the Puritan side, there appeared in this year an anonymous refurbishing of a *Defence* of the Millenary Petition, which (as the Preface states) 'hath lien hid . . . about 14 yeares'. It was divided into two sections, entitled respectively 'The Anatomie of the Ceremonies' and 'Bellum Ceremoniale'; and it carried a slighting reference to 'M. Sprint' and his *Cassander Anglicanus*.

> 87. *A True, Modest, and Iust Defence of the Petition for Reformation, exhibited to the Kings most excellent Maiestie. Containing an Answere to the Confutation published under the names of some of the Universitie of Oxford. Together with a full Declaration out of the Scriptures, and practise of the Primitive Church, of the severall points of the said Petition.* 1618 (STC 14434)

Another Puritan work, in two separate parts, was presented as a *Plain Discourse of an Unlettered Christian* by Thomas Dighton, a layman, stating his reasons for refusing to kneel at communion. The first part he published in 1618, and the second the following year, without reference to any of the books on the Episcopal side – though one of them may well have provided him with the occasion.

88. *Certain Reasons of a Private Christian against Conformitie to kneeling in the very act of receiving the Lords Supper. By Tho: Dighton Gent.* 1618   (STC 6876)

89. *The Second Part of a Plain Discourse of an Unlettered Christian. Wherein by way of demonstration hee sheweth what the reasons bee which hee doth ground upon, in refusing conformity to kneeling in the act of receiving the Lords Supper. By Tho: Dighton.* 1619 (STC 6877)

Two other books followed on the Episcopal side, but without specifying any adversaries by name. In 1620 John Denison, one of the King's chaplains, published a sermon, entitled *Beati Pacifici*, in which he criticized 'certaine contentious brethren' as 'Peace-breakers'. The following year a minister in Kent, James Wats, discussed *The Controversie debated* about kneeling at communion and praised the attitude of John Sprint as a guide for Puritans to follow.

90. *Beati Pacifici. The Blessednes of Peace-makers: And the Advancement of Gods Children. In Two Sermons preached before the King, by Iohn Denison Doctor of Divinity, and one of his Maiesties Chapleynes.* 1620   (STC 6583)

(The relevant sermon is the first, and longest of the two.)

91. *The Controversie debated About the Reverend gesture of Kneeling, in the Act of Receiving the Holy Communion. By Iames Wats, Minister of Gods Word at Woodnosborough in Kent: And sometime fellow of Magdalene Colledge in Cambridge.* 1621   (STC 25109)

In Scotland, however, the controversy was much keener than in England, partly because the tradition of the Scottish Church was more presbyterian, and partly because that tradition found an energetic spokesman in a minister named David Calderwood — although, or rather because, he had been banished by the King in 1617 and had taken refuge in Holland. In the first place, the five articles of the Perth Assembly were defended by two ministers, soon to be made bishops: David Lindsay, whose *Reasons of a Pastors Resolution* was published in London in 1619; and John Michaelson, whose *Lawfulnes of Kneeling* was published in Saint Andrews the following year. In his Dedication the latter mentions that 'amongst all the five Articles agreed upon, and concluded, in the last Generall Assemblie, none is so much hated, & spoken against, as Kneeling at the Communion' — since it had been the Scottish custom to receive seated.

92. *The Reasons of a Pastors Resolution, touching the Reverend receiving of the holy Communion: Written by David Lindesay, D. of Divinitie, in the Universitie of Saint Andrewes in Scotland, and Preacher of the Gospell at Dundy.* 1619 (STC 15656)

93. *The Lawfulnes of Kneeling, in the Act of receiving the Sacrament of the Lordes Supper. Written by M. Iohn Michælson, Preacher of Gods Word, at Burnt-Yland.* 1620 (STC 17856)

They were followed in 1620 by the Archbishop of Saint Andrews, John Spottiswoode himself, who had to deal (as he describes in his *History of the Church of Scotland*, subsequently published in 1655) with 'a relation of the Government of the Scottish Church' directed by 'the troublers of our Church' (David Calderwood and his friends) to the Synod of Dort in Holland (then being held to condemn the ideas of Arminius). Since the relation had been in Latin, he wrote his *Refutatio* also in Latin to justify the position of the Perth Assembly in the eyes of continental readers.

94. *Refutatio Libelli de Regimine Ecclesiae Scoticanae.* 1620 (STC 23103)

On the other hand, a fierce series of attacks on the Assembly came from Holland, chiefly from the pen of David Calderwood. To begin with, he presented his own account of the *Perth Assembly* in 1619, in two parts: first, describing 'The Proceedings' from his viewpoint; and then, proving (against Morton) the unlawfulness of kneeling at communion. He went on in the following year to publish a free Latin translation of this account (the first part), entitled *Parasynagma Perthense*, adding satirical verses by the presbyterian leader, Andrew Melville, *Anti-tami-cami-categoria* (accusation of Thames and Cam, i.e. the doctors of Oxford and Cambridge), originally composed in 1604 against the attitude of the two universities to the Millenary Petition.

95. *Perth Assembly. Containing 1. The Proceedings thereof. 2. The Proofe of the Nullitie thereof. 3. Reasons presented thereto against the receiving the five new Articles imposed. 4. The oppositenesse of it to the proceedings and oath of the whole state of the Land. An. 1581. 5. Proofes of the unlawfulnesse of the said five Articles, viz. 1. Kneeling in the act of Receiving the Lords Supper. 2. Holy daies. 3. Bishopping. 4. Private Baptisme. 5. Private Communion.* 1619 (STC 4360)

(The two parts are entitled:

The Proceedings of the Assemblie holden at Perth in August, Anno Dom. 1618.

Kneeling in the act of receiving the sacramentall elements of Bread and Wine, proved unlawfull.)

96. *Parasynagma Perthense et Iuramentum Ecclesiae Scoticanae et A. M. Antitamicamicategoria.* 1620 (STC 4361)

(The full title of Melville's satire is as follows:

Pro Supplici Evangelicorum Ministrorum in Anglia Ad Serenissimum Regem contra Larvatam geminae Academiae Gorgonem Apologia, sive Anti-tami-cami-categoria. Authore A. M.)

Calderwood then proceeded to deal with the individual defenders of ceremonies in Scotland: with Lindsay, in *A Solution of Doctor Resolutus* in 1619; and with Michaelson, in *A Defence of our Arguments* in 1620. Explaining his former title, he says: 'Seeing the Doctor stileth arrogantly his reasons Resolutions; let him be called Doctor Resolutus for Scotland.' His complaint is that 'We are become so Apish in the imitation of the English patterne'. In the latter book he particularly notes how Michaelson depends for his arguments on the English writers, Morton and Denison.

97. *A Solution of Doctor Resolutus, His Resolutions for kneeling.* 1619 (STC 4364)

98. *A Defence of our Arguments against kneeling in the act of receiving the Sacramentall elements of bread and wine impugned by Mr. Michelsone.* 1620 (STC 4354)

There followed a brief exchange of words between Calderwood and the continental divine, Daniel Tilenus. The latter published a *Paraenesis ad Scotos* in 1620, defending the five Articles one by one on behalf of what he calls 'violati a turbulentis ingeniis, Ecclesiastici regiminis'. In reply, Calderwood wrote his *Speach of the Kirk of Scotland* and published it in the same year, with slighting reference to 'Tilenus . . . his Palinod'.

99. *Paraenesis ad Scotos, Genevensis Disciplinae Zelotas. Autore Dan. Tileno Silesio.* 1620 (STC 24070)

(The chapters from XII to XVI deal particularly with each of the five Articles:

XII. De Ingeniculatione in suscipienda sacra coena.
XIII. An Eucharistia ad Clinicos deferenda.
XIIII. An Baptismus quovis tempore & loco cum necessitas postulat sit administrandus.
XV. De Baptizatorum Confirmatione.
XVI. De Festorum dierum observatione.)

100. *The Speach of the Kirk of Scotland to her beloved children.* 1620 (STC 4365)

Calderwood went on to publish his *Altar of Damascus* in 1621, comparing the Anglican hierarchy which was being imposed on the Scottish Church to the pagan altar which so fascinated King Achaz in Damascus that he had a copy made of it for the Temple of Jerusalem (II Kings xvi. 10). For his description of the Anglican hierarchy he largely relied on Richard Mocket's recent work, *Doctrina et Politia Ecclesiae Anglicanae*, which had got the author into serious trouble with the King in 1617. Again, he was opposed by Tilenus, who published a treatise *De Disciplina Ecclesiastica* for the Scottish Church in the following year. Without mentioning Calderwood by name, the author is evidently thinking of him and his book when he remarks:

'Nuntiant illi . . . quod scilicet Achaz Altare Domini removeat a Templo . . . quae est apud Damascenos . . . hoc est, sacra omnia denuo ad Romanenses ritus effingi.'

In reply, Calderwood brought out a bulky Latin translation of the *Altar of Damascus* with many additions and amplifications, including a new chapter, 'De rebus Adiaphoris & ceremoniis', under the assumed name of Edward Didoclavius (an anagram of David Calderwood). The amplifications largely took the form of a refutation of Tilenus' *Paraenesis*. In an appendix he added that relation on the Scottish Church sent in the name of Hieronymus Philadelphus to the Synod of Dort which had provoked the Archbishop of Saint Andrews to pen his *Refutatio*. He also took this opportunity of answering the *Refutatio*.

101. *The Altar of Damascus or The Patern of the English Hierarchie, And Church-Policie obtruded upon the Church of Scotland.* 1621
    (STC 4352)

102. *Doctrina, et Politia Ecclesiae Anglicanae, a Beatissimae Memoriae Principibus Edouardo Sexto, Regina Elizabetha stabilitae, et a Religiosissimo, & Potentissimo Monarcha Iacobo, Magnae Britan. &c. Rege continuatae. Quibus eiusdem Ecclesiae Apologia praefigitur pro sua discessione in utraque a gravissimis Romanae Ecclesiae corruptelis, Tyrannide, Idololatria, Erroribus, & quod ad Concilium Tridentinum non accesserit.* 1616   (STC 17991)

(The contents include the following items:

Apologia Ecclesiae Anglicanae. (Jewel)
Doctrina Catechetica Ecclesiae Anglicanae: magis succincta . . . magis ampla. (Nowell)
Ecclesiae Anglicanae Doctrina: Articuli. Homiliae. (summaries)
Liber Precum Publicarum.
Ecclesiae Anglicanae Disciplina et Politia. (Mocket))

103. *De Disciplina Ecclesiastica Brevis & modesta dissertatio, ad Ecclesiam Scoticam. Autore Gallo quodam Theologo, Verbi Divini Ministro.* 1622 (STC 24067)

(The place of publication is Aberdeen.)

104. *Altare Damascenum ceu Politia Ecclesiae Anglicanae obtrusa Ecclesiae Scoticanae, a formalista quodam delineata, illustrata & examinata studio & opera Edwardi Didoclavii Cui Locis suis interserta Confutatio Paraeneseos Tileni ad Scotos Genevensis, ut ait, disciplinae zelotas Et adjecta Epistola Hieronymi Philadelphi de Regimine Ecclesiae Scoticanae. Eiusque Vindiciae contra Calumnias Iohannis Spotsuodi Fani Andreae Pseudoarchiepiscopi per anonymum.* 1623   (STC 4353)

(After 953 pages of main text, followed by an index, there come 108 pages of supplementary material, with new pagination:

Pro Supplici . . . Anti-tami-cami-categoria. Authore A. Melvino 1604. De Regimine Ecclesiae Scoticanae Epistola . . . Hieronymus Philadelphus. Epistolae Philadelphi Vindiciae contra calumnias Iohannis Spotsuodi Fani Andreae Pseudo-archiepiscopi. Authore Anonymo.)

Meanwhile, other anonymous writings were being published in Holland to the same effect, and possibly by the same author, or at least under his auspices. In 1620 there appeared *A Dialogue betwixt Cosmophilus and Theophilus*, that is, between 'a lover of the World' and 'a lover of God' – the one being addressed as 'precise', and the other as 'politick'. The next year saw the publication of the Scottish *Booke of Discipline* (of 1560), with a commentary to show how 'in these last daies some dangerous Dalilah have betrayed Sampson', with 'Apostolicall discipline abolished, and Popish policie exalted'. Thirdly, there appeared a pamphlet on *The Course of Conformitie*, directed not so much against the Perth Assembly as against the Parliament of 1621 which ratified its proceedings.

105. *A Dialogue betwixt Cosmophilus and Theophilus anent the Urging of new ceremonies upon the Kirke of Scotland.* 1620   (STC 5826)

(This is also attributed to John Murray.)

106. *The First and Second Booke of Discipline. Together with some Acts of the Generall Assemblies, Clearing and confirming the same: and An Act of Parliament.* 1621   (STC 22015)

(The book is in three parts:

Actes of the Generall Assembly
The First Booke of Discipline (1560)
The Second Booke of Discipline (supplementary to the first))

107. *The Course of Conformitie, As it Hath proceeded, Is concluded, Should be refused.* 1622   (STC 21874)

(This is attributed in STC to W. Scot.)

In 1624 two more books came from the prolific pen of Calderwood: *A Dispute* and *An Exhortation*, both dealing with the Perth Assembly again – the former concentrating once more on Lindsay's *Reasons*, and commending 'the Replyer to Morton' on the disputed question of kneeling.

108. *A Dispute upon Communicating at our Confused Communions.* 1624 (STC 4356)

109. *An Exhortation of the Particular Kirks of Christ in Scotland to their Sister Kirk in Edinburgh.* 1624   (STC 4358)

Finally, as an interesting postscript to all these controversial writings emanating from the Dutch presses, there appeared in 1625 a book entitled *Vox Vera* by the Scotsman Patrick Scot on the Episcopal side. Describing a visit to Amsterdam, he refers to 'the huge Chaos of those infamous libels' he encountered there.

> 'There, I did behold, every Bookesellers shop, and most Pedlers stalles, loaden with the nullitie of Perthes assembly; the Altar of Damascus, the Dialogue betwixt Theophilus and Cosmophilus, the Speech of the Church of Scotland to her beloved Children, and the course of Conformitie ioyned with all these (severally printed before) reprinted in one volume . . . Secondly, did come to my hand the petition of the Kirke of Scotland to the heigh Parliament of England . . . next was offered to me, Speculum belli sacri, or the mirrour of holy warre . . . next to my greater admiration, did I behold Altare Damascenum . . . These were closed up with a malicious Satirisme against a learned grave Treatise written by the Archbishop of Saint Andrewes.'

110. *Vox Vera: or, Observations from Amsterdam. Examining The late Insolencies of some Pseudo-Puritans, separatists from the Church of Great Brittaine. And closed up with a serious three-fold Advertisement for the generall use of every good Subiect within his Maiesties Dominions, but more especially of those in the Kingdome of Scotland. By Patricke Scot, North-Brittaine.* 1625   (STC 21863)

(The author notes the anagram of Edwardi Didoclavii for Davidis Calderwodi, in the genitive form.)

The outcome of this controversy, among other things (including the Civil War), was the publication of two *Histories* of the Scottish Church by the two protagonists, Spottiswoode and Calderwood. The former succeeded in bringing his version of the events out first, strangely enough in London under the Commonwealth in 1655. Being on the Episcopal side, he took his story back to the first coming of Christianity to the country and so presented the Reformation from 1560 onwards as but an episode in that history. Calderwood followed him (from the grave) some twenty years later in 1678, with what he professed to be *The True History* of events, though he characteristically began his story in 1560 with the Parliament that ratified the presbyterian 'Confession of Faith' and concluded with 'The nullitie of Perth Assemblie'.

111. *The History of the Church of Scotland, Beginning the Year of our Lord 203, and continued to the end of the Reign of King James the VI of ever blessed Memory. Wherein are described, The Progress of Christianity; The Persecutions and Interruptions of it; The Foundations of Churches; The Erecting of Bishopricks; The Building and Endowing Monasteries, and other Religious Places; The Succession of Bishops in their Sees: The Reformation of Religion, and the frequent Disturbances of that Nation, by Wars, Conspiracies, Tumults, Schisms. Together with great variety of other Matters, both Ecclesiasticall and Politicall. Written by that grave and Reverend Prelate, and wise Counsellor, John Spotswood, Lord Archbishop of S. Andrews, and Privy Counsellor to King Charles the I. that most Religious and blessed Prince.* 1655 (Wing S5022)

112. *The True History of the Church of Scotland, From the beginning of the Reformation, unto the end of the Reigne of King James VI . . . Written by That learned and laborious Servant of Christ Mr David Calderwood . . .* 1678 (Wing C279, GS 247)

h) *The Arminian Controversy*

Meanwhile, the development of the Anglican Church under James I was being affected no less by events in Holland than by those in Scotland. Already in the previous reign of Elizabeth the orthodox Calvinistic interpretation of the Thirty-Nine Articles, particularly that relating to predestination, had begun to be called into question at the university of Cambridge. This had led to the formulation of the Lambeth Articles in 1595, which had been drawn up by the Puritan professor of divinity, William Whitaker, and accepted (with some reservations) by the Archbishop of Canterbury, John Whitgift. The Queen, however, had refused to give them the royal sanction; and so they remained a dead letter. Not only that, but her refusal provided an implicit encouragement to those who opposed them, men such as Peter Baro (the Lady Margaret professor of divinity), John

Overall (Whitaker's successor as Regius professor of divinity), Lancelot Andrewes (Master of Pembroke, and soon to become Bishop of Chichester), and Richard Bancroft (Bishop of London, and soon to become Archbishop of Canterbury). After Bancroft's death in 1610, however, the Calvinist party in the Church of England took heart at the appointment of one of their leaders, George Abbot, as Archbishop of Canterbury in the following year. Then in 1615 the Calvinist John Prideaux was appointed Regius professor of divinity at Oxford. Under their influence the King's own sympathies, for all his anti-Puritanism, came to move in that direction, especially as the problem now facing him was not so much one of discipline as one of doctrine.

It was about this time in Holland that a movement of reaction against Calvin's theology of predestination was being led by the Dutch divine, Jacob Harmensen (or Arminius), who had been appointed professor of divinity at the university of Leyden in 1603. From then onwards, till his death in 1609, he was involved in controversy with his Calvinist colleague, Franciscus Gomarus. Interestingly enough, it was also to some extent against the writings of the English Puritan William Perkins – his *Armilla Aurea* of 1590, and his treatise *De Praedestinationis Modo et Ordine* of 1598 – that he came to elaborate his ideas, as stated in his *Examen Modestum Libelli* (a criticism of Perkins' latter treatise), published after his death in 1612. This *Examen* was in turn criticized by Perkins' disciple, John Yates, in his book, *Gods Arraignement of Hypocrites*, in 1615.

113. *Iacobi Arminii Veteraquinatis Batavi, S. Theologiae Doctoris eximii, Examen Modestum Libelli, quam D. Gulielmus Perkinsius apprime doctus Theologus, edidit ante aliquot annos De Praedestinationis modo & ordine, itemque de Amplitudine gratiae divinae. Addita est propter argumenti convenientiam Analysis Cap. IX ad Roman. ante multos annos ab eodem ipso D. Arminio delineata. Cum indice rerum contentarum.* 1612

114. *Gods Arraignement of Hypocrites: with an Inlargement concerning Gods decree in ordering sinne. As likewise a Defence of Mr. Calvine against Bellarmine; and of Mr. Perkins against Arminius.* 1615 (STC 26081)

Soon after the death of Arminius his followers drew up a *Remonstrance* as a statement of their theological position to be presented to the States-General of Holland – whence they came to be known, not only as Arminians, but also as Remonstrants. But their position was seriously endangered when the successor of Arminius at Leyden, Konrad Vorst (or Vorstius), was accused of Socinian heresy and dismissed from his professorial chair in 1612 by the States-General. This was largely due to the personal intervention of James I, who in that year published a *Declaration* against Vorstius (in three languages), terming him 'a wretched Heretique, or rather Atheist'. This was because Vorstius had ventured to send two of his books, *Tractatus Theologicus de Deo* (1610) and *Apologetica Exegesis* (1611), to the King for his royal approval. But at that time James was in no mood to condone what he saw as heresy, after having just had two men of Arian views, Bartholomew Legate and Edward Wightman, burnt for heresy.

115. *Tractatus Theologicus De Deo, Sive de Natura & Attributis Dei. Omnia fere ad hanc materiam pertinentia (saltem de quibus utiliter & religiose disputari potest) decem Disputationibus antehac in Illustri Schola Steinfurtensi, diverso tempore, publice habitas, breviter & methodice comprehendens. Accesserunt etiam seorsim Annotationes, (de quibus vide infra Admonitiunculam ad Lectorem) ad uberiorem eorum exegesim, quae in thesibus haud satis explicata esse videbantur. Auctore Conrado Vorstio S. Theol. D. & Professore.* 1606

(The second edition, a copy of which he submitted to King James, was dated 1610.)

116. *Doct. Conradi Vorstii Apologetica Exegesis sive Plenior Declaratio Locorum Aliquot Quae ex libro eiusdem de Deo, sive de Natura & Attributis Dei excerpta, eique pro erroneis imposita, hoc titulo late in vulgus emanaverunt: ab eodem ipso Auctore scripta, & in lucem edita. Accessit in fine Appendix brevicula adversus iniquas M. Becani Iesuitae criminationes.* 1611

(The reference in the Appendix is to a work of the Jesuit theologian, Martin Van der Beeck (Becanus), *Quaestiones Miscellaneae De Fide Haereticis servanda. Contra Quendam Calvinistam Batavum*, published in 1609.)

117. *His Maiesties Declaration concerning His Proceedings with the States generall of the United Provinces of the Low Countreys, In the cause of D. Conradus Vorstius.* 1612   (STC 9233)

118. *Declaration Du Serenissime Roy De La Grand'Bretaigne sur les actions devers les Etats Generaux des Pais bas unis touchant le faict de Conradus Vorstius.* 1612   (STC 9229)

119. *Declaratio Serenissimi Magnae Britanniae Regis, Qua quid cum Generalibus foederatarum Belgii Provinciarum Ordinibus super re Vorstii actum tractatumque sit, singillatim explicatur.* 1612 (STC 9232)

Following in James' footsteps, an English Puritan resident in Holland, Matthew Slade, came out with a series of attacks on Vorstius by way of a scholastic disputation in Latin between 1612 and 1614.

120. *Matthaei Sladi Anglo-Britanni Cum Conrado Vorstio Theol. Doct. De blasphemiis, haeresibus & Atheismis a Sereniss. Sapientissimoque Magnae Britanniae Franciae & Hiberniae Rege Iacobo, hujus nominis Primo, Christanae Fidei defensore Potentissimo, in ejusdem Vorstii de Deo Tractatu & Exegesi apologetica, nigro Theta notatis, Scholasticae Disputationis Pars Prima. Ad Nobiliss. ac praepotentes DD. Ordines foederatarum Belgii Regionum Generales. In qua Fides Orthodoxa, de vera Immensitate & infinitate trin-uni Dei, opponitur heterodoxiae Augustini Steuchi Episcopi Kisami, & Vorstii supra nominati, statuentium Deum & finitum esse, & Domicilio quodam non suo habitare. Ostenditurque, Serenissimum Regem gravissimas ob caussas Vorstii Doctrinam de finitudine, localitate, quasi-Corporalitate & quasi-Compositione Essentiae Dei condemnasse: multaque in iisdem Vorstii Apologiis Latinis atque Belgicis fraudulenta Sophismata & aperta mendacia deteguntur. Addita est venerabilis senis D. Dav. Parei ad Vorstium epistola, nuper scripta. 1612*

121. *Matthaei Sladi Anglo-Britanni Disceptationis cum Conrado Vorstio Theol. Doctore Pars Altera. De immutabilitate & simplicitate Dei. Qua docetur Serenissimus ac Sapientissimum Magnae Britanniae, Franciae & Hiberniae Regem Iacobum hujus nominis Primum, Christianae Fidei Defensorem Θεόχριστον, juste ac merito notasse blasphemum Vorsti dogma, Deum esse mutabilem & accidentibus subjectum adserentis. Ad illustres, nob. amplissq. Hollandiae et West-Frisiae Ordines. Praefixa est Prioris Disceptationis Appendix, cujus capita hac aversa Pagina commonstrantur, Appositum C. Vorstii & F. Socini Concentus sive Bicinii exemplum: Cum Rerum, verborum atque Testium Syllabo. 1614*

After him came William Ames, who engaged another of the Dutch Remonstrants, Nicholas Grevinchovius, in a Latin disputation between 1615 and 1617, on the more central point at issue.

122. *Dissertatio theologica de duabus quaestionibus hoc tempore controversis, quarum prima est de reconciliatione per mortem Christi impetrata omnibus ac singulis hominibus: altera, de electione ex fide praevisa. Sermone primum inchoata, postea vero scripto continuata, inter Guilielmum Amesium theologum Anglum, & Nicolaum Grevinchovium, ecclesiastem Roterodamensem. Non qualem ille eam edidit cum suo, quod agnoscit, auctario; sed genuina illa atque integra: cui accessit ejusdem Grevinchovii responsio ad Amesii instantias. 1615*

123. *Guilielmi Amesii rescriptio scholastica & brevis. Ad Nicolai Grevinchovii responsum illud prolixum, quod opposuit dissertationi, de redemptione generali. 1615*

124. *Guil. Amesii ad Responsum Nic. Grevinchovii Rescriptio Contracta.*
Accedunt ejusdem assertationes Theologicae de Lumine Naturae &
Gratiae. 1617

(Printed by William Brewster's Pilgrim Press at Leyden.)

On the other hand, in view of the royal attitude, few English divines – apart
from the followers of Smyth and Helwys, who came to be known as 'General
Baptists' for their Arminian assertion of the general extent of Christ's
redemption to all men (cf. Ch. II) – dared to express support for the ideas of
Arminius, though there were not a few sympathisers among the Anglican
bishops. The only spokesman was Richard Thomson, 'the grand propagator
of Arminianism', who published his *Diatriba de Amissione et Intercisione*
Gratiae et Justificationis from the safety of Leyden in 1616. He was answered
by Robert Abbot in an *Animadversio* appended to a collection of Oxford
lectures *De Gratia, et Perseverantia Sanctorum* in 1618.

125. *Diatriba de Amissione et Intercisione Gratiae et Justificationis.* 1616

126. *De Gratia, Et Perseverantia Sanctorum, Exercitationes aliquot habitae*
in Academia Oxoniensi, Authore Roberto Sarisburiensi iam Episcopo,
Theologiae tunc in eadem Academia Professore Regio. Quibus accessit
eiusdem in Richardi Thomsoni Anglo-Belgici Diatribam de amissione &
intercisione Iustificationis, & Gratiae, animadversio brevis. 1618
(STC 46)

Judgment was finally passed on the Arminians at the Synod of Dort (or
Dordrecht) in 1618–19; and the Calvinist orthodoxy was duly vindicated
against them. From England the King sent four official representatives, from
the Calvinist party in the Anglican Church: George Carleton (Bishop of
Llandaff), John Davenant (Master of Queens' College, Cambridge, and Lady
Margaret Professor of Divinity), Samuel Ward (Master of Sidney Sussex
College, Cambridge), and Joseph Hall (Dean of Worcester). In addition, the
King also decided to send a Scotsman, Walter Balcanquhall (Master of the
Savoy, London); and Joseph Hall had to be replaced during the Synod by
Thomas Goad (Chaplain to the Archbishop of Canterbury) on account of ill
health. In 1619 the results of the Synod, reaffirming the doctrine of
predestination against the five Articles of the Remonstrants, were published
both in Latin and in English translation, as well as *A Catalogue of the*
Deputies. The original *Acta* in Latin were published at Dort in the following
year. The speech of Joseph Hall, delivered in Latin on that occasion,
appeared both in Dutch and in French translation in 1621. George Carleton
also published his *Oration* made before the States-General of Holland,
containing a general exhortation to peace and concord, away from the past
'iangling disputes'. The part taken by the English divines in the outcome of

the Synod was subsequently published, in both Latin and English, on the occasion of the controversy which broke out in England at the end of the reign.

127. *Iudicium Synodi Nationalis, Reformatarum Ecclesiarum Belgicarum, habitae Dordrechti, Anno 1618 & 1619. Cui etiam interfuerunt plurimi insignes Theologi Reformatarum Ecclesiarum Magnae Britanniae, Palatinatus Electoralis, Hassiae, Helvetiae, Correspondentiae Wedder-avicae, Genevensis, Bremensis, & Emdanae, De Quinque Doctrinae Capitibus in Ecclesiis Belgicis Controversis. Promulgatum VI May MDCXIX.* 1619

128. *The Iudgement of the Nationall Synode of the Reformed Belgique Churches, assembled at Dort, Anno 1618 and 1619. In which Synode were admitted many Divines of note, being of the Reformed Churches. Of Great Britaine, Of the Countie Palatine of Rhene, Of Hassia, Of Helvetia, Of the Correspondence of Weterav, Of Geneva, Of Breme, and Of Embden, Concerning the five Articles controverted in the Belgique Churches: Published (by reading in Latine in the great Church at Dort) May 6, 1619. stylo novo. Englished out of the Latine copie.* 1619   (STC 7066)

(The 'five notorious controverted Articles' are given as:

1. 'Of Divine Predestination'.
2. 'Of Redemption' – i.e. the extent of the efficacy of Christ's death on the cross.
3. 'Of Conversion' – i.e. the extent of free will in the state of man's corruption.
4. 'Of Conversion' – i.e. the manner of man's conversion to God.
5. 'Of the perseverance of the Saints'.

The presentation ended with two conclusions:

1. 'The Sentence of the Synod concerning the Remonstrants'.
2. 'The Sentence . . . Concerning the doctrine of Conradus Vorstius'.)

129. *Acta Synodi Nationalis, In nomine Domini nostri Iesu Christi, Auctoritate illustr. et praepotentum DD. Ordinum Generalium Foederati Belgii Provinciarum, Dordrechti habitae Anno MDCXVIII et MDCXIX. Accedunt Plenissima, de Quinque Articulis, Theologorum Judicia.* 1620

130. *A Catalogue of the Deputies of the High and Mightie States Generall of the United Provinces. And of the Reverend and Learned Divines, who now are met in the Nationall Synode, Celebrated in the Citie of Dordrecht in Holland. Translated out of the Latin and Dutch Copies.*

with A Short Narration of the occasions, and Introduction of the said
Synodicall Assembly. 1618   (STC 7065)

(From Great Britain the four names given are those of Carleton, Hall,
Davenant and Ward.)

131. *Harangue ou Exhortation, prononcee en Latin, au Synode de Dordrecht*
en Hollande, le xxix. de Novembre 1618. Par M Joseph Hall, docteur
Anglois, Doyen de Wigorne. Nouvellement mise en Francois. 1621

(The Latin original is given in the *Acta Synodi* above, p. 38:
Sessione Decima-sexta. xxix. Novembris, die Iovis ante meridiem. a D.
Iosepho Hallo Wigorniensi Decani . . . exhortatio Latina, ex
Ecclesiastae Salomonis cap. septimo vers. 16. Ne sis justus nimis, neque
sis sapiens nimis, &c.)

132. *An Oration made at the Hage, before the Prince of Orenge, and the*
Assembly of the High and Mighty Lords, the States Generall of the
United Provinces: By the Reverend Father in God, the Lord Bishop of
Landaff, one of the Commissioners sent by the Kings most Excellent
Maiesty to the Synod of Dort. 1619   (STC 4638)

133. *Suffragium Collegiale Theologorum Magnae Britanniae de Quinque*
controversis Remonstrantium Articulis, Synodo Dordrechtanae
exhibitum Anno MDCXIX. Judicio Synodico praevium. 1626
(STC 7067)

(It is subscribed by the five English participants, according to their
titles at the (subsequent) time of publication:

'Ita attestamur Georgius Cicestrensis, Iohannes Sarisburiensis, Gualterus
Balcanquall, Samuel Ward, Thomas Goad.')

134. *The Collegiat Suffrage of the Divines of Great Britaine, Concerning the*
Five Articles controverted in the Low Countries. Which Suffrage was by
them delivered in the Synod of Dort, March 6. Anno 1619. Being their
vote or voice foregoing the joint and publique judgment of that Synod.
1629   (STC 7070)

A prominent French Calvinist divine, Peter Du Moulin (Molinaeus), who had
also taken part in the Synod, published his *Anatomy of Arminianism* in the
immediate aftermath of the Synod. It was at once translated from its original
Latin into English in 1620.

135. *Anatome Arminianismi Seu, Enucleatio Controversiarum quae in Belgio*
agitantur, super doctrina De Providentia: De Praedestinatione, De
morte Christi, De natura & Gratia. Authore Petro Molinaeo Pastore
Ecclesiae Parisiensis. 1619

136 *The Anatomy of Arminianisme: or The opening of the Controversies lately handled in the Low-Countryes, Concerning the Doctrine of Providence, of Predestination, of the Death of Christ, of Nature and Grace. By Peter Moulin, Pastor of the Church at Paris. Carefully translated out of the originall Latine Copy.* 1620   (STC 7307)

Meanwhile the English sympathisers with the Dutch Arminians – though they rejected the name of 'Arminian' – prudently refrained from raising a voice against the condemnation. Yet they were supported by many of the most influential bishops and divines: John Buckeridge (Bishop of Rochester), Samuel Harsnet (Bishop of Chichester), Richard Neile (Bishop of Durham), William Laud (President of St. John's College, Oxford), and Richard Montague (one of the royal chaplains). It was not till several years later, in 1623, on the occasion of a Catholic book of controversy that Richard Montague ventured to give indirect expression to his feelings on the matter and so brought on himself a storm of Puritan protest. The book in question (which has been ascribed to Matthew Kellison, but is now recognized as the work of John Heigham, the publisher) was provocatively entitled *The Gagge of the New Gospel.* A second edition, published in the same year and 'augmented throughout the whole', bore the altered title of *The Gagge of the Reformed Gospell*; while later editions in the reign of Charles I changed *Gagge* to *Touchstone*. This was countered by Richard Montague in *A Gagg for the new Gospell?* in 1624.

137. [= 675] *The Gagge of the New Gospel: contayning a briefe abridgement of the errors of the Protestants of our time. With their refutation, by expresse texts of their owne English bible.* 1623   (Not in STC, AR 422)

(The second edition of 1623 has the altered title:

The Gagge of the Reformed Gospell. Briefly Discovering the errors of our time. With The Refutation by expresse textes of their owne approoved English Bible. The Second Edition; Augmented throughout the whole, by the Author of the first.   (STC 14907, AR 423, ERL 336))

138. *A Gagg for the new Gospell? No: A New Gagg for An Old Goose. Who would needes undertake to stop all Protestants mouths for ever, with 276. places out of their owne English Bibles. Or An Answere to a late Abridger of Controversies, and Belyar of the Protestants Doctrine. By Richard Mountagu. Published by Authoritie.* 1624   (STC 18038)

Though Montague was by no means polite to his Papist opponent, sneering at him as 'this Gagger', he ventured to express a moderate view on the vexed subject of Antichrist – with a glance at 'some' who were not so moderate. On page 74 of his work he says:

'Whether the Pope bee that Antichrist or not, the Church resolveth not, tendreth it not to be beleeved any way. Some I grant are very peremptory; too peremptory indeed, that he is . . . But they that are so resolute, peremptory, and certaine; let them answere for themselves, they are old enough: the Church is not tyed, nor any man that I know, to make good their private imaginations.'

Some of the Calvinist party were not slow in recognizing themselves in these words, or in answering for themselves against Montague. They were, in particular, Samuel Ward and John Yates (both of Cambridge), who did not hesitate (as he complained) to traduce him to the world 'for a Papist and an Arminian'. He accordingly defended himself against their (unpublished) criticism in a further book, published in 1625, with the title *Appello Caesarem* and a Dedication to the new King, Charles I. While defending himself against the charges of Popery and Arminianism, with the formal approbation of the Dean of Carlisle, Francis White, he came out even more into the open — with counter-charges against 'your Divines, the commonly called Calvinists', and specifically against their 'desperate doctrine of Predestination'. He recalled how Queen Elizabeth had refused to ratify the Lambeth Articles, and how Archbishop Bancroft had referred to them, when pressed by the Puritans at the Hampton Court Conference, as 'a Desperate doctrine'. As for the Church of Rome, he professed his readiness (with Hooker) to take it for 'a true, though not a sound Church of Christ' and 'a part of the Catholick, though not the Catholick Church'.

139. *Appello Caesarem. A Iust Appeale from Two Uniust Informers. By Richard Mountagu.* 1625   (STC 18030)

   (The book is divided into two parts:

   1. The First Part touching Arminianisme.

   2. The Second Part touching Popery.)

This work of Montague's immediately stirred up a Puritan hornets' nest, and an unprecedented number of indignant refutations, all of which came out in 1626. First came his former accusers: John Yates, with his *Ibis ad Caesarem* in English; and Samuel Ward, with a Latin sermon preached in St. Mary's Church, Cambridge, on the subject of *Gratia Discriminans*.

140. *Ibis ad Caesarem. Or A Submissive Appearance before Caesar. In Answer to Mr. Mountagues Appeale, in the points of Arminianisme and Popery, maintained and defended by him, against the Doctrine of the Church of England.* 1626   (STC 26083)

   (The author signs himself Iohn Yates at the end of his Dedication — also to King Charles.)

141. *Gratia Discriminans. Concio ad Clerum, Habita Cantabrigiae in Ecclesia B. Mariae, Ian. 12. 1625. Per Sa: Wardum Sae Theologiae Doctorem, Professorem Theologicum Dnae Margaretae, Collegiiq; Sidneiani in eadem Academia Praefectum.* 1626 (STC 25026)

The position of the Anglican divines attending the Synod of Dort was now clarified by their leader, George Carleton (now Bishop of Chichester) in *An Examination*, affirming that the doctrine there defined was perfectly consonant with that of the Anglican Church from Elizabethan times, whereas it is now the author of the Appeal who 'hath troubled the Church of England with strange Doctrines'. The Puritans merely differed from the main body of the Church in matters of discipline, not in doctrine. The Scots representative at Dort, Walter Balcanquhall (now Dean of Rochester), added *A Ioynt Attestation* to those of the other English representatives. This was published as an appendix to Carleton's *Examination*, though with a new title-page and pagination. It was also in this context that the above-mentioned *Suffragium Collegiale Theologorum* was published in the same year, to prove that the decisions at Dort corresponded to the orthodox position of the Anglican Church.

142. *An Examination of those things wherein the Author of the late Appeale holdeth the Doctrines of the Pelagians and Arminians, to be the Doctrines of the Church of England. Written by George Carleton Dr. of Divinitie, and Bishop of Chichester.* 1626 (STC 4633)

(A second edition came out in the same year, with the following addition to the original title:

The second Edition, Revised, and enlarged by the Author. Whereunto also there is annexed a Joynt Attestation, avowing that the Discipline of the Church of England was not impeached by the Synod of Dort. (STC 4634)

143. *A Ioynt Attestation, Avowing that the Discipline of the Church of England was not impeached by the Synode of Dort.* 1626 (STC 1239)

Still in the same year, the Puritan politician, Francis Rous, was inspired by a sermon of Balcanquhall to bring out his *Testis Veritatis*, to prove that the Calvinist doctrine of predestination was indeed that of the Anglican Church. Two other Puritan divines added their contributions: Anthony Wotton, with his *Dangerous Plot Discovered* against both of Montague's books; and Henry Burton, with his *Plea to An Appeale* against what he termed 'Pontifician Idolatry' — thereby entering on his troubled career of anti-episcopal agitation. Yet another answer is said to have come from the pen of the ageing Matthew Sutcliffe; but it was either not published or has not come down to us.

144. *Testis Veritatis. The Doctrine of King Iames our late Soveraigne of famous Memory. Of the Church of England. Of the Catholicke Church. Plainely shewed to bee one in the points of Predestination, Free-will, Certaintie of salvation. With a discovery of the Grounds both Naturall and Politicke of Arminianisme. By F. Rous.* 1626 (STC 21347)

145. *A Dangerous Plot Discovered. By a Discourse, Wherein is proved, That, Mr: Richard Mountague, in his two Bookes; the one, called A new Gagg; the other, A iust Appeale: Laboureth to bring in the faith of Rome, and Arminius: under the name and pretence of the doctrine and faith of the Church of England. A Worke very necessary for all them which have received the truth of God in love, and desire to escape errour. The Reader shall finde: 1. A Catalogue of his erroneous poynts annexed to the Epistle to the Reader. 2. A demonstration of the danger of them. cap. 21, num. 7 &c. pag. 178. 3. A list of the heads of all the Chapters contained in this Booke.* 1626 (STC 26003)

(The book is dedicated 'To the High and Honorable Court of Parliament' then in session, by way of a 'humble supplication'.)

146. *A Plea to An Appeale: Traversed Dialogue wise. By H. B.* 1626 (STC 4153)

(In his 'Preface to the Reader' the author refers with approval to the above-mentioned books by Carleton and Rous.)

In these writings Montague was criticized not only for his Arminianism and Popery, but also for a revival of what Burton called 'that wicked heresy of the Pelagians'. This accusation was now developed (still in 1626), to somewhat eccentric lengths, by an anonymous author, commonly identified as Daniel Featley, who had recently been associated with Francis White against the Jesuit John Percy (alias Fisher), but now took the opposite side in this controversy. He first published a book in Latin entitled *Parallelismus nov-antiqui erroris Pelagiarminiani*. To this he provided his own English translation, entitled *A Parallel: of Newe-old Pelagiarminian Error*, in which he lamented that 'Many men have too much free-will, and take to themselves too free liberty nowadayes to advance and maintaine free-will'. A second edition of this translation, without reference to the Latin original, came out shortly afterwards with the altered title, *Pelagius redivivus. or Pelagius Raked out of the Ashes*. Finally, before the year was out the same author brought out *A Second Parallel*, in which he proposed 'to take the line of Pelagius which is already brought downe to Arminius, and from Arminius to draw it out even to the Appealer' — despite the fact that 'the Appealer disclaimes all kinred or affinitie with Arminius'.

147. *Parallelismus nov-antiqui erroris Pelagiarminiani.* 1626 (STC 10734)

148. *A Parallel: of Newe-old Pelagiarminian Error.* 1626   (STC 10735)

>   (The second edition is entitled:

>   *Pelagius redivivus. or Pelagius Raked out of the Ashes by Arminius and his Schollers.* 1626   (STC 10736))

149. *A Second Parallel Together with A Writ of Error sued against the Appealer.* 1626.   (STC 10737)

i) *The Sabbatarian Controversy*

A somewhat subordinate controversy, that was carried on fitfully during the reign between Anglicans and Puritans, was on the question of the Sabbath: whether its observance was based on the Old Law as still binding on Christians, or on a custom instituted by the Church now liberated from the Old Law; and whether or not its observance was compatible with lawful pastimes and other forms of recreation. The Puritans naturally tended to regard it as derived from the Word of God in the Old Testament, and to insist on its strict observance — even to the extent of prohibiting even lawful forms of recreation. Already in the preceding reign of Elizabeth there had grown up a literature on this subject, without however arousing any theoretical opposition. As early as 1572 Humphrey Roberts had published *An earnest Complaint of divers vain, wicked and abused Exercises, practised on the Saboth day.* In 1579 John Northbrooke brought out *A Treatise wherein Dicing, Dauncing, Vaine plaies or Enterludes . . . commonly used on the Sabboth day, are reprooved.* In 1583 Philip Stubbes touched upon the same question in his famous *Anatomie of Abuses*, with a chapter on 'The Maner of sanctifying the Sabaoth in Ailgna' (or Anglia backwards). In the same year John Field published *A godly exhortation* on the occasion of an accident at Paris garden on a Sunday, when many people were killed as a divine warning to others 'concerning the keeping of the Sabboth day'. Subsequently, Richard Greenham wrote his 'Treatise of the Sabboth' against even lawful recreations on the Sabbath, and this was first published in his collected *Works* in 1599. None of these writings, however, met with any strong opposition until Nicholas Bownde brought out his *Doctrine of the Sabbath* in 1595, when his Puritan severity incurred the severe disapproval of Archbishop Whitgift in 1599 and of the Chief Justice, Sir John Popham, in 1600. The controversy arising out of his book began in the reign of James I, especially when it was brought out in a second edition under a new title, *Sabbathum Veteris et Novi Testamenti*, in 1606.

150. *The Doctrine of the Sabbath, Plainely layde forth, and soundly proved by testimonies both of holy Scripture, and also of olde and new ecclesiasticall writers. Declaring first from what things God would have*

us straightly to rest upon the Lords day, and then by what meanes we ought publikely and privatly to sanctifie the same: Together with the sundry abuses of our time in both these kindes, and how they ought to bee reformed. Divided into two Bookes, by Nicolas Bownde, Doctor of Divinitie. 1595   (STC 3436)

151. *Sabbathum Veteris et Novi Testamenti: Or The true doctrine of the Sabbath, held and practised of the Church of God, both before, and under the Law; and in the time of the Gospell: plainly laid foorth and soundly prooved by testimonies both of holie Scripture, and also of old and new ecclesiasticall Writers: Fathers and Councels, and lawes of all sorts, both Civill, Canon, and Common. Declaring first from what things God would have us straitly to rest upon the Lords day: and then by what meanes we ought publikely and privately to sanctifie the same. Together with the sundrie abuses of men in both these kindes: and how they ought to be reformed. Divided into two Bookes by Nicolas Bownd, Doctor of Divinitie: And now by him the second time perused, and inlarged with an interpretation of sundrie points belonging to the Sabbath: and a more ample proofe of such things, as have bin gainsaid, or doubted of by some Divines of our time: and a more full answere unto certaine obiections made against the same: with some other things not impertinent to this argument.* 1606   (STC 3437)

(The Preface 'ad pium lectorem' was contributed by Andrew Willet.)

Moreover, in between these two editions there appeared in 1604 yet another book with the same title, *The Doctrine of the Sabbath*, from the pen of another Puritan minister, George Widley. He, too, regarded pastimes as 'unlawfull upon the Sabbath', though he did not go so far as to maintain that 'al recreations at all times' were to be strictly prohibited. In his book, however, he makes no reference to Bownde or to any controversy on the subject.

152. *The Doctrine of the Sabbath, handled in foure severall Bookes or Treatises. The first of which intreateth of the day of rest. The second, of the duties of the day. The third, of the persons whom these duties concerne. And the fourth, the reasons used to perswade all persons to the practise of these duties upon that day. Written by G. W. Master of Arts, and Minister of the word of God in Portsmouth.* 1604 (STC 25610)

The first published statement of the Anglican position on this question, following on the practical measures taken by Archbishop Whitgift, came from the pen of Robert Loe, of Exeter, in a Latin treatise entitled *Effigiatio Veri Sabbathismi*, which appeared in 1605. Without naming his opponent,

Loe declared: 'Convivia publica diebus dicatis Deo nec ratio prohibet nec religio', and 'Non omnis Sabbatho condemnenda est animorum recreatio'. He significantly dedicated his work to King James.

153. *Effigiatio Veri Sabbathismi. Authore Roberto Loeo, Exoniensis Ecclesiae Thesaurario.* 1605   (STC 16692)

More sharply combative, however, was Thomas Rogers in the Preface to his above-mentioned treatise on *The Faith, Doctrine, and religion ... of England* (54), which appeared in 1607 after the second edition of Bownde's work. He strongly criticized the Puritans for having 'set up a newe Idoll, their Saint Sabbath', which he saw as a subtle stratagem to regain their influence without coming into open conflict with the State. But he claimed to have been 'the man, and the meanes that these Sabbatarian errors, and impieties are brought into light, and knowledge of the State'.

In that same year, 1607, however, the Puritan Sabbath was again upheld by John Sprint in his book of *Propositions*, though he made no explicit mention either of Bownde or of Rogers. He even claimed that the truth of the Christian Sabbath had been specially revealed by God 'unto this age of ours'.

154. *Propositions tending to prove the necessarie use of the Christian Sabbaoth, or Lords Day; and that it is commaunded unto us in Gods Word. Whereunto is added the Practice of that sacred Day, framed after the rules of the same Word. By Iohn Sprint, an unworthie Minister of the Gospell of Iesus Christ, at Thornebery in Gloucester shire.* 1607 (STC 23109)

This idea was taken to extreme lengths by John Traske, in asserting an even more general application of Jewish customs besides those of the Sabbath to Christians; and his followers were known as Traskites. His fancies were criticized by a Jesuit priest, John Falconer, in *A Briefe Refutation* in 1618. But two years later Traske himself retracted his teaching and published *A Treatise of Libertie from Iudaisme,*

155. *A Briefe Refutation of Iohn Traskes Iudaical and Novel Fancyes. Stiling himselfe Minister of Gods Word, imprisoned for the Lawes eternall Perfection, or Gods Lawes perfect Eternity. By B. D. Catholike Devine.* 1618   (STC 10675, AR 299, ERL 68)

156. *A Treatise of Libertie from Iudaisme, Or An Acknowledgement of true Christian Libertie, indited and published By Iohn Traske: Of late stumbling, now happily running againe in the Race of Christianitie.* 1620   (STC 24178)

Traske's ideas were, however, continued into the following reign by one Theophilus Braborne.

A practical outcome of the spread of the Puritan Sabbath, with its prohibition even of lawful recreation, was the controversial *Declaration* proclaimed by James I in 1618, after having experienced the effects of the Puritan teaching in the county of Lancashire. He particularly lamented how the Papists were profiting from it, as it enabled them to portray Protestantism as a joyless religion.

157. *The Kings Maiesties Declaration to His Subiects, Concerning lawfull Sports to be used.* 1618   (STC 8566)

This proclamation was later supported by the Regius professor of divinity at Oxford, John Prideaux, in a public Act of 1622. This was first published with other lectures in the original Latin in 1625, and later separately translated into English and published in 1634.

158. *Lectiones novem de totidem religionis capitibus praecipue hoc tempore controversis prout publice habebantur Oxoniae.* 1625   (STC 20356)

159. *The Doctrine of the Sabbath. Delivered in the Act at Oxon. Anno 1622. By Dr. Prideaux his Maiesties Professour for Divinity in that University. And now translated into English for the benefit of the common People.* 1634   (STC 20348)

A contemporary account of these controversies on the Sabbath was given a few years later, in the reign of Charles I, by Peter Heylin from the Anglican point of view.

160. *The History of the Sabbath. In Two Bookes. By Pet. Heylyn.* 1636 (STC 13274)

(He comes to the controversies of his time in Book II, chap. VIII.)

CHAPTER 2

Schisms among Separatists

a) *The Brownists and the Millenary Petition*

At the time of James' accession to the English throne, the small community of English separatists at Amsterdam – also known as Brownists or Barrowists – were united in a single group under Francis Johnson as pastor and Henry Ainsworth as teacher. Yet they had experienced many internal problems, which came to a climax when Francis Johnson excommunicated both his father and his brother George; and the latter published his *Discourse of some troubles* in the very year 1603. The new reign now encouraged them to hope, with the millenary petitioners in England, not so much for toleration as for their long desired reformation of the Church of England according to the pattern of God's Word. Johnson himself therefore set out for London to present a petition of their own to the King. This petition was drawn up in three different forms, together with a summary of their 'humble suit', and later published in 1604 in their *Apologie or Defence*. This was largely the work of Johnson himself, with the assistance of his friend Ainsworth (as the latter subsequently confessed in 1613). While incorporating their previous *Confession of faith* of 1596, it also presented their reply to those university doctors who had published their *Answere* to the Millenary Petition in 1604 together with some criticism of the 'absurd Brownists'.

161. *An Apologie or Defence of such true Christians As are commonly (but uniustly) called Brownists: Against such imputations as are layd upon them by the Heads and Doctors of the University of Oxford, In their Answer To the humble Petition of the Ministers of the Church of England, desiring reformation of certayne Ceremonies and abuses of the Church.* 1604   (STC 238)

(After the Dedication 'To the High and Mighty Prince, King Iames our Soveraigne Lord', there follows:

The Confession of faith of certayne English people, living in exile/ in the Low countreys.

The three petitions are entitled:

The humble petition of certayne poore Christians, your Maiestyes loyall
Subiects.
The humble Supplication of sundry your Maiesties faithfull Subiects,
who have now a long tyme ben constreyned eyther to live as exiles
abroad, or to endure other grievous persecutions at home, for bearing
witnesse to the truth of Christ against the corruptions of Antichrist yet
remayning.
To the Kings most excellent Maiesty. (14 Positions))

Not only did their petition prove unavailing, but after the return of their
representatives to Holland they had to suffer further attacks — of a similar
nature to George Johnson's *Discourse*. The first of these was Thomas White's
exposure of financial and sexual scandals within their community in his
Discoverie of Brownisme in 1605. White was one of those Puritans who had
joined the Brownists on the failure of the Millenary Petition, but found
himself out of sympathy with their ideals and their manner of life. Johnson
himself undertook to answer him in *An Inquirie*, published the following
year, in which he charged this apostate with 'despitefully reviling us, and
wickedly blaspheming the Name and tabernacle of the Lord'.

162. *A Discoverie of Brownisme: or, A briefe declaration of some of the*
     errors and abhominations daily practised and increased among
     the English company of the separation remayning for the present at
     Amsterdam in Holland. 1605   (STC 25408)

     (The name of Tho. White is signed at the end of the text. There is also
     an Appendix giving:

     Certaine briefe reasons prooving the use of the Lords prayer as a
     Prayer.)

163. *An Inquirie and Answer Of Thomas White his Discoverie of Brownisme.*
     By Francis Iohnson Pastor of the exiled English Church at Amsterdam
     in Holland. 1606   (STC 14662)

     (At the end of this work Johnson adds:

     An Answer to the Reasons alledged to prove the use of the Lords
     prayer as a Prayer.)

In the same year, however, there appeared yet another *Recantation of a*
Brownist by Peter Fairlambe — though in his criticism of 'these phanatick
spiritted Reformers' he looks back from Johnson's group to their
schismatical predecessors, Browne, Harrison, Barrow, Greenwood and Penry.
His book is valuable for three comprehensive lists: a) 'bookes in defence of

the pretended discipline which conteyne in them, the grounds of Brownisme'; b) 'bookes in defence of Brownisme, grounded upon the former'; c) 'bookes in defence of the Church of Englandes government, by Bishops, fully confuting all the former'. Johnson, however, apparently decided to leave this book unanswered.

164. *The Recantation of a Brownist. Or A Reformed Puritan. Written by one that hath altogether, bin led in the same erronious opinions for many yeeres together: And now since his conversion, hath measured the pretended holy Discipline, by Pastors, Doctors, Elders and Deacons, (which the Disciplinarian malecontents would obtrude upon our Church,) and hath found it far shorter, then the Discipline used either in the Primitive Church, or in this our Church of England: if all antiquitie be not reiected.* 1606   (STC 10668)

b) *Exodus from England*

The situation of Johnson's little group of separatists at Amsterdam was profoundly altered by the outcome of the Hampton Court Conference in 1604 and the consequent persecution of Puritans in England. In particular, two Puritan groups in Nottinghamshire and Lincolnshire — centring on John Smyth, of Gainsborough, and John Robinson, of Scrooby — came to the decision to emigrate with all their followers to the Low Countries for religious freedom. Smyth arrived there first, about the year 1607, with Thomas Helwys and other followers. After making contact with Johnson's group, he decided to maintain a separate identity and to form a second separatist Church at Amsterdam — especially as he was unable to agree with Johnson's views, in spite of having formerly studied under him at Cambridge. Their differences soon appeared in published form, as will be seen in due course. Meanwhile Robinson followed Smyth after an interval of about a year; and his scattered flock were eventually reunited in Amsterdam over the winter of 1608–9. But he, too, decided to keep separate from Johnson's group; and for the sake of peace he led his followers to Leyden, where they continued peaceably for many years — till some of them decided to sail westwards in search of a new home in New England.

This considerable exodus from England did not pass unnoticed at home. No fewer than eight publications came out in the years 1607–8 against this new wave of separation, mostly from former friends and acquaintances. A minor controversy now took place between Joseph Hall, the future Bishop of Exeter and adversary of Milton, and his former pupil, John Robinson. Hall had addressed an epistle 'To Mr. Smith, and Mr. Rob. Ring-leaders of the late separation; at Amsterdam', with the sub-heading: 'Setting foorth their iniurie done to the Church, the iniustice of their cause, and fearfulnesse of their offence, Censuring and advising them.' This epistle was soon after published in the second of two volumes of Hall's collected *Epistles*, as the first of the 'third decade'. To this Robinson responded with an anonymous *Answer to a censorious Epistle*, which was the immediate occasion of Hall's *Common Apologie of the Church of England* in 1610. It is only from Hall's work that we have Robinson's *Answer* in printed form.

165. *Epistles, The Second Volume: Conteining two Decads. By Ioseph Hall.*
    1608   (STC 12662)

166. *Answer to a censorious Epistle.* 1608?   (167)

167. *A Common Apologie of the Church of England: Against the uniust*
    Challenges of the over-iust Sect, commonly called Brownists. Wherein
    the grounds and Defences, of the separation are largely discussed:
    occasioned, by a Late Pamphlet published under the name, Of an
    Answer to a censorious Epistle, Which the Reader shall finde in the
    Margent. By J. H. 1610   (STC 12649)

Besides Hall, a number of Puritan ministers added their criticism of the separatists. The first was Edward James, whose *Retraite sounded* only remains as a title on the *Stationers' Register* for 1607 (*Arber* III, p. 153). In the same year John Sprint, of Gloucestershire, published his *Considerations* and *Arguments*, which are likewise known only from the reply they provoked from the pen of Henry Ainsworth. More impressive was the criticism of Smyth's former acquaintance, Richard Bernard, vicar of Worksop in Nottinghamshire, who published his *Disswasions from the Separatists Schisme* in 1608 against the Brownists – in two parts, of which the first had the title *Christian Advertisements,* while the second was the main part of the book. In the first part he makes a distinction which was later taken up by his opponents, between the 'Atheisticall Securitane', the 'Anabaptisticall Puritane', the 'carelesse Conformitant' and the 'preposterous Reformitant'. A third attack came from William Crashaw, father of the poet, who preached a *Sermon* at Paul's Cross on 14 February 1608, as well against the Papists as the Brownists, and published it the following May. In particular he asked four questions of the Brownists:

> 'Wherein are wee deadly or incurably wounded? . . . Are they
> healed? . . . If they be healed, and we still deadly wounded, . . . How
> have they sought, and sufficiently endevoured our healing? . . . If they
> will needes leave our Church, whither will they go?'

To these one may also add a couple of works by the former separatist, Henoch Clapham, who in 1608 returned to his attack on them with a pair of pamphlets in dialogue form, entitled *Errour On the Right Hand* and *Errour on the Left Hand.* In the former he directed his main criticism against the 'flyer', the Brownist who must needs take refuge in Holland; and in the latter, against the 'mal-content', the Puritan who remains within the Church of England while rejecting her ceremonies.

168. *A retraite sounded to certen brethren latelye seduced by the schismaticall Brownistes to forsake the Churche, wrytten by Edward Iames Master in the Artes and Mynister of Gods Worde.* 1607

169. *Considerations touching the poynts in difference, between the godly ministers and people of the Church of England, and the seduced brethren of the separation.* 1607?

170. *Arguments: That the best Assemblies of the present Church of England, are true visible Churches; That the Preachers in the best assemblies of England, are true ministers of Christ . . .* 1607?

(Both these works are known only from H. Ainsworth's refutation of them in his *Counterpoyson*, vid. inf.)

171. *Christian Advertisements and Counsels of Peace. Also disswasions from the Separatists schisme, commonly called Brownisme, which is set apart from such truths as they take from us and other Reformed Churches, and is nakedly discovered, that so the falsitie thereof may better be discerned, and so iustly condemned and wisely avoided. Published for the benefit of the humble and godlie lover of the trueth. By Richard Bernard, Preacher of Gods Word.* 1608   (STC 1927)

(Mention is made of several other books against the Brownists, as awaiting an answer:

'Master Gyshops booke, Master Bradshawes challenge, Doctor Allisons confutation, certaine Ministers reioynder to Master Smith.')

172. [= 546] *The Sermon preached at the Crosse, Feb, xiiij. 1607. By W. Crashawe, Batchelour of Divinitie, and preacher at the Temple; Iustified by the Authour, both against Papist, and Brownist, to be the truth: Wherein, this point is principally followed –, that the religion of Rome, as now it stands established, is worse then ever it was.* 1608 (STC 6027)

173. *Errour On the Right Hand, through a preposterous Zeale. Acted by way of Dialogue. Betweene Mal-content and Flyer. Flyer and Anabaptist. Anabaptist & Legatine-arrian. Flyer and Legatine-arrian. Flier, Legatine-arrian & Familist. Flyer and Familist. Flyer and Mediocritie. Whereto is also added, certaine Positions touching Church and Antichrist: as without the true holding thereof, it is impossible for a*

zelous soule, to avoyde either Schisme or Faction. By Henoch Clapham.
1608   (STC 5341)

174. *Errour on the Left Hand. Through a frozen Securitie: howsoever hot in*
opposition, when Satan so heats them. Acted by way of Dialogue.
Betw. Malcontent and Romanista. Malcontent Romanista & Libertinus.
Malcontent and Libertinus. Malcontent and Atheos. Malcontent and
Atheos. Malcontent & the good & bad spirit. Malcontent and
Mediocrity. By Henoch Clapham. 1608   (STC 5342)

In response to this chorus of criticism, Johnson merely reaffirmed his
position with regard to the Church of England, in the form of *Certayne*
Reasons and Arguments drawn for the most part from the recent writings of
'the silenced & deprived Ministers', particularly Bradshaw's *Twelve Argu-*
ments. But he attacked no individual author by name; and so his own book
remained unanswered – till Robinson took it up in another connection some
six years later. The refutation of the recent attacks he entrusted to his
assistant, Henry Ainsworth, who in the same year, 1608, brought out his
Counterpoyson to Sprint, Bernard and Crashaw together. In his 'fore-speech
to the Christian reader' he summed up these adversaries as follows:

'The Considerations and Arguments first answered, were written by
M. Spr. a Minister in Glocestershire; and in them (as I suppose) the
summ and weight of that which may be sayd for that church, is
comprised. Mr. Bernards book hath rather shew than weight of reason,
as the judicious reader may perceiv . . . Mr. Crashawes questions are
rather to stumble at, then to direct the ignorant.'

175. *Certayne Reasons and Arguments Proving that it is not lawfull to heare*
or have any spirituall communion with the present Ministerie of the
Church of England. 1608   (STC 14660)

176. *Counterpoyson. Considerations touching the points in difference*
between the godly Ministers & people of the Church of England, and
the Seduced brethren of the Separation. Arguments That the best
assemblies of the present Church of England are true visible Churches.
That the Preachers in the best assemblies of Engl. are true Ministers of
Christ. Mr Bernards book intituled The Separatists Schisme. Mr
Crashawes Questions propounded in his Sermon preached at the Crosse.
Examined and answered by H. A. 1608   (STC 234)

c) *The Impact of Anabaptism*

This controversy was now further complicated by divisions among the
separatists themselves; with the result that, while answering their many

critics in England, they also became engaged in criticism of one another. The main problem arose out of the developing views of John Smyth, who first published a statement of his separatist principles in 1607 in a book which only survives today in a single copy at York Minster: *Principles and Inferences*. It was not long, however, before he revised his position as here stated, as he came to realize his deep 'differences from the auncyent brethren of the Seperation', particularly with respect to 'the liturgy, presbytery, and treasury of the Church'. He agreed with Johnson in rejecting the validity of the Church and Ministry of England; but he now went further in rejecting the validity of their baptism. His new position he expressed in *The Differences of the Churches of the seperation*, published in 1608. He went on in the following year to publish his own refutation of Bernard's *Separatists Schisme*, while at the same time voicing his disagreement with Ainsworth's *Counterpoyson*. He entitled his book *Paralleles, Censures, Observations*.

177. *Principles and Inferences concerning The visible Church*. 1607   (Not in STC, printed in T. Whitley, ed. *Works of John Smyth*, I 249–268)

178. *The Differences of the Churches of the seperation: Contayning, A Description of the Leitourgie and Ministerie of the visible Church: Annexed: as a correction and supplement to a litle treatise lately published, bearing title: Principles and Inferences, concerning the visible Church, Published, 1. For the satisfaction of every true lover of the truth especially the Brethren of the Seperation that are doubtfull. 2. As also for the removing of an Uniust calumnie cast uppon the Brethren of the Seperation of the second English Church at Amsterdam. 3. Finally for the cleering of the truth: & the discovering of the mysterie of iniquitie yet further in the worship & offices of the Church. Divided into two parts 1. Concerning the Leitourgie of the Church 2. Concerning the Ministerie of the Church. which hath two sections One of the Eldership: Another of the Deacons office wherto apperteineth the Treasury. By Iohn Smyth.* 1608   (STC 22876)

179. *Paralleles, Censures, Observations. Aperteyning: to three several writinges. 1. A Lettre written to Mr. Ric. Bernard, by Iohn Smyth. 2. A Book intituled, The Seperatists Schisme published by Mr. Bernard. 3. An Answer made to that book called the Sep. Schisme by Mr. H. Ainsworth. Whereunto also are adioyned. 1. The said Lettre written to Mr. Ric. Bernard divided into 19. Sections. 2. Another Lettre written to Mr. A.S. 3. A third Lettre written to certayne Brethren of the Seperation. By Iohn Smyth.* 1609   (STC 22877)

Smyth was now answered by Ainsworth, as teacher of Johnson's congregation, in *A Defence of the Holy Scriptures*, which came out in 1609.

This was directed mainly against *The Differences*, but also in some measure against that part of the *Censures* which dealt with Ainsworth's *Counter-poyson*. In the next year Bernard responded to both his separatist critics in *Plaine Evidences*, referring to Smyth (for the first recorded time) as 'the Anabaptisticall Se-baptist'. For Smyth had now come to hold an anabaptist position, and had taken the extraordinary step of baptizing himself first and then his followers. Bernard also speaks of another answer to his book from Robinson, adding, 'if it had come in, hee should also have been replyed upon'. This work of Robinson's was, in fact, published soon after Bernard's, under the title, *A Iustification of Separation* — allowing the author to touch on his opponent's 'second treatise' (as he notes at the end of his *Iustification*).

180. *A Defence of the Holy Scriptures, Worship, and Ministerie, used in the Christian Churches separated from Antichrist: Against the challenges, cavils and contradictions of M. Smyth: in his book intituled The differences of the Churches of the Separation. Hereunto are annexed a few observations upon some of M. Smythes Censures; in his answer made to M. Bernard. By Henry Ainsworth, teacher of the English exiled Church in Amsterdam.* 1609   (STC 235)

181. *Plaine Evidences: The Church of England is Apostolicall, the seperation Schismaticall. Directed against Mr. Ainsworth the Separatist, and Mr. Smith the Se-baptist: Both of them severally opposing the Booke called the Separatists Schisme. By Richard Bernard, Preacher of the word of God at Worsop.* 1610   (STC 1958)

182. *A Iustification of Separation from the Church of England. Against Mr Richard Bernard his invective, intituled; The Separatists schisme. By Iohn Robinson.* 1610   (STC 21109)

(Robinson here ridicules Bernard for his 'rhyming Rhetorick'.)

The first clear manifesto by Smyth of his anabaptist position appeared in 1609 with the publication of his book, *The Character of the Beast*, in which he clarified 'the controversy now betwixt us, & the Seperation commonly called Brownists'. This arose out of a private correspondence between him and a former companion of his in Nottinghamshire, Richard Clifton, who was now a member of Johnson's congregation at Amsterdam. The main points of difference no longer concerned the organization of the Church, but the question of infant baptism and the rebaptism of converts from Antichrist.

183. *The Character of the Beast: or The False Constitution of the Church. Discovered in certayne passages betwixt Mr. R. Clifton and Iohn Smyth, concerning true Christian baptisme of New Creatures, or New*

> borne Babes in Christ: &nd false Baptisme of infants borne after the
> Flesh. Referred to two Propositions: 1. That infants are not to bee
> Baptised. 2. That Antichristians converted are to bee admitted into the
> true Church by baptisme. 1609   (STC 22875)

This challenge was first met in general terms (according to his usual custom)
by Francis Johnson, who published *A Brief Treatise* against the anabaptists,
without so much as naming Smyth or any of his friends, but leaving the
formal answer 'to such as are specially interessed and imployed therein'.
That answer came out the following year, 1610, from the pen of Clifton,
who was the obvious person to undertake the task, and who now published
The Plea for Infants. In the same year another answer to Smyth came from
London, with the title *A Description of the Church of Christ*, under the
initials I. H. (Joseph Hall?)

184. *A Briefe Treatise conteyning some grounds and reasons, against two
errours of the Anabaptists: 1. The one, concerning baptisme of infants.
2. The other, concerning anabaptisme of elder people. By Francis
Iohnson, Pastor of the exiled English Church at Amsterdam. 1609*
(STC 14659)

185. *The Plea for Infants and Elder People, concerning their Baptisme. Or A
Processe of the Passages betweene M. Iohn Smyth and Richard Clyfton;
Wherein, first is proved, That the baptising of Infants of beleevers, is an
ordinance of God. Secondly, That the rebaptising of such, as have been
formerly baptised in the Apostate Churches of Christians, is utterly
unlawful. Also, The reasons and obiections to the contrarie, answered.
Divided into two principal heads. I. Of the first Position, concerning the
baptising of infants. II. Of the second Position, concerning the
rebaptising of Elder people. 1610   (STC 5450)*

186. *A Description of the Church of Christ, with her peculiar Priviledges,
and also of her Commons, and Entercommoners. With some
Oppositions and Answers of Defence, For the maintenance of the Truth
which shee professeth: Against certaine Anabaptisticall and erronious
opinions, Verie hurtfull and dangerous to weake Christians. Maintained
and practised By one Master Iohn Smith, sometimes a Preacher in
Lincolneshire, and a Companie of English people with him now at
Amsterdam in Holland. Whome he hath there with himselfe Rebaptised.
By I. H. 1610   (STC 12567)*

It was about this time that a further schism took place among Smyth's
followers, whom he had persuaded to accept rebaptism with himself. For he
had soon afterwards heard of a group of Dutch anabaptists, known as New
Frisians or Waterlanders, and related to the Mennonites, from whom he
thought he should have sought rebaptism in the first place. Many of his

followers, led by Thomas Helwys, disagreed with him; while others joined him in seeking admission to the Dutch group, under Hans de Ries, though they were kept waiting till the time of his premature death (from consumption) in 1612. Meanwhile, Helwys took up his pen and issued a series of pamphlets to explain what came to be known as the General Baptist position – not only on the subject of infant baptism, but also on religious toleration and on the Arminian ideas which he and Smith had come to accept in contrast to the strict Calvinism of Robinson and the other separatists. (Hence the name 'General', referring to the general relevance of Christ's redemption for all men.) He first published *A Declaration of Faith* in twenty-seven articles in 1611. He then followed it up with his *Short and Plaine proofe* of the universality of Christ's redemption in the same year. In his Preface he refers to his 'little treatise/ intituled a Declaration off Faith, of English people remayning at Amsterdam' as providing a brief statement of what is now to be proved in more detail. He also published *An Advertisement* to the New Frisians, calling on Hans de Ries and his followers to admit their errors which had led his former leader astray.

187. *A Declaration of Faith of English People Remaining at Amsterdam in Holland: being the remainder of Mr. Smiths company. With an Appendix, giving an account of his sickness and death.* 1611   (York Minster)

188. *A Short and Plaine proofe by the Word/ and workes off God/ that Gods decree is not the cause off anye Mans sinne or Condemnation. AND That all Men are redeemed by Christ. As also That no Infants are Condemned.* 1611   (STC 13055)

(The Dedication is signed, Tho: Helwys.)

189. *An Advertisement or admonition, unto the Congregations, which men call the New Fryesers, in the lowe Countries, written in Dutche. And Publiched in Englis. Wherein is handled 4. Principall pointes of Religion. 1. That Christ tooke his Flesh of Marie, haveing a true earthly, naturall bodie. 2. That a Sabbath or day of rest, is to be kept holy everie First day of the weeke. 3. That ther is no Succession, nor privilege to persons in the holie thinges. 4. That Magistracie, being an holie ordinance of God, debarreth not anie from being of the Church of Christ. After these followes certen demandes concerning Gods decree of salvation and condemnation.* 1611   (STC 13053)

(There is some uncertainty about the correct reading of the name given here as 'New Fryesers'. It may also be read as 'New Fryelers', presumably for 'Free-willers', with reference to the Arminian ideas of this group; but there are no other instances of this word. What appears as an l in the title is probably a simple misprint for the long s.)

Helwys went on to publish *A Short Declaration of the mistery of iniquity* in 1612, with a criticism of 'The false profession of Brownisme' in general and of 'Some perticuler errors in Mr. Robinsons book of iustification of Separation' – considering that he recognizes the validity of baptism in a false Church. It was also under his auspices that there appeared about 1613 a book mentioned by Robinson as *The Confession of Fayth*, including *The Last Booke* of John Smyth (being a retractation of his errors), the *Confession* itself in one hundred articles, and an account of *The Life and Death of John Smith* by another of his followers, Thomas Piggott. Both books were answered two years later by Robinson, in his treatise *Of Religious Communion*, in which he complains of 'the unreasonable provocations of Mr. Thomas Helwis'.

190. *A Short Declaration of the mistery of iniquity.* 1612 (STC 13056)

191. *The confession of fayth published in certayn Conclusions by the remaynders of Mr Smithes company.* 1613? (York Minster)

(This is the title as given by Robinson, since the only surviving copy is without a title-page. The contents have the following titles:

The Last Booke, Called the retractation of his Errours, and the Confirmation of the Truth.

Propositions and Conclusions concerning true Christian Religion, containing A Confession of Faith of certain English people, living at Amsterdam.

The Life and Death of John Smith.)

192. *Of Religious Communion Private & Publique. With the silenceing of the clamours raysed by Mr. Thomas Helwisse agaynst our retayning the baptism receaved in Engl: & administering of Bapt: unto Infants. As also a Survey of the confession of fayth published in certayn Conclusions by the remaynders of Mr Smithes company. By Iohn Robinson.* 1614 (STC 21115)

d) *Further Schism among the Separatists*

It was partly owing to his reaction against the anabaptism of Smyth and his followers that Johnson came to adopt a position on the validity of baptism in the Roman Church and on the ultimate authority of elders in disputes, which was unacceptable to his colleague Henry Ainsworth and many of his congregation. This led to a schism between them in December 1610, and to his subsequent departure with some faithful followers for Emden in 1612. It was not till much later, however, that their difference of opinion was

expressed in published form. For the time being Johnson contented himself
with a direct presentation of his ideas in *A short Treatise*, in 1611, without
so much as a mention of Ainsworth — though he has a passing criticism of
the 'straunge opinions, and aberrations' of Smith (with reference to his
Differences and *Paralleles*).

193. *A short Treatise Concerning the exposition of those words of Christ,*
    Tell the Church, &c. Matt. 18.17. Written by Francis Iohnson, Pastor of
    the English exiled Church at Amsterdam in the low Countreyes. 1611
    (STC 14663)

Yet another source of disaffection among Johnson's little group was the
existence in Amsterdam of an English Reformed Church, as part of the
Dutch Reformed Church, of which John Paget had been minister since 1607.
In July 1611 four members of Johnson's group withdrew from him. One of
them, Christopher Lawne, returned to England and to communion with the
Anglican Church; while his three companions remained with Paget in
Amsterdam. The following year Lawne published *The Prophane Schisme of*
the Brownists in the name of himself and his companions, as yet another
exposure of what he called 'that impure Sect'. He followed this up in 1613
with *Brownisme turned The In-side out-ward*, to show up the contrast
between the profession and the practice of his former coreligionists,
remarking that 'the strictest in separation' were 'the leaudist in conversation'.

194. *The Prophane Schisme of the Brownists or Separatists. With the*
    Impietie, Dissensions, Lewd, and Abhominable Vices of that impure
    Sect. Discovered by Christopher Lawne, Iohn Fowler, Clement Sanders,
    Robert Bulward. Lately returned from the Companie of M. Iohnson,
    that wicked Brother, into the bosome of the Church of England, their
    true Mother. 1612   (STC 15324)

    (Reference is here made to 'a booke intituled, The first part of the
    hunting of the Fox', by 'master Thorpe a deacon of master Ainsworths
    Church', in which the notorious elder of Johnson's Church, Daniel
    Studley, is 'traced up and downe'. This was Giles Thorpe, whose book
    was probably never published, though it is also mentioned in other
    writings of the time.)

195. *Brownisme turned The In-side out-ward. Being a Paralell betweene the*
    Profession and Practise of the Brownists Religion. By Christopher
    Lawne, lately returned from that wicked Separation. 1613
    (STC 15323)

    (Other books mentioned, which are not otherwise known, are 'Cut.
    Huttons worke. Generation of slanders. Mr. Halies Intrustion. Saund.

Artic. proph. schism . . . Ainsworths answer to Mr. Stone. Iohn
Iohnsons 14 Article.')

The first of these books was, however, immediately repudiated by Lawne's
companions, who were outraged to find him misusing their names on his
title-page. They published a *Declaration,* dissociating themselves from his
publication, while however admitting: 'Such a booke indeed we sent by one
of us to be printed there (in London), but in the publishing thereof great
iniury hath beene done unto us.' This they prefixed to another book, *A
Shield of Defence*, which was published in 1612 to defend the Puritan
Thomas Brightman's recent *Revelation of the Apocalyps* (1611) against the
criticisms of Jean de l'Ecluse (or Delacluse), a French elder of Ainsworth's
Church at Amsterdam. These criticisms were contained in a book entitled *An
Advertisement*, which has survived in a unique copy in the Congregational
Library, London. Its author (according to the *Shield*) 'labours to conclude
their separation from certaine speeches of Mr. Brightman, testifying against
the corruptions of the church of England.' Brightman's book will come up
for consideration later, in connection with other commentaries on the
Apocalypse (454).

196. *An Advertisement to Everie Godly Reader of Mr. Thomas Brightman
his book. namely, A Revelation of the Apocalyps. In which advertisement is shewed how corruptly he teacheth, that notwithstanding all the
sinns & abhominations that are in the Church of England, and by him
shewed, yet that it is blasphemous to separate from it.* 1612

(The unique copy is in the Congregational Library, London. It has been
reprinted in *Transactions of the Congregational Historical Society*, VI
(1913–15), pp. 251–64)

197. *A Shield of Defence against the Arrowes of Schisme Shot abroad by
Iean de L'escluse in his advertisement against Mr. Brightman. Here unto
is prefixed a declaration touching a booke intituled, The prophane
schisme of the Brownistes. By Iohn Fowler, Clement Saunders, Robert
Bulwarde.* 1612   (STC 11212)

Writing of the official reply to Lawne's book on behalf of the separated
brethren, however, fell to Richard Clifton, as teacher. He now published *An
Advertisement* against Lawne in 1612, comparing his book to White's
scurrilous *Discoverie of Brownisme*, which had been sufficiently answered by
Johnson in 1606. As Lawne had made much of the dissensions leading to
Ainsworth's withdrawal from the group in 1610, Clifton presented some of
the documents relating to that affair, including 'A Copie of the writing,
touching the division made among us, which was sent to a friend in England,
By Mr. H.A.' and 'An Answer to the writing and exceptions aforesaid, sent

to the same partie, by Mr. Fr. Io.' This had the effect of drawing Ainsworth into the controversy; and he responded with *An Animadversion* in 1613, in which he made public for the first time his views on the unfortunate schism between Johnson and himself.

198. *An Advertisement concerning a book lately published by Christopher Lawne and others, against the English exiled Church at Amsterdam. By Richard Clyfton Teacher of the same Church.* 1612 (STC 5449)

199. *An Animadversion to Mr Richard Clyftons Advertisement. Who under pretense of answering Chr. Lawnes book, hath published an other mans private Letter, with Mr Francis Iohnsons answer therto. Which letter is here iustified; the answer therto refuted: and the true causes of the lamentable breach that hath lately fallen out in the English exiled Church at Amsterdam, manifested, By Henry Ainsworth.* 1613 (STC 209)

A new development in this controversy took place with the publication in 1614 of an anonymous examination of Johnson's *Reasons*, which had been published six years before. This work was entitled *The Unreasonablenesse of the separation*, as though in answer to Robinson's *Iustification of Separation* (though, in fact, no mention is made of the book); and its authorship has been attributed to William Bradshaw, on whose *Twelve Arguments* Johnson had freely drawn for his *Reasons*. At the same time, the author warned his readers in the Preface that 'It is not Mr. Iohnson that is dealt with alone, for change the name onely, and put in Mr. Ainsworth, or any such.' The application of all this to Robinson came in a brief appendix entitled *A Manuduction for Mr. Robinson*, in which some have seen the hand of William Ames, appealing to the separatist leader to return to public communion with the Anglican Church, seeing how ready he was to accept private communion.

200. *The Unreasonablenesse of the separation. Made apparant, by an examination of Mr. Iohnsons pretended reasons, published an. 1608. Wherby hee laboureth to iustifie his schisme from the Church Assemblies of England.* 1614 (STC 3532)

201. *A Manuduction for Mr. Robinson, and such as consent with him in privat communion, to lead them on to publick. Breifly comprized in a letter written to Mr. R. W.* 1614 (STC 3532)

(This appendix has a separate title-page and pagination.)

Robinson, however, remained unconvinced by the arguments or persuasions of the other, whether Bradshaw or Ames, and responded in 1615 with *A Manumission to a Manuduction*, to clarify his stand on private and public communion – which was admittedly less uncompromising than that of Johnson or Ainsworth. This provoked an immediate rejoinder from his anonymous adversary, in *A Second Manuduction*; and there this little controversy came to an end.

202. *A Manumission to a Manuduction, or Answer to a letter inferring publike communion in the parrish assemblies upon private with godly persons there. By Iohn Robinson.* 1615   (STC 21111)

203. *A Second Manuduction for Mr. Robinson. Or the confirmation of the former, in an answer to his manumission.* 1615   (STC 3520)

At least, it came to an end between Robinson and his anonymous adversary; but Paget soon stepped in to urge the latter's main contention, and to call for a satisfactory reply to *The Unreasonablenesse of the separation*. He entitled his book, *An Arrow Against the Separation of the Brownists* – with a possible reflection on an earlier book by Ainsworth against the 'pseudo-catholik Church', entitled *An Arrow against Idolatrie* (1611), to which he makes allusion. Still, he waited three years before publishing it in 1618, to see if Robinson would make any reply. It is an interesting work, for the insight it reveals into all these controversies and into the shades of difference between the separatist groups in Holland:

> 'Of the Brownists also there are sundry sects: Some separate from
> the Church of England for corruptions; and yet confesse both it &
> Roome also to be a true Church, as the followers of Mr. Iohnson:
> Some renounce the Church of England as a false Church; and yet allow
> private communion with the godly therein, as Mr. Robinson and his
> followers: Some renounce all Religious communion both publique
> and private with any member of that Church whosoever, as Mr.
> Ainsworth and such as hearken unto him, being deepest and stiffest in
> their Schisme.'

As for his own group in the Reformed Church, Paget says:

> 'Our Church is a distinct body from the Church of England . . . (yet)
> the members of our Church do not renounce the communion thereof
> but communicate with them as occasion is given.'

204. *An Arrow Against the Separation of the Brownists. Also an Admonition touching Talmudique & Rabbinical allegations. By Iohn Paget.* 1618   (STC 19098)

Hitherto, despite the exchange between Clifton and Ainsworth, there had been no published confrontation between Johnson and his former assistant. Rather, they seemed to be exercising a certain restraint towards each other, out of regard for their former collaboration. In 1617, however, they at last came into collision over a book by Johnson, entitled *A Christian Plea*, in which he attempted to clarify his stand in relation to the other groups of separatists – namely, the Anabaptists, the Arminians, and those of the Reformed Church. This book contained three treatises, against three different groups, none of them directly involving that of Ainsworth; but in his preface 'To the Christian Reader' he mentioned the latter on two occasions. On the one hand, he commends him for having once written well – 'if he could have kept unto it' – 'in his plea against Mr. Smyth, about the Ministerie, worship, & government of the Church', i.e. in his *Defence of Holy Scriptures*. On the other, he accuses him of having published 'sundrie manifest untruths' in his *Animadversion*. This was enough to elicit a strongly worded *Reply to a Pretended Christian Plea* from Ainsworth in 1618 (though it was not actually published till 1620); for he considered that his old pastor had become too indulgent towards the Church of Rome. There the controversy between them ended, as Johnson himself died in 1618.

205. *A Christian Plea Conteyning three Treatises. I. The first, touching the Anabaptists, & others mainteyning some like errours with them. II. The second, touching such Christians, as now are here, commonly called Remonstrants or Arminians. III. The third, touching the Reformed Churches, with whom my self agree in the faith of the Gospel of our Lord Iesus Christ. Made by Francis Iohnson, Pastour of the auncient English Church, now sojourning at Amsterdam in the Low Countreyes.* 1617 (STC 14661)

206. *A Reply to a Pretended Christian Plea for the Antichristian Church of Rome: published by Mr. Francis Iohnston a^o 1617. Wherin the weakness of the sayd Plea is manifested, and arguments alleaged for the Church of Rome, and Baptisme therein, are refuted; By Henry Ainsworth. Anno 1618.* 1620 (STC 236)

Finally, mention may be made of a book that appeared in 1617 against the Brownists in general, though it seems to have been prompted by Ainsworth's *Counterpoyson* which had come out a decade earlier. This was *A Treatise of the Church* by the former Puritan exorcist, now conforming minister, John Darrell. In it he claimed to have answered the Brownist arguments proving the Anglican Church to be a false Church, particularly 'those which lately and at large are by M. Ainsworth enforced against us in his Counterpoyson.' But no reason was given for the long delay of publication. Even when the book was published, it was ignored – and perhaps unnoticed – by his opponents.

207. *A Treatise of the Church. Written against them of the Separation, commonly called Brownists. Wherein the true Doctrine of a visible*

> *Church is taught, and the Church of England, proved to be a true*
> *Church. The Brownists false doctrine of the visible Church is*
> *convinced: their shamefull perverting of the holy Scriptures discovered,*
> *their Arguments to prove the Church of England a false Church*
> *answered.* 1617   (STC 6286)

e) *Anabaptism in England*

About the time of Smyth's death in 1612 it was decided by Thomas Helwys
and his colleague John Murton that the time had come for them to return to
England, despite the great danger of persecution. It was, in fact, not long
after their return that Helwys was arrested and put in prison, where he died
some time later, before 1616. His place was taken by John Murton, who also
continued his literary labours and elicited responses from both Robinson and
Ainsworth. While himself a prisoner in London, Murton wrote to the pastor
of a separatist group in Colchester, John Wilkinson, in the hope of
establishing relations with him; but the response was unfavourable.
Originally written in 1613, this response was eventually published in 1646,
under the title of *The Sealed Fountaine*. It was presented as 'A reproof of
some things written by John Morton, and others of his company and
followers, to prove that Infants are not in the state of condemnation, And
that therfore they are not to be baptised'.

208. *The Sealed Fountaine opened to the Faithfull, and their Seed. Or, A*
     short Treatise, shewing, that some Infants are in the state of Grace, and
     capable of the seales, and others not. Being the chief point, wherein the
     Separatists doe blame the Anabaptists. By John Wilkinson, Prisoner at
     Colchester, against John Morton, Prisoner at London. 1646
     (Wing W2243)

In addition to their Anabaptist and Arminian doctrines, these early
Baptists were among the first to call for religious toleration — not only for
themselves, but for all denominations, even the Papists. This ideal had been
touched on in Helwys' *Mistery of iniquity* in 1612, and in Smyth's
Confession of fayth about the same time. But it was developed more fully in
a couple of books two or three years later. The first to appear was Leonard
Busher's *Religious Peace* in 1614, in the form of a supplication to King and
Parliament, presenting 'certayne reasons against perseqution'. Little is known
of the author, save that he represented a third group of Anabaptists, separate
from those of Smyth and Helwys; but his work is said to be 'the earliest
known publication pleading for full liberty of conscience' (Masson, *Milton*,
iii. 102). This was followed in 1615 by Murton's own *Obiections: Answered*
by way of Dialogue. It was also from Murton's group that *A Most Humble*
Supplication was presented to the King and Parliament, and (presumably)

published in 1620. The issue did not really become controversial at this time, though it was partly developed out of the previous controversy between Helwys and Robinson. For the pleas for toleration were simply ignored by those to whom they were addressed.

209. *Religious Peace Or A reconciliation, between princes & Peoples, & Nations (by Leonard Busher: of the County of Gloucester, of the towne of Wotton, and a Citticen, of the famous and most honorable Citty London, and of the second right worshipfull Company) Supplicated (unto the hygh and mighty King of great Brittayne: etc: And to the Princely and right Honorable Parliament) with all loyalty, humility and carefull Fidelity.* 1614 (STC 4189)

210. *Obiections: Answered by way of Dialogue, wherein is proved By the law of God: By the Law of our Land: And by his Maties many testimonies That no man ought to be persecuted for his religion, so he testifie his allegeance by the Oath, appointed by Law.* 1615 (STC 13054 — where it is attributed to Helwys)

(A second edition was published in 1662 under the altered title, *Persecution for Religion Judged and Condemn'd.*)

211. *A Most Humble Supplication of many of the Kings Maiesties Loyal Subiects ready to testify all civil obedience by the Oath of Allegiance, or otherwise, and that of Conscience; who are persecuted (only for differing in religion) contrary to divine and human testimonies.* 1620

(The only surviving form of this *Supplication* was published in 1662, where it is described as 'presented, 1620'.)

It was in the aftermath of the Synod of Dort that Murton finally came into open conflict with Robinson. In *A Discription of what God hath Predestinated*, published in 1620, he developed his ideas on predestination, on election and reprobation, on falling from grace, on free will, on the original state of man, and on Christ's redemption. He also added an appendix, replying to a small pamphlet (no longer extant) by John Robinson, 'who laboureth to prove, that none may baptise but Pastors or Elders of a Church'.

212. *A Discription of what God hath Predestinated Concerning Man, In his Creation, Transgression, & Regeneration. As also an Answere to Iohn Robinson, touching Baptisme.* 1620 (STC 6773)

(This may have been the original edition of a book entitled *Truth's Champion*, mentioned by Thomas Grantham in his *Christianismus Primitivus* of 1678 as in its third edition. Its full title reveals contents similar to those of *A Description*:

Truth's Champion: Wherein are made plain these Particulars, That Christ died for all Men, Of Predestination, of Election, Free-will, Falling-away, Of Baptism, of Original-Sin. The Copy of this Book was found hid in an Old Wall near Colchester in Essex. The third Edition.)

It was not, however, till four years later that Robinson brought out his reply. Meanwhile, in 1623, there appeared no fewer than three works against the English Anabaptists. Two were of a more general nature: I. P.'s *Anabaptisme's Mysterie of Iniquity Unmasked* (with an implicit reference to Helwys' book of 1612), and Edmund Jessop's *Discovery of the Errors of the English Anabaptists.* Ainsworth, too, wrote *A Censure upon a Dialogue of the Anabaptists*, which remained unfinished at his death in 1622 but was published by his followers a year later. Finally, in 1624 Robinson came out with his *Defence of the Doctrine propounded by the Synode at Dort*, and an attack on the 'new Gospell of Anabaptistry and Free-will'. This was followed in the same year by yet another answer to Murton by the Puritans, Robert Cleaver and John Dod, entitled *The Patrimony of Christian Children.*

213. *Anabaptisme's Mysterie of Iniquity Unmasked.* 1623   (STC 19068)

(This was directed against an unidentified letter, expressing opinions like those of Murton, dated May 1622.

I. P. is variously identified as John Preston (Dexter) and John Paget (Burrage).)

214. *A Discovery of the Errors of the English Anabaptists. As also an Admonition to all such as are led by the like spirit of error. Wherein is set downe all their severall and maine points of error, which they hold. With a full answer to every one of them severally, wherein the truth is manifested. By Edmond Iessop who sometime walked in the said errors with them.* 1623   (STC 14520)

215. *A Censure upon a Dialogue of the Anabaptists, Intituled, A Description of what God hath Predestinated concerning man. &c. By Henry Ainsworth.* 1623   (STC 226)

(This work was republished in 1644 with the altered title:

A Seasonable Discourse, or, A Censure upon a Dialogue of the Anabaptists, Intituled, A Description of what God hath Predestinated concerning Man, Is tryed and examined, Wherein these seven points are handled & Answered, viz. 1. Of Predestination 2 Of Election 3 Of Reprobation 4 Of Falling away 5 Of Freewill 6 Of Originall sinne 7 Of Baptizing Infants. By Henry Ainsworth. 1644   (Wing A818)

216. *A Defence of the Doctrine Propounded by the Synode at Dort: against*

John Murton and his Associates, in a Treatise intuled; A Description
what God, &c. With the Refutation of their Answer to a Writing
touching Baptism. By Iohn Robinson. 1624   (STC 21107a)

217. *The Patrimony of Christian Children: Or, A Defence of Infants*
Babtisme prooved to be consonant to the Scriptures and will of God
(against the erroneous positions of the Anabaptists). By Robert Cleaver,
with the ioynt consent of Mr. Iohn Dod. 1624   (STC 5389)

(In his Preface Cleaver speaks of 'the assaults especially of the Papists,
the Arminians, the Familists, and the Anabaptists' in these days.)

By way of postscript to these separatist controversies, there appeared in
1630 a composite volume containing unpublished works of Ainsworth and
Robinson, reflecting in different ways on their past troubles. The first item
consisted of *Certain Notes* of Ainsworth's last sermon in 1622, appealing for
unity among brethren. The second was *An Appeale on Truths Behalf*,
written by Robinson in 1624 as 'The judgment of the Church of Leyden
upon the present differences occasioned by our opposites themselves'.
Before he, too, died in 1625, he also republished an English translation of *A*
Iust and Necessarie Apologie, which he had previously brought out in Latin
in 1619.

218. *Certain Notes of M. Henry Aynsworth his Last Sermon. Taken by pen*
in the publique delivery by one of his flock a little before his death.
Anno 1622. Published now at last by the said writer, as a love token of
remembrance to his brethren, to inkindle their affections to prayer,
that scandalls (of manie years continuance) may be removed, that are
barrs to keep back manie godly wise and judicious from us, wherby we
might grow to farther perfection again. 1630   (STC 227)

219. *An Appeale on Truths Behalf.* 1630   (STC 21107)

(This is without a title-page, being a continuation from the above with
consecutive pagination and only an inner title. It is signed: Iohn
Robinson Leyden Sept. 18. 1624.)

220. *Apologia Iusta, et Necessaria Quorundam Christianorum, aeque*
contumeliose ac communiter dictorum Brownistarum sive
Barrowistarum. per Iohannem Robinsonum Anglo-Leidensem, suo &
Ecclesiae nomine, cui præficitur. 1619

221. *A Iust and Necessarie Apologie of certain Christians, no lesse*
contumeliously then commonly called Brownists or Barrowists. By Mr.
Iohn Robinson, Pastor of the English Church at Leyden, first published
in Latin in his and the Churches name over which he was set, after

translated into English by himself, and now republished for the speciall and common good of our own Countrimen. 1625   (STC 21108)

(No earlier edition of this English translation is extant.)

f) *Scattered Controversies*

There yet remain a few more controversies involving the separatists not so much with one another as with a common adversary. In the first place, the adversary they all had in common was the Church of Rome, which they all regarded as Antichrist — though there were degrees in their opposition. Yet they were rarely in direct conflict with that Church, since their immediate quarrel was with the Church of England, and then with their schismatical opponents in Holland. Ainsworth, however, published two works against the Papists: one on a general level against 'this pseudocatholik Church or false ecclesiastical Monarchie', entitled *An Arrow against Idolatrie* (1611); and the other against an individual Catholic priest of the same name as himself, entitled *The Trying out of the Truth*. The latter work was a controversy in one volume, consisting of 'certayn Letters or Passages between Iohn Aynsworth and Henry Aynsworth' (though unrelated to each other); and it was put together by one E. P., who professed a certain impartiality in his Preface 'to the Christian reader':

> 'And whereas the controverters are so different in iudgment, and yet both of them for conscience sake suffer affliction, being separated from the Ch: of Eng: the one, to the practise of a Romane Catholik; the other to a way, thereunto most opposite; and both of them being leaders & men of note, in their so much different religions . . . .'

222. *An Arrow against Idolatrie. Taken out of the quiver of the Lord of hosts. By H. Ainsworth.* 1611   (STC 221)

223. *The Trying out of the Truth: begunn and prosequuted in certayn Letters or Passages between Iohn Aynsworth and Henry Aynsworth; the one pleading for, the other against the present religion of the Church of Rome. The chief things here handled, are: 1. Of Gods word and scriptures, whither they be a sufficient rule of our faith. 2. Of the Scriptures expounded by the Church; and of unwritten traditions. 3. Of the Church of Rome, whither it be the true Catholike Church, and her sentence to be received, as the certayn truth. Published for the good of others by E. P. in the yeare 1615.*   (STC 240)

Another controversy in which Johnson was briefly engaged was with a former Catholic priest, John Carpenter, who had reverted to the Church of

England. This was on the vexed question of the use of fixed prayers in the liturgy, particularly the Lord's Prayer; Johnson (as a follower of Barrowe) maintaining the negative, while Carpenter (as an Anglican and a former Catholic priest) maintained the affirmative. After carrying on their dispute in letters (in Latin), they published their respective contributions in a single volume in 1610.

224. *Quaestio de Precibus et leiturgiis, ab hominibus praescriptis: Utrum in cultu divino licitum sit, eiusmodi leiturgiis uti, illasque pro precibus nostris ad Deum ex libro legere et recitare; an non: Duabus epistolis tractata: Quarum altera scripta erat, Per Iohannem Carpenterum Anglum, nuper Ecclesiae Romanae, nunc Anglicanae, Presbyterum. Altera, Per Franciscum Iohnsonum, Pastorem Ecclesiae Anglo-Amsterodamensis.* 1610

In two further unrelated controversies the separatists endeavoured to refute particular attacks by Anglican ministers (of Puritan tendencies) against their position. In each case, oddly enough, the book attacking them is no longer extant, and only the separatist reply remains. John Yates, of Norwich, had written a book entitled *Monopolie*, against the separatist use of 'prophesying', in which he also criticized Robinson for his failure to answer Hall's *Common Apologie of the Church of England* (1610). Robinson, therefore, replied in 1618 with a book entitled *The Peoples Plea* (with an echo of Johnson's *Christian Plea* of the preceding year).

225. *The Peoples Plea for the Exercise of Prophesie. Against Mr. Iohn Yates his Monopolie. By Iohn Robinson.* 1618   (STC 21115a)

(The inner title is as follows:

An Answere to the Arguments laid down by Mr. Iohn Yates, Preacher in Norwich, to prove ordinary Prophesie in publick, out of office, unlawfull: answered by Iohn Robinson.)

About the same time, a minister in Essex, Thomas Drakes (or Draxe), published his *Ten Counter-Demands* in belated response to the 'Seven Questions' which Francis Johnson had appended as long ago as 1595 to his *Treatise of the Ministery*. On behalf of 'the poore Separatists' one of Johnson's group, William Euring, published *An Answer* in 1619.

226. *Seven Questions which have ben propounded to divers of the Ministers of these assemblyes, with request that they would aunswer them directly and syncerely from the Scriptures. Which also still is desired at theyr hands.* 1595

(Appendix to *A Treatise of the Ministery of the Church of England.* (STC 13464).

227. Αντερωτηματα *Thomae Draks. Ten Counter-Demands Propounded to those of the Separation, (or English Donatists) to be directly, and distinctly answered.* c.1618—19   (STC 7186a)

228. *An Answer to the Ten Counter Demands propounded by T. Drakes, Preacher of the Word at H. and D. in the County of Essex. By Wil. Euring.* 1619   (STC 10567)

Another small controversy between the English separatists in Holland and an individual in Norwich was not published till many years later in 1657, as *A Seasonable Treatise for This Age.* 'One Mr. Woolsey prisoner in Norwich' had written a letter to Johnson's group, on a particular point concerning the New Law; and Francis Johnson as pastor, with his teacher Henry Ainsworth and other elders, felt it necessary to refute the opinions expressed in the letter. The date is given as 7 December 1602.

229. *A Seasonable Treatise for This Age: Occasioned by a Letter written by one Mr. Woolsey prisoner in Norwich, to the then-exiled Church at Amsterdam; in which he endeavours to prove it unlawful to eat blood, things strangled, and things offered to idols, now in the times of the Gospel. Which Letter is by the consent of the said Church answered; the Grounds and Reasons therein, examined and refuted; and the contrary thereunto proved from Scripture; By Francis Iohnson Pastor, Henry Ainsworth Teacher, Daniel Studley, Stanshal Mercer Elders Of the same Church. Written long since, but never published till now.* 1657   (Wing S2245)

Also, on certain minor matters of Biblical exegesis there arose a controversy between Ainsworth, who was no mean Scriptural scholar, and the eccentric Hugh Broughton. The latter, though fiercely critical of the Anglican establishment in questions of Biblical interpretation, never joined the separatists, though he published most of his criticisms from the safety of the Low Countries. Early in James' reign, he published *An Advertisement of Corruption* in the official attitude to Biblical translation; and this apparently involved him in an exchange of correspondence with Ainsworth, which was published by one F. B. in 1605 under the title of *Certayne Questions* — one of them concerning 'The forme of Prayer, commonly called the Lords prayer'.

230. *An Advertisement of Corruption in our Handling of Religion. To the Kings Majestie. By Hugh Broughton.* 1604   (STC 3843)

231. *Certayne Questions Concerning 1. Silk, or wool, in the High Priests Ephod. 2. Idol temples, commonly called Churches. 3. The forme of Prayer, commonly called the Lords prayer. 4. Excommunication, &c.*

Handled between Mr Hugh Broughton remayning of late at Amsterdam
in the Low countreyes. And Mr Henry Ainsworth Teacher of the exiled
English Church at Amsterdam aforesayd. 1605   (STC 3848)

Finally, the separatists were also involved in a minor controversy with the
Family of Love. The continuing existence of the Family into the reign of
James is attested by *A Supplication* which they drew up and presented to
the King 'for grace and favour'. This was examined and refuted by an
anonymous author, presumably an Anglican, in 1606. Two years later
Ainsworth also came out against the Familists, in a refutation of *An Epistle*
sent unto two daughters of Warwick from H.N. (who had founded the
Family half a century earlier). On this point at least the Anglican and the
separatist were perfectly at one, in rejecting the Family as 'a vile secte' and a
fit religion 'for Atheists and carnal hypocrites'.

232. *A Supplication of the Family of Love (said to be presented into the*
Kings royall hands, knowen to be dispersed among his Loyall Subiectes)
for grace and favour. Examined, and found to be derogatorie in an hie
degree, unto the glorie of God, the honour of our King, and the
Religion in this Realme both soundly professed & firmly established.
1606   (STC 10683)

233. *An Epistle sent unto two daughters of Warwick from H. N. The oldest*
Father of the Familie of Love. With a refutation of the errors that are
therin; by H. A. 1608   (STC 18553)

CHAPTER 3

Catholics and the King

a) *Catholic Petitions*

The Catholics, no less than the Puritans, were filled with renewed hope at the accession of James in 1603. The more sanguine among them even looked for an immediate reconversion of England, as it were under a second Constantine; while the more realistic at least expected some measure of toleration and the suspension of the cruel penal laws that had been passed against them by the successive parliaments of Elizabeth. After all, James was the son of the Catholic Mary Stuart, who had been unjustly sentenced to death by her royal cousin in 1587. He was also known to be out of sympathy with the presbyterians, under whom he had suffered much in Scotland. In fact, though they did not know it, James had entered into secret negotiations with Pope Clement VIII during the last years of Elizabeth's reign, in the hope of securing Catholic support for his claim to the English succession. This was subsequently revealed by Cardinal Bellarmine, when he came to write against the King in 1608 on the Oath of Allegiance. It had been this hope of toleration which had largely motivated the 'appellant' priests in their controversy against the Jesuits during the last years of Elizabeth's reign; but they had met with an unexpected rebuff from the Queen in her last royal proclamation, dated 5 November 1602. At that time a Catholic priest, Richard Broughton, had addressed *An Apologicall Epistle* (in 1601) to the lords of the Privy Council, appealing for an 'attonement', which, he said, would be 'the most honourable and renowned thing our age hath seene'. This *Epistle* he intended as an introduction to a larger work, entitled *The Resolution of Religion*, whose *First Part* he published in 1603 'against all Atheists, and Epicures'. He reserved his more controversial material for a second part, which never appeared as such. He was, however, immediately answered by the Puritan Andrew Willet in *An Antilogie*. The latter appealed to the King 'as another Constantine, to reconcile the Church-ministers', who had presented the Millenary Petition, but deplored any measure of toleration for the Catholics.

234. *An Apologicall Epistle: Directed to the right honorable Lords, and others of her Maiesties privie Counsell. Serving aswell for a Praeface to a Booke entituled, A Resolution of Religion: as also, containing the Authors most lawfull Defence to all estates, for publishing the same.* 1601   (STC 3893, AR 152, ERL 94)

235. *The First Part of the Resolution of Religion, divided into two bookes, conteyning a demonstration of the necessitie of a divine and supernaturall worshippe. In the first, against all Atheists, and Epicures: In the seconde, that Christian Catholicke Religion is the same in particuler, and more certaine in every article thereof, then any humane or experimented knowledge, against Iewes, Mahumetans, Pagans, and other external enemies of Christ. Manifestly convincing al their sects and professions, of intollerable errors, and irreligious abuses.* 1603 (STC 3896, AR 161, see ERL 281)

236. *An Antilogie or Counterplea to an Apologicall (he should have said) Apologeticall Epistle published by a Favorite of the Romane separation, and (as is supposed) one of the Ignatian Faction: Wherein two hundred untruths and slaunders are discovered, and many politicke obiections of the Romaines answered. Dedicated to the Kings most excellent Maiestie by Andrew Willet, Professor of Divinitie.* 1603   (STC 25672)

About this time a series of Catholic petitions and supplications to the same effect were being addressed to the new King. Though few of them were printed, they were all promptly attacked by Protestant writers, who thus gave them their first and only printed form. The first of these to be noticed was an anonymous *Catholiques Supplication unto the Kings Maiestie*, beginning with the words, 'Most puissant Prince, and orient Monarch'. It was immediately pounced on by two Protestant divines: Christopher Muriel, with his *Answer*, and Gabriel Powell, who added a *Supplicatorie Counterpoyse of the Protestants*.

237. *The Catholiques Supplication.* 1603

(The text is given in full by Christopher Muriel, below.)

238. *An Answer unto the Catholiques Supplication, presented unto the Kings Maiestie, for a tolleration of Popish religion in England. Wherein is contained a confutation of their unreasonable petitions, and slaunderous lyes against our late Soveraigne Queene Elizabeth, whose happie and gratious governement, the Papists in their said supplication do so peremptorilie traduce. Together with an information unto his Maiestie of divers their wicked and treasonable practises, attempted in*

the life time of our late Queene his worthy predecessor, whose life they
alwayes sought meanes to extinguish. Whereunto is annexed the
Supplication of the Papists, word for word as it was presented unto the
Kings Maiestie: With some necessarie annotations thereupon. Written
by Christopher Muriell the elder. 1603   (STC 18292)

239. *The Catholikes Supplication unto the Kings Maiestie; for Toleration of
the Catholike Religion in England; with short notes or animadversions
in the margine. Whereunto is annexed Parallel-wise, a Supplicatorie
Counterpoyse of the Protestants, unto the same most excellent
Maiestie. Together with the reasons of both sides, for and against
toleration of divers Religions.* 1603   (STC 20141)

(The Preface is signed Gabriel Powel.)

In the following year one of the former 'appellant' priests, John Colleton,
addressed another *Supplication to the Kings most excellent Maiestie* – 'this
fourth Supplication' (Powell) – beginning with the words, 'Most high and
mightie Prince'. It was presented to the King by the French Ambassador, but
only served to arouse his wrath. Published secretly in England, it included a
further appeal to 'the present Parliament', but that Parliament only increased
the severity of the existing penal laws. Again, two Protestant divines brought
out confutations in the same year, as if determined to give the Catholics no
chance to be heard. The first was the Dean of Exeter, Matthew Sutcliffe,
who dismissed the *Supplication* as patched out of Bristow's *Motives* and
Stapleton's invectives. His book went into two editions in that year. He was
followed by Gabriel Powell, who published *A Consideration of the Papists
Reasons* in the same year and mentioned Sutcliffe as having already 'amated
these importunate & shamelesse Petitioners' – though he had not yet seen
his book.

240. *A Supplication to the Kings most excellent Maiestie, Wherein, severall
reasons of State and Religion are briefely touched: not unworthie to be
read, and pondered by the Lords, Knights, and Burgesses of the present
Parliament, and other of all estates. Prostrated At his Highnes feete by
true affected Subiects.* 1604   (STC 14432, AR 247, ERL 247)

241. *The Supplication of Certaine Masse-Priests falsely called Catholikes.
Directed to the Kings most excellent Maiestie, now this time of
Parliament, but scattered in corners, to moove mal-contents to mutinie.
Published with a Marginall glosse, for the better understanding of the
Text, and an answer to the Libellers reasons, for the cleering of all
controversies thereof arising.* 1604   (STC 14430)

(This book is anonymous; but its author is identified as Sutcliffe from
Powell's mention of his name. The second edition of 1604 bore the
revised title:

. . . Published with a Marginall glosse, and an answer to the Libellers reasons againe revewed and augmented, and by Sections applied to the severall parts of the supplicatory declamation. (STC 14431))

242. *A Consideration of the Papists Reasons of State and Religion, for toleration of Poperie in England, Intimated in their Supplication unto the Kings Maiestie, & the States of the Present Parliament.* 1604 (STC 20144)

That October, 'a certayne Petition or Apologie of the lay Catholikes of England', which had been presented to the King 'about the later end of the parliament', was published by one John Lacey under the title of *A Petition Apologeticall* (perhaps recalling Willet's correction of Broughton's title). It also contained 'a Coppie of the banished Priestes Letter, to the Lordes of his Maiesties most honourable privy Councell'. A vigorous protest was included against Sutcliffe's 'clamorous calumnious invective, published in this present session of Parliament, against a most modest, learned, and submissive supplication'. So it was naturally Sutcliffe who undertook the reply to this *Petition*, though his *Briefe Examination* did not appear till 1606. Again, his book went into two editions in one year, with a revised title for the second edition, *The Petition . . . examined.*

243. *A Petition Apologeticall, presented to the Kinges most excellent Maiesty, by the Lay Catholikes of England, in Iuly last.* 1604 (STC 4835, AR 646, ERL 234)

244. *A Briefe Examination of a Certaine Peremptorie Menacing and Disleal Petition presented, as is pretended, to the Kings most excellent Maiestie, By certaine Laye Papistes, calling themselves, The Lay Catholikes of England, and now lately Printed, and divulged by a busy compagnion, called John Lecey.* 1606 (STC 23452)

(The title of the second edition of 1606 reads:

The Petition Apologeticall of Lay papists, calling themselves the lay Catholikes of England, Presented, as is sayd, to his Maiestie, Wherein presumptuously they demaund a toleration of their popish and Antichristian religion, and offer proofes of their loyalty, and pledges for their Massepriests; contradicted, examined, glozed, and refuted. (STC 23452a))

Yet another *Epistle, or Apologie*, tending to the same end, was written by one who gave himself out to be a 'brother of the reformed Church'; but Gabriel Powell, who undertook his *Refutation* in 1605, saw him as 'a Puritane-Papist' (i.e. a Jesuit) in disguise. The *Epistle* itself has not apparently survived; but its title and contents are given by Powell in his answer.

245. *An Epistle, or Apologie of a true and charitable brother of the reformed Church in favour of Protestants, Papists, and those of the Reformation, for a more moderat course of proceeding in matters of Religion, by searching the Scriptures, and examining their Spirits for the sense, and true meaning of them by a peaceable conference, and such easy meanes as were practised in the Apostolicall, and Primitive Church for planting the faith, and rooting out of errour, tending to unitie of Religion, loyaltie to the Kings Maiestie, increase of honour to him and his posterity, and good of the Common-wealth.*

(The title as given in Powell's *Refutation*, below.)

246. *A Refutation of an Epistle Apologeticall written by a Puritan-Papist to perswade the Permission of the promiscuous use and Profession of all Sects and Heresies: Wherein the unlawfulnesse and danger of such wicked Licence is fully declared by auctoritie of Scriptures, Canons, Councels, Fathers, Lawes of Christian Emperours, and iudgement of Reason. Together with the Punishment of Heretiques and Idolaters.* 1605 (STC 20149)

(The Preface is signed Gabriel Powel.)

Finally, in the aftermath of the Gunpowder Plot of 1605 and the renewal of persecution it occasioned against the Catholics, there appeared another *Petition*, dated September 1606, and addressed 'To the Bishops, Preachers, and Gospellers'. This, too, has only survived in the *Answere* undertaken by the Protestant minister, Francis Bunny, in 1607. He refers to it as 'more reasonable then their former supplications have beene', seeing that 'it requireth not a Toleration of Poperie, or immunitie from penalties by law imposed', but only a relaxation of their extreme rigour.

247. *A Petition to the Bishops, Preachers, and Gospellers.* 1606

(The title as given in Bunny's *Answere*, below.)

248. *An Answere to a Popish Libell intituled A Petition to the Bishops, Preachers, and Gospellers, lately spread abroad in the North partes. By Francis Bunny Prebendary of Durham; sometimes fellow of Magdalen Colledge in Oxford.* 1607 (STC 4097)

b) *Conversion v. Subversion*

Meanwhile the controversy between the Jesuit Robert Persons and the Dean of Exeter, Matthew Sutcliffe, which had arisen in Elizabeth's reign over the *Watchword* of Sir Francis Hastings in 1598, took a new turn with the accession of James and the renewal of Catholic hopes. It was out of his seventh 'Encounter' with Hastings in his *Temperate Ward-word* (1599) that Persons first developed the idea of his *Treatise of Three Conversions of England*, which soon grew into three volumes containing three parts (two parts in Vol. I, and the third part divided between Vols. II and III). The first two parts, combined in Vol. I, developed the main thesis of 'three conversions' (in the time of the apostles, of King Lucius, and of Pope St. Gregory I, respectively) against Sir Francis Hastings in his seventh 'Encounter', followed by an examination of John Foxe's presentation of the growth of the Protestant religion in his *Book of Martyrs*. They had already been penned in the reign of Elizabeth and dedicated 'to the Catholiques of England', when news came of the Queen's death and the accession of the Scottish King. So Persons inserted an Addition into his Dedicatory Epistle, acclaiming the new King as another Constantine and expressing the hope of delivery from persecution, and published the volume in 1603. The third part, divided owing to its excessive length between Vols. II and III, consisted of a detailed examination of Foxe's *Calendar of Protestant Saints*. Both volumes were published in 1604, the second being dedicated 'to the Protestants of England', with the addition of *A Relation of the Triall* (first published in 1600), and the third 'To the glorious Company of English Sainctes in heaven', with the addition of *A Review of Ten Publike Disputations*.

249. *A Treatise of Three Conversions of England from Paganisme to Christian Religion. The First under the Apostles, in the first age after Christ: The Second under Pope Eleutherius and K. Lucius, in the second age. The Third, under Pope Gregory the Great, and K. Ethelbert in the sixth age; with divers other matters thereunto apperteyning. Divided Into three partes, as appeareth in the next page. The former two whereof are handled in this booke, and dedicated to the Catholikes of England. With a new addition to the said Catholikes, upon the news of the late Q. death and succession of his Maiestie of Scotland, to the crowne of England. By N. D. author of the Ward-word.* 1603
    (STC 19416, AR 640, ERL 304)

250. *The Third Part of a Treatise, Intituled: of three Conversions of England: conteyninge. An Examen of the Calendar or Catalogue of Protestant Saints, Martyrs and Confessors, divised by Iohn Fox, and prefixed before his volume of Acts and Monuments. With a Paralell or Comparison therof to the Catholike Roman Calendar, and Saints therin conteyned. The first six monethes. Wherunto in the end is annexed a defence of a certaine Triall, made before the King of France upon the yeare 1600. betweene Monsieur Peron Bishop of Evreux, and Monsieur Plessis Mornay Governour of Saumur, about sundry points of Religion. By N. D.* 1604 (STC 19416, AR 640, ERL 305)

(The title of the book appended is given on a new title-page:

A Relation of the Triall Made before the King of France, upon the yeare 1600 betweene the Bishop of Evreux, and the L. Plessis Mornay. About Certayne pointes of corrupting and falsifying authors, wherof the said Plessis was openly convicted. Newly revewed, and sett forth againe, with a defence therof, against the impugnations both of the L. Plessis in France, and of O. E. in England. By N. D. 1604 (STC 19413, AR 637, see ERL 305))

251. *The Third Part of a Treatise Intituled Of Three Conversions of England. Conteyninge an examen of the Calendar or Catalogue of Protestant Saintes, Martyrs and Confessors, devised by Fox, and prefixed before his huge Volume of Actes and Monuments: With a Paralel or Comparison therof to the Catholike Roman Calendar, and Saintes therin conteyned. The last six monethes. Wherunto is annexed in the end, another severall Treatise, called: A re-view of ten publike Disputations, or Conferences, held in England about matters of Religion, especially about the Sacrament and Sacrifice of the Altar, under King Edward and Queene Mary. By N. D.* 1604 (STC 19416, AR 640, ERL 306)

(The title of the book appended is given on its own title-page as follows:

A Review of Ten Publike Disputations Or Conferences held within the compasse of foure yeares, under K. Edward & Qu. Mary, concerning some principall points in Religion, especially of the Sacrament & sacrifice of the Altar. Wherby, May appeare upon how weake groundes both Catholike Religion was changed in England; as also the fore-recounted Foxian Martyrs did build their new opinions, and offer themselves to the fire for the same, which was chiefly upon the creditt of the said Disputations. By N. D. 1604 (STC 19414, AR 638, see ERL 306))

It was natural for Sutcliffe to undertake the official Anglican reply to Persons; and this he did not in one, but in three stages — as complicated as those of his adversary. First, in his *Ful and Round Answer to N. D.*, published in 1604 and dedicated to King James as 'Defender of the true, auncient, and Catholike faith', he devoted most of his attention to Persons' *Warn-word* of 1602, by way of defending 'our late Queene for her heroical vertues and happy government' impugned by the Jesuit. But in an 'Advertisement to the Reader' he added a preliminary criticism of the recent *Treatise of Three Conversions* set forth by Persons 'under the old stampe of N. D.' — an author, he noted, 'alwaies more studious of the subversion, then of the conversion of England'. This comment he applied to his subsequent answer to Persons' first volume, entitling it *The Subversion of Robert Parsons*. Already 'in making' in 1604, this book did not appear till 1606; but he followed it up in the same year with his *Threefold Answer* dealing with Persons' other volumes.

252. *A Ful and Round Answer to N. D. alias Robert Parsons the Noddie his foolish and rude Warne-word. Comprised in three Bookes, Whereof, the first containeth a defence of Queene Elizabeths most pious and happie government, by him maliciously slaundered. The second discovereth the miserable estate of Papists, under the Popes irreligious and unhappy tyrannie, by him weakely defended. The third, toucheth him for his uncivill termes and behavior, and divers other exorbitant faults and abuses, both here and elsewhere by him committed, and cleareth his vaine obiections and cavils.* 1604   (STC 23465)

(Two subsequent editions of this work were published in the reign of Charles I, in 1625 and n.d. That of 1625 was entitled: *The blessings on Mount Gerizzim* (STC 23466, see 726); and the other, *A True Relation of Englands Happinesse* (STC 23467).)

253. *The Subversion of Robert Parsons His confused and worthlesse worke, Entituled, A treatise of three Conversions of England from Paganisme to Christian Religion.* 1606   (STC 23469)

(The Dedication is signed Matthew Sutcliffe.)

254. *A Threefold Answer unto the third part of a certaine Triobolar Treatise of Three supposed Conversions of England to the moderne Romish Religion published by Rob. Parsons under the continued Maske of N. D. The first Part whereof conteineth a defence of the Martyrs and Confessors of the true faith against the heresies and impieties of Poperie, and of their acts, sayings, and sufferings by him wickedly traduced. The second examineth some part of the Romish Martyr-ologies and Legends, and of the impious doctrine and practise of Papists in worshipping of Saints and Angels, by him weakely defended. The third refuteth his exorbitant Discourses, relations, and observa-tions, and discovereth his grosse leasings, falsities, fooleries and other enormities.* 1606   (STC 23470)

(The Dedication is signed Matt Sutcliffe.)

Two other Protestant attacks on Persons followed shortly after. In 1606 William Attersoll published his *Badges of Christianity*, in which he professed to unmask 'the insolent bragging of the late Warn-word'. But after three hundred and ninety-two pages of discussion on the sacraments, with not a mention of Persons, he merely added a Corollary against 'this odious mak-bate N. D.' for his boast of unity in the Roman Church. Two years later the learned librarian of the Bodleian, Thomas James, published *An Apologie for Iohn Wicliffe* against Persons' criticisms of Foxe's account of the English Lollards, contained in the third part of the *Treatise of Three Conversions*.

255. *The Badges of Christianity. or A Treatise of the Sacraments fully declared out of the word of God: Wherein the truth itselfe is proved, the doctrine of the reformed Churches maintained, and the errors of the church of Rome are evidently convinced: by perusing wherof the discreet Reader may easily perceive, the weake and unstable grounds of the Roman religion, and the iust causes of our lawfull separation. Divided into three Bookes: 1. Of the Sacraments in generall. 2. Of Baptisme. 3. Of the Lords Supper. Hereunto is annexed a Corollarie or necessary advertisement, shewing the intention of this present worke, opening the differences among us about the question of the Supper, discovering the Idolatry and divisions of the Popish Cleargy, and unmasking the insolent bragging of the late Warn-word, touching the supposed and pretended unity thereof. By William Attersoll, Minister of the Word of God.* 1606   (STC 889)

256. *An Apologie for Iohn Wicliffe, shewing his conformitie with the now Church of England; with answer to such slaunderous obiections, as have beene lately urged against him by Father Parsons, the Apologists, and others. Collected chiefly out of diverse works of his in written hand, by Gods speciall providence remaining in the Publike Library at Oxford, of the Honorable foundation of Sr. Thomas Bodley Knight: By Thomas James keeper of the same.* 1608   (STC 14445)

(The 'Apologists' mentioned here come together in the anonymous author of *The Apologie of the Romane Church* (1604), John Brereley, often identified as Lawrence Anderton – see 512.)

Closely related to this controversy was another in which Persons opposed no less an adversary than the Attorney General, Sir Edward Coke, on a legal question. In his famous series of *Reports* on 'the auncient and excellent Lawes of England' Coke had dealt with the reign of Elizabeth in *The Fift Part*; and he had praised her for her overthrow of 'all usurped and forraine power, and authoritie, spirituall and temporall'. This work, originally published in 1605, became particularly popular, and was reprinted no fewer than four times in James' reign – in 1606, 1607, 1612 and 1624. Persons, however, ventured to take up Coke's challenge in 1606 under the name of 'A Catholick Devyne', and undertook to prove that the Papal jurisdiction was fully 'conforme to the ancient lawes of England in former times'. His *Answere* was subsequently referred to by Thomas James in the above-mentioned *Apologie*, which was significantly dedicated to Coke himself. In the same work James also alludes to 'an other book wherin your Lordship is most uniustly produced, or rather traduced for an egregious falsarie'; but its identity is not clear.

257. *The Fift Part of the Reports of Sr. Edward Coke Knight, the Kings Attorney Generall: Of divers Resolutions and Iudgements given upon great deliberation, in matters of great importance & consequence by the reverend Iudges and Sages of the Law; together with the reasons and causes of the Resolutions and Iudgements. Published in the yeare of the most happie and prosperous raign of King Iames, of England France and Ireland the 3. and of Scotland the 39. and in al humblenesse, of right, dedicated to his most excellent Maiestie, being the fountaine of Iustice, and the life of the Law.* 1605   (STC 5504)

(The volume has a parallel title in Latin:

Quinta Pars Relationum Edwardi Coke Equitis aurati, Regii Attornati Generalis . . .)

258. *An Answere to the Fifth Part of Reportes Lately set forth by Syr Edward Cooke Knight, the Kings Attorney generall. Concerning The ancient & moderne Municipall lawes of England, which do apperteyne to Spirituall Power and Iurisdiction. By occasion wherof, & of the principall Question set downe in the sequent page, there is laid forth an evident, plaine & perspicuous Demonstration of the continuance of Catholicke Religion in England, from our first Kings christened, unto these dayes. By a Catholicke Devyne.* 1606   (STC 19352, AR 611, ERL 245)

Coke himself, however, disregarded Persons' objections, and went on to publish a sixth and a seventh part of his *Reports*, in 1607 and 1608, with the title this time phrased in legal French. But in his Preface to *La Sept Part* he uttered a general warning against 'those bookes of late written (which I have seene) from Rome or Romanists' as having incurred the danger of Praemunire and high treason. Persons responded in 1609 with 'a peece of a Reckoning with Syr Edward Cooke', which he added to his *Quiet and Sober Reckoning with M. Thomas Morton* – to be dealt with in the following controversy.

259. *La Size Part des Reports Sr. Edw. Coke Chivaler, chiefe Justice del Common banke; des divers Resolutions & Iudgements dones sur solemne arguments, & avec grand deliberation & conference des tresreverend Iudges & Sages de la Ley, de cases en ley queux ne fueront unques resolve ou adiudges par devant: Et les raisons & causes des dits Resolutions & Iudgements. Publies en le cinq' An de treshaut & tresillustre Iaques Roy Dengl. Fr. & Irel. & de Escoce le 41. Le fountaine de tout Pietie & Iustice, & la vie de la Ley.* 1607 (STC 5509)

260. *La Sept Part des Reports Sr. Edw. Coke Chivaler, chiefe Justice del Common Banke: des divers Resolutions & Iudgements done sur*

solemne arguments & avec grand deliberation & conference des tresreverend Iudges & Sages de la Ley, de cases en les queux ne fueront unques resolve ou adiudges par devant: Et les raisons & causes des dits Resolutions & Iudgements. Publies en le Size An de treshaut & tresillustre Iaques Roy Dengl. Fr. & Irel. & de Escoce le 42. Le fountaine de tout Pietie & Iustice, & la vie de la Ley. 1608 (STC 5511)

c) *Controversy on Conspiracy and Equivocation*

The above-mentioned book of Persons against Thomas Morton, then Dean of Gloucester, has its place in another controversy on which the busy Jesuit was also engaged. It was Morton who began this controversy in 1605, with an anonymous work entitled *An Exact Discoverie of Romish Doctrine*. It was his aim to prove 'Romish schooles to be Seminaries of Rebellions in all Protestants government: and Popish priests, as also their adherents, to be worthily executed for seditious and traiterous persons'. In the course of his work he took particular exception to the teaching of Cardinal Toletus and Gregory Martin ('in libr. Resolutionis Casuum', also attributed to Allen) on equivocation. In the following year an anonymous Catholic answer, commonly attributed to the seminary priest, Richard Broughton, appeared under the title of *A iust and moderate Answer*. Published after the exposure of the Gunpowder Plot, it was dedicated to the King with a strong disclaimer of any part in that 'late intended Conspiracy'.

261. *An Exact Discoverie of Romish Doctrine in the case of Conspiracie and Rebellion, by pregnant observations: Collected (not without direction from our Superiours) out of the expresse dogmaticall principles of Popish Priests and Doctors.* 1605   (STC 18184)

262. *A iust and moderate Answer To a most iniurious, and slaunderous Pamphlet, intituled, An exact Discovery of Romish doctrine in case of Conspiracie and Rebellion. Wherein the innocency of Catholike religion is proved, and every obiection returned upon the Protestant Accuser, and his owne profession. With licence of Superior.* 1606   (STC 18188, AR 164, ERL 93)

Morton now came out into the open with a defence entitled *A Full Satisfaction*, dedicating it (like his anonymous adversary) to the King. Publishing it as he did in 1606, in the aftermath of the Gunpowder Plot and its related trials, he dwelt at length on the topical question of equivocation, with special reference to 'the booke intituled, Resolution of English cases'. It was now in answer to Morton that Persons came into the controversy, for once under his own initials P. R., with *A Treatise tending to Mitigation*, which appeared in 1607. After refuting both of Morton's books, he proceeded to give examples (as a *retorsio argumenti*) of 'the use of equivocation in some Protestant English Bishops', with special reference to John Jewel in his famous controversy with Thomas Harding in the early years of Elizabeth's reign.

263. *A Full Satisfaction concerning a double Romish Iniquitie; hainous Rebellion, and more then heathenish Aequivocation. Containing three Parts: The two former belong to the Reply upon the Moderate Answerer; the first for Confirmation of the Discoverie in these two points, Treason and Aequivocation: the second is a Iustification of Protestants, touching the same points. The third Part is a large Discourse confuting the Reasons and grounds of other Priests, both in the case of Rebellion, and Aequivocation. Published by Authoritie.* 1606   (STC 18185)

264. *A Treatise tending to Mitigation towardes Catholicke-Subiectes in England. Wherin is declared, That it is not impossible for Subiects of different Religion, (especially Catholickes and Protestantes) to live togeather in dutifull obedience and subiection, under the government of his Maiesty of Great Britany. against The seditious wrytings of Thomas Morton Minister, & some others to the contrary. Whose two false and slaunderous groundes, pretending to be drawne from Catholicke doctrine & practice, concerning Rebellion and Equivocation, are overthrowne, and cast upon himselfe. Dedicated to the learned Schoole-Devines, Cyvill and Canon Lawyers of the two Universities of England. By P. R.* 1607   (STC 19417, AR 641, ERL 340)

It took some time for Morton to come out with his full answer to Persons' book. Instead, in 1608 he published a provisional answer entitled *A Preamble Unto an Encounter*, calling his adversary 'the Mitigator', as he had called his previous adversary 'the Moderator'. Without waiting for his final reply, Persons immediately countered with the above-mentioned *Quiet and Sober Reckoning* in 1609. The Moderator, presumably Broughton, also brought out his *Plaine Patterne of a Perfect Protestant Professor* about the same time. At last, in 1610 Morton produced his *Encounter against M. Parsons* in fulfilment of his promise. There the controversy ended, partly because Morton had (it was said) been so discomfited that he 'resolved to write no more books' (cf. Foley VII 1015), partly because Persons himself died that year – though, as Morton commented on hearing the news, 'yet will not our Adversary die, as long as his bookes, or cause shall live in the handes and hartes of his favorites'.

265. *A Preamble Unto an Incounter with P. R. the Author of the deceitfull Treatise of Mitigation: Concerning the Romish doctrine both in*

question of Rebellion and of Aequivocation: By Thomas Morton.
Published by Authoritie. 1608   (STC 18191)

266. *A Quiet and Sober Reckoning with M. Thomas Morton somewhat set in choler by his Adversary P. R. concerning Certaine imputations of wilfull falsities obiected to the said T. M. in a Treatise of P. R. intituled Of Mitigation, some part wherof he hath lately attempted to answere in a large Preamble to a more ample Reioynder promised by him. But heere in the meane space the said imputations are iustified, and confirmed, & with much increase of new untruthes on his part returned upon him againe: So as finally the Reckoning being made, the Verdict of the Angell, interpreted by Daniell, is verified of him. Daniel 5. vers. 27. You have byn weighed in the ballance, & are found to want weight. There is also adioyned a peece of a Reckoning with Syr Edward Cooke, now L. Chief Iustice of the Common Pleas, about a Nihil dicit, & some other points uttered by him in his two late Preambles, to his sixt and seaventh Partes of Reports.* 1609   (STC 19412, AR 635, ERL 259)

267. *A Plaine Patterne of a Perfect Protestant Professor: which is, to be a false corrupter, perverter, and abuser of Authorities, &c. Taken forth of the first, chiefest, and principal part, of the gloriously intituled booke: (A ful satisfaction) written by a man of great sincerity, and integrity, (by his owne and other Protestant friendes judgement) M. Thomas Morton, Doctor in Divinity, and Deane of Glocester, published with privilege, and in their time of Convocation.* 1608–10   (STC 18185a, AR 167, ERL 247)

268. *The Encounter against M. Parsons, by A Review of his last Sober Reckoning, And his Exceptions urged in the Treatise of his Mitigation. Wherein moreover is inserted: 1. A Confession of some Romanists, both concerning the particular Falsifications of principall Romanists, as Namely, Bellarmine, Suarez, and others: As also concerning the Generall fraude of that Church, in corrupting of Authors. 2. A Confutation of Slaunders, which Bellarmine urged against Protestants. 3. A Performance of the Challenge, which Mr. Parsons made, for the examining of sixtie Fathers, cited by Coccius for proofe of Purgatorie; to shew thirtie one of them to have beene either Apocrypha, or corrupted, or wrested. 4. A Censure of a late Pamphlet, Intituled, The Patterne of a Protestant, by one once termed the Moderate Answerer. 5. An handling of his Question of Mentall Equivocation (After his boldnesse with the L. Cooke) upon occasion of the most memorable, and feyned Yorkshire Case of Equivocating; and of his raging against D. Kings Sermon. Published by Authoritie.* 1610   (STC 18183)

During this controversy, Morton was assisted by two other writers, whom he quotes in his *Encounter*, Thomas James and William Crashaw. They both sought to produce evidence of the 'Generall fraude' of the Roman Church, as connected with the charges of conspiracy and equivocation. Already in 1600 James had published in Latin his *Bellum Papale*, accusing the Papists of tampering with the text of the Latin Vulgate; and this he now followed up with a similarly entitled *Bellum Gregorianum*, published in 1610 to draw attention to alterations made to the writings of St. Gregory the Great.

269. *Bellum Papale, Sive Concordia Discors Sixti Quinti, et Clementis Octavi, circa Hieronymianam editionem. Praeterea, in quibusdam locis gravioribus habetur comparatio utriusq; editionis, cum postrema & ultima Lovanensium; ubi mirifica industria Clementis, & Cardinalium super castigationem Bibliorum deputatorum, notas dumtaxat marginales Lovanensium in textum assumendo, clare demonstratur. Auctore Thoma Iames, Novi Collegii in alma Academia Oxoniensi socio, & utriusq; Academiae in Artibus Magistro.* 1600   (STC 14447)

270. *Bellum Gregorianum sive corruptionis Romanae in operibus D. Gregorii M. Jussu Pontificum Rom. recognitis atq; editis, ex Typographia Vaticana, loca insigniora observata a theologis ad hoc officium deputatis.* 1610   (STC 14446)

As for Crashaw, he had in 1606 brought out a book, in Latin and English (mixed), on *Romish Forgeries and Falsifications*, accusing the Roman Church and 'her Indices expurgatorios' of having 'razed the records' and resorted to 'corruption and forgerie in the highest degree'. After prefixing 'A Treatise, wherein is briefly discovered the foulnesse and unlawfulnesse of Popish purging of Autors', he illustrated his argument with particular reference to the alterations made in the text of the German friar John Ferus, *In Epistolam Primam Iohannis*. He went on in 1611 to publish a *Manuale Catholicorum*, a mediaeval book of prayers, which he claimed as a proof that Anglican piety existed in the darkest of the dark ages – in a document that had escaped the meddling intervention of 'Popish policy'.

271. [= 522] *Romish Forgeries and Falsifications: Together with Catholike Restitutions. The first Booke of the first Tome. Observed, collected, and now discovered for the use and honour of the Catholike Church, and to the iust rebuke of the Romish Sinagogue, by W. Crashaw Bachelor in Divinitie, and Preacher at the Temples. This first Booke is set forth in Latine and English for the use of the English Reader, whether he be a true Catholike or a Romish.* 1606   (STC 6014)

(There is also a Latin title on a separate title-page:

Falsificationum Romanarum: et Catholicarum Restitutionum. Tomi primi Liber primus. Ad Ecclesiae Catholicae usum & honorem, &

85

> *synagogae Romanae iustum opprobrium, observavit & detexit*
> *W. Crashavius in Theologia Bacchal. & verbi divini apud Templ. Lond.*
> *Praedic. Cum Indice Controversiarum.* 1606)

272. *Manuale Catholicorum. A Manuall For True Catholickes. Enchiridion*
     Piarum Precum et Meditationum. Ex vetustissimis Manuscript.
     pergamenis descripta. Ex Bibliotheca W. Crashavi. Theol. Bacchal. &
     verbi Div. Mnistir. apud Temp. Lond. A Handful: or Rather a Heartfull
     of holy meditations and Prayers. Gathered out of certaine ancient
     Manuscripts, written 300 yeares ago, or more. By William Crashaw
     Batchelour of Divinity, and Preacher at the Temple. 1611   (STC 6018)

Meanwhile, the anonymous author of *A Treatise of the Groundes of the
Olde and Newe Religion* (Edward Mayhew) had come out in 1608 with his
reply to Crashaw and James, among other Anglican writers. He was now
answered by James in *A Treatise of the Corruptions* in 1611, together with
two continental Jesuits, James Gretser and Anthony Possevinus, who had
challenged James' *Bellum Papale.* The librarian went on in the following year
to attack the Society of Jesus in general in his *Iesuites Downefall*, and to cast
particular aspersions on 'The Life of Father Rob. Parsons'.

273. [= 519] *A Treatise of the Groundes of the Old and Newe Religion.*
     Devided into two parts, Whereunto is added an Appendix, containing a
     briefe Confutation of William Crashaw his first Tome of Romish
     forgeries and falsifications. 1608   (STC 24247, AR 493, ERL 124)

274. [= 524] *A Treatise of the Corruptions of Scripture, Councels, and*
     Fathers, by the Prelats, Pastors, and Pillars of the Church of Rome, for
     maintenance of Popery and irreligion. By Thomas Iames, Student in
     Divinitie, and chiefe Keeper of the Publique Librarie in the Universitie
     of Oxford; of the Honorable foundation of Sir Thomas Bodley, Knight.
     Together with a sufficient answere unto James Gretser, and Antonie
     Possevine Iesuites, and the unknowne Author of the Grounds of the old
     religion & the new. Divided into V. Parts. 1611   (STC 14462)

275. *The Iesuites Downefall, Threatned against them by the Secular Priests*
     for their wicked lives, accursed manners, Hereticall doctrine, and more
     then Matchiavillian Policie. Together with the Life of Father Parsons
     An English Iesuite. 1612   (STC 14459)

d) *Repercussions of the Gunpowder Plot*

The foregoing controversy between Morton and Persons, while it was
initiated by the former before the discovery of the Gunpowder Plot in 1605,

was a significant commentary on the implications of that Plot from the opposing sides. Other controversies, too, inevitably arose out of the discovery. An early echo of the issues involved was expressed by Sir John Hayward, the former critic of Doleman's *Conference* (1595), in his anonymous *Reporte of a Discourse* in 1606. While reasserting the royal claim to supremacy in affairs of religion, he attacked the 'perfidious Aequivocation' of the Jesuits as 'the bane of civill Societie, the overthrow of all humane Commerce'. After a second edition in 1607, a third was published in 1624 with the author's name and a new title, *Of Supremacie in Affaires of Religion*. It elicited no Catholic response.

276. *A Reporte of a Discourse concerning supreme powers in affaires of Religion. Manifesting That this power is a right of Royaltie, inseparably annexed to the Soveraigntie of every State: and that it is a thing both extreamely dangerous, and contrarie to the use of all auncient Empires and Commonwealths, to acknowledge the same in a forraine Prince.* 1606   (STC 13001)

(The third edition of 1624 is entitled:

Of Supremacie in Affaires of Religion. By Sir Iohn Hayward, Knight, Doctor of Lawe   (STC 13003).)

A vigorous controversy, however, arose out of the trial of the conspirators and particularly of the English Jesuit superior, Father Henry Garnet, in 1606. During the latter's trial, under the prosecution of the Attorney General, Sir Edward Coke, emphasis was laid on Garnet's use of equivocation to conceal his knowledge of the Plot, which he had obtained from Robert Catesby under the seal of confession. The full details of this trial were immediately published as *A True and Perfect Relation*, which was referred to by the Jesuit Richard Blount as 'the Kings book of Mr. Garnetts death and arraignment' (Foley I 65). It was shortly afterwards translated into Latin by the great antiquary and historian, William Camden.

277. *A True and Perfect Relation of the proceedings at the severall Arraignments of the late most barbarous Traitors.* 1606   (STC 11618)

(A second edition, which came out in the same year, has the enlarged title:

A True and Perfect Relation of the whole proceedings against the late most barbarous Traitors, Garnet a Iesuite, and his Confederats: Contayning sundry Speeches delivered by the Lords Commissioners at their Arraignments, for the better satisfaction of those that were hearers, as occasion was offered; The Earle of Northamptons Speech having bene enlarged upon those grounds which are set downe. And lastly all that passed at Garnets Execution. 1606   (STC 11619))

278. *Actio In Henricum Garnetum Societatis Iesuiticæ in Anglia*
  Superiorem, Et cæteros qui proditione longe immanissima Sereniss.
  Britanniae Magnae Regem, & Regni Angliae Ordines pulvere fulminali e
  medio tollere coniurarunt: Una cum Orationibus Dominorum
  Delegatorum. Adiectum est supplicium de Henrico Garneto Londini
  sumptum. Omnia ex Anglico a G. Camdeno Latine versa. 1607
  (STC 11620)

A particular incident connected with Garnet's execution, the alleged
appearance of a miraculous straw on which a drop of the martyr's blood was
seen to form the face of a crowned child, was the subject of a mocking
pamphlet by Robert Pricket, entitled *The Iesuits Miracles*, which appeared in
1607.

279. *The Iesuits Miracles, or new Popish Wonders. Containing the Straw, the*
  Crowne, and the Wondrous Child, with the confutation of them and
  their follies. 1607 (STC 20340)

The controversy that followed was conducted largely in Latin, though
Persons defended his fellow Jesuit in a lengthy 'Epistle Dedicatory to Syr
Edward Cooke Knight', which he appended to his *Answere* of 1606. It was a
Cretan Jesuit, Andreas Eudaemon-Joannes, or André l'Heureux, who took
up the detailed defence of Garnet with his *Apologia Pro R. P. Henrico
Garneto Anglo* in 1610, against the speech for the prosecution given by Sir
Edward Coke. He also added an engraving of the 'miraculosa effigies R. P.
Henrici Garneti' as a frontispiece, with an explanation of its meaning and
circumstances.

280. *R. P. Andreae Eudaemon-Ioannis Cydonii e Societate Iesu, Ad*
  Actionem Proditoriam Edouardi Coqui, Apologia Pro R. P. Henrico
  Garneto Anglo, eiusdem Societatis Sacerdote. 1610

This elicited a reply, after an interval of three years, from the Regius
professor of divinity at Oxford, Robert Abbot, with his *Antilogia adversus
Apologiam* in 1613. He added a further criticism of the legendary 'Spica
Iesuitica'. Another answer came from the eminent Huguenot scholar, Isaac
Casaubon, who had settled in England in 1610. In his lengthy criticism of
the *Annales* of Cardinal Baronius, *De Rebus Sacris et Ecclesiasticis
Exercitationes*, published in 1614, he included a 'Digressio adversus
Andream Eudaemono-Iohannem', referring to his opponent as 'animosis-
simus ille parricidarum patronus'. Yet another attack came from the pen of
John Prideaux, soon to succeed Abbot as Regius professor at Oxford. In his
Castigatio cuiusdam Circulatoris, published in 1614, he had one chapter 'De
rebus Anglis' and another 'De doctrina Garneti'.

281. *Antilogia adversus Apologiam Andreae Eudaemon-Ioannis Iesuitae pro Henrico Garneto Iesuita Proditore. Qua mendacissimi Monachi adversus Ecclesiam & remp. Anglicanam violatae religionis & iustitiae nomine calumniae refutantur; & Iesuitarum, Garneti vero maxime, Proditoria consilia & coniurationes exploratissima veritate referuntur. Authore Rob. Abbotto sacrae Theologiae in Academia Oxoniensi Professore Regio.* 1613   (STC 45)

282. *Isaaci Casauboni De Rebus Sacris et Ecclesiasticis Exercitationes XVI. Ad Cardinalis Baronii Prolegomena in Annales, & primam eorum partem, de Domini Nostri Iesu Christi Nativitate, Vita, Passione, Assumtione. Ad Iacobum, Dei gratia, Magnae Britanniae, Hiberniae, &c. Regem Serenissimum.* 1614   (STC 4745)

(The title of his digression against Eudaemon-Joannes is:

Digressio adversus Andream Eudaemono-Iohannem, origine Christi- anum, sed quem facta quovis pagano deteriorem arguant: in qua mendacia infanda scelestissimi Iesuitae solide refutantur.)

283. [= 418] *Castigatio cuiusdam Circulatoris, qui R. P. Andream Eudaemon-Iohannem Cydonium e Societate Iesu seipsum nuncupat. Opposita ipsius calumniis in Epistolam Isaaci Casauboni ad Frontonem Ducaeum. Per Iohannem Prideaux SS. Theologiae Doctorem & Collegii Exoniensis Rectorem.* 1614   (STC 20344)

(This was more directly a reply to the Jesuit's *Responsio ad Epistolam Isaaci Casauboni* (1612) against Casaubon's *Ad Frontonem Ducaeum S. J. Theologum Epistola* (1611) — to be considered later in another context; cf. 416–18.)

Finally, in answer to both Casaubon and Abbot, Eudaemon-Joannes published his *Responsio* in 1615.

284. *R. P. Andreae Eudaemon-Ioannis Cydonii e Societate Iesu Responsio ad Caput IV Primae Exercitationis Isaaci Casauboni, Et Ad Antilogiam Roberti Abbatis adversus Apologiam P. Garneti.* 1615

e) *The King v. the Jesuit Cardinal*

The main outcome of the Gunpowder Plot for the Catholics in England was the passing of an 'Act for the better discovery and repressing of Popish Recusants' by the Parliament of 1606. This included the imposition of a newly framed Oath of Allegiance (said to have been devised by a former Jesuit, Sir Christopher Perkins), in which they were required to 'detest and abjure, as impious and heretical, this damnable doctrine and position that princes which be excommunicated or deprived by the Pope may be deposed or murdered by their subjects.' Though this Oath was twice condemned by Pope Paul V, the English Archpriest, George Blackwell, expressed his approval of it and even wrote a letter to his clergy advising them to take it. One has to remember, however, that Blackwell was imprisoned at the time, and subjected to considerable pressure from Lambeth Palace – as appears from a series of *Examinations* held there in June and July 1607, which were published soon afterwards. On 28 September Cardinal Bellarmine wrote him a letter of admonition, pointing out the main objections to the Oath from a Catholic viewpoint. But so far from accepting these objections, Blackwell wrote a strong reply in defence of his position. This exchange was published, together with an additional letter of Blackwell's 'to the Romish Catholickes in England', under the title of *A Large Examination taken at Lambeth*. It was subsequently translated into Latin by John Wilson, and published in 1609.

285. *Mr. George Blackwel, (Made by Pope Clement 8. Arch-priest of England) his Answeres upon sundry his Examinations: Together, with his Approbation and taking of the Oath of Allegeance: And his Letter written to his Assistants, and brethren, mooving them not onely to take the said Oath, but to advise all Romish Catholikes so to doe.* 1607 (STC 3105)

286. *A Large Examination taken at Lambeth, according to his Maiesties direction, point by point, of M. George Blakwell, made Arch-priest of England, by Pope Clement 8. Upon occasion of a certaine answere of his, without the privitie of the State, to a Letter lately sent unto him from Cardinall Bellarmine, blaming him for taking the oath of Allegeance. Together with the Cardinals Letter, and M. Blakwels said answere unto it. Also M. Blakwels Letter to the Romish Catholickes in England, aswell Ecclesiasticall, as Lay.* 1607   (STC 3104)

287. *In Georgium Blacvellum Angliae Archipresbyterum A Clemente Papa Octavo designatum Quaestio bipartita: Cuius Actio prior Archipresbyteri iusiurandum de Fidelitate praestitum. Altera eiusdem iuramenti Assertionem, contra Cardinalis Bellarmini Literas, continet.* 1609   (STC 3103)

(The documents contained in this volume are as follows:

a) *In Archipresbyterum recens comprehensum Quaestio prior, ad eius de Fidelitate iusiurandum perducta.*
b) *Eiusdem ad Sacerdotes Pontificios Epistola, de licito illius iuramenti usu.*
c) *Cardinalis Bellarmini literae ad Archipresbyterum, quem de praestito Fidelitatis sacramento, gravius reprehendit.*

d) *Archipresbyteri ad easdem Responsum.*

e) *Hinc nata est in Archipresbyterum altera Quaestio.*

f) *Archipresbyteri ad Pontificios secunda, de admittendo Fidelitatis iuramento, Epistola.*

g) *Visum est (ut affines huic argumento) ex Archivis addi:*
    1. *Quaestionem habitam Anno 1570 . . . de Bulla Anathematis, contra Reginam Elizabetham.*
    2. *Fidelitatis quamdam formulam, quam ante octennium scripto conceptam Sacerdotes e Pontificiis Saeculares . . . subscripta manu frequentes sunt professi.)*

Towards the end of 1607 there appeared an anonymous defence of the Oath against the two breves of Pope Paul V and Bellarmine's Letter to Blackwell. It bore the Latin title, *Triplici nodo, triplex cuneus*, though its contents were in English, and it was published by the royal printer, Robert Barker, and 'by royal authority'. From the first its royal authorship was an open secret. It also appeared soon afterwards in French and Latin translation.

288. *Triplici nodo, triplex cuneus. or An Apologie for the Oath of Allegiance, Against the two Breves of Pope Paulus Quintus, and the late Letter of Cardinal Bellarmine to G. Blackwel the Arch-priest. Authoritate Regia.* 1607   (STC 14400)

289. *Triplici nodo triplex cuneus. Sive Apologia pro Iuramento Fidelitatis. Adversus duo Brevia P. Pauli Quinti, & Epistolam Cardinalis Bellarmini, ad G. Blackvellum Archipresbyterum nuper scriptam. Authoritate regia.* 1607   (STC 14403)

290. *Triplici nodo, triplex cuneus. ou Apologie pour le Serment de Fidelite, que le Roy de la grand Bretagne veut estre faict par tous ses sujets, Contre les deux Brefs du Pape Paul cinquième, & l'Epistre, ou Lettre, nagueres envoyee par le Cardinal Bellarmin à G. Blackwel Archiprestre. Traduict de l'Anglois, par P. P. Advocat au Parlement de Paris.* 1608 (STC 14408)

At the Pope's expressed wish Bellarmine undertook the reply to this *Apology*, using not his own name, but that of his chaplain, Matteo Torti. His *Responsio* was published at Cologne in the following year; but its authorship, too, was soon generally known.

291. *Matthaei Torti Presbyteri, & Theologi Papiensis Responsio ad Librum Inscriptum, Triplici Nodo, triplex cuneus, sive Apologia pro Iuramento fidelitatis: adversus duo Brevia Papae Pauli V. & recentes litteras*

> *Cardinalis Bellarmini ad Georgium Blacuellum Angliae Archi-presbyterum: Qua ostenditur, Iuramentum illud ab hostibus fidei Catholicae excogitatum, iniquissime a subditis Catholicis, sub gravissima bonorum omnium amissionis, perpetuorumq. carcerum poena, postulari atq. exigi.* 1608

James responded to this book by calling in all copies of the first edition of his *Apologie*, and publishing a new edition – without the opening Latin words of the former title – under his royal name, with the addition of a 'Premonition', or 'Praefatio Monitoria'. This was also translated into Latin and published in 1609, at the same time as the English original.

292. *An Apologie for the Oath of Allegiance. First set foorth without a name: And now acknowledged by the Authour, the Right High, and Mightie Prince, Iames, by the Grace of God, King of Great Britaine, France and Ireland; Defender of the Faith, &c. Together with a Premonition of his Maiesties, to all most Mightie Monarches, Kings, free Princes and States of Christendome.* 1609   (STC 14401)

293. *Apologia pro Iuramento Fidelitatis, Primum quidem ΑΝΩΝΥΜΟΣ: Nunc vero ab Ipso Auctore, Serenissimo ac Potentiss. Principe, Iacobo Dei gratia, Magnae Britanniae, Franciae & Hiberniae Rege, Fidei Defensore, denuo edita. Cui praemissa est Praefatio Monitoria Sacratiss. Caesari Rodolpho II. Semper Augusto, Caeterisque Christiani Orbis Sereniss. ac Potentiss. Monarchis ac Regibus: Illustriss. Celsissimisque Liberis Principibus, Rebus publicis atque Ordinibus inscripta, eodem Auctore.* 1609.   (STC 14405)

The King now commissioned the Bishop of Chichester, Lancelot Andrewes, to undertake a full reply to the Cardinal. This came out in 1609, under a title playing on the pseudonym used by Bellarmine: *Tortura Torti*. Bellarmine, meanwhile, reacted to James' admission of his authorship with a new edition of the *Responsio* in 1610, giving his real name and adding an 'Admonitio ad Lectorem' to explain the situation. He also published an *Apologia* in reply to James' 'Praefatio Monitoria', and had it bound with a third edition of the *Responsio* in the same year.

294. *Tortura Torti: Sive, Ad Matthaei Torti Librum Responsio, qui nuper editus contra Apologiam Serenissimi Potentissimique Principis, Iacobi, Dei Gratia, Magnae Britanniae, Franciae, & Hiberniae Regis, Pro Iuramento Fidelitatis.* 1609   (STC 626)

295. *Roberti S. R. E. Cardin. Bellarmini, Responsio ad Librum inscriptum, Triplici nodo, triplex cuneus, sive Apologia pro Iuramento fidelitatis:*

*Adversus duo Brevia Papae Pauli V, & recentes literas Cardinalis
Bellarmini. Ad Georgium Blakuellum Angliae Archipresbyterum.* 1610

296. *Apologia Roberti S. R. E. Cardinalis Bellarmini, pro Responsione sua ad
Librum Iacobi Magnae Britanniae Regis, cuius titulus est, Triplici nodo
triplex cuneus: in qua Apologia refellitur Praefatio Monitoria Regis
eiusdem. Accessit eadem ipsa Responsio, iam tertio recusa, quae sub
nomine Matthaei Torti Anno superiore prodierat.* 1610

Andrewes was, therefore, again commissioned to reply to Bellarmine's
Apologia; and again he had his answer, entitled *Responsio ad Apologiam*, out
within a year. In this work he also glanced at some of the many continental
theologians who had joined in the controversy against the King: Cristanovis,
Pacenius, Becanus, Persons, Coquaeus, Eudaemon-Joannes, Schioppius,
Capellus and Gretser. (Here we can only deal with those whose criticisms
provoked some substantial response in England.)

297. *Responsio ad Apologiam Cardinalis Bellarmini, Quam nuper edidit
contra Praefationem Monitoriam Serenissimi ac potentissimi Principis
Iacobi, Dei Gratia Magnae Britanniae, Franciae, & Hiberniae Regis,
Fidei Defensoris, Omnibus Christianis Monarchis, Principibus, atque
Ordinibus inscriptam.* 1610   (STC 604)

A somewhat eccentric postscript to this particular stage of the controversy
was provided by the Scottish Dean of Salisbury, John Gordon. In the three
years from 1610 to 1612 he brought out three small books, defending the
King against the Cardinal, and making outrageous play on the pseudonym of
Tortus: *Antitortobellarminus* (1610), *Orthodoxo-Iacobus: et Papapostaticus*
(1611), and *Anti-Bellarmino-tortor* (1612). In this he was, no doubt,
following the example of his fellow countryman, Andrew Melville, in his
Antitamicamicategoria of 1604. Of these works the first was noticed by the
German Jesuit, James Gretser, who published his *Antitortor Bellarminianus*
in 1611.

298. *Antitortobellarminus, Sive Refutatio Calumniarum, mendaciorum, et
Imposturarum Laico-Cardinalis Bellarmini, contra iura omnium Regum,
et sinceram, illibatamque famam, Serenissimi, Potentissimi, piissimique
Principis, Iacobi, Dei gratia, magnae Britanniae, Franciae, et Hiberniae
Regis, Fidei Catholicae antiquae defensoris, et propugnatoris: per
Ioannem Gordonium, Scoto-Britannum, Theol. Doctorem, et Decanum
Ecclesiae Cathedralis Sarisburiensis in Anglo-Britannia. In Torto-
Bellarminum. Dogmata torta prius torsisti nomine torti,/ Nomine quae
proprio nunc male torta vomis:/ Torto-Bellarmini ergo tibi nomina
sume:/ Danda etenim Tortis Nomina torta strophis:/ Ut tibi pro recto*

tortum: indirecta potestas/ Sic papae in Reges, fictio torta tua est.
1610   (STC 12054)

299. *Orthodoxo-Iacobus: et Papapostaticus. Sive Theses Confirmatae testi-*
moniis Graecorum, et Latinorum Patrum, qui vixerunt usque ad
millesimum a Christo annum; quibus probatur Serenissimum Regem
maximae Britanniae &c. esse Catholicae fidei, verum Defensorem &
Propugnatorem: Papasq. Cardinalitios defecisse a fide Sanctae Trini-
tatis, & Iuramento Baptismi. Per Ioannem Gordonium, Sacrae Theo-
logiae Doctorem, et Ecclesiae Sarisburiensis in Anglo Britannia,
Decanum. 1611   (STC 12060)

300. *Anti-Bellarmino-tortor, sive Tortus Retortus & Iuliano-papismus. Et*
Theses confirmatae doctrina antiquorum Symbolorum, et Patrum
Graecorum & Latinorum testimoniis, quibus probatur adorationem
Paparum per Osculationem Crucis Sandalio pedis assutae, & lagani
Missalis levati supra caput Papae missificantis, & in solemni pompa equo
albo vecti, & adorationem imaginis Dei Patris Infulis Pontificiis amictae,
esse Arianam creaturae adorationem, Anthropolatriam, Necrolatriam &
Ethnicam idololatriam, & Imitationem Iulianae Apostatae, qui se cum
Idolis suis a Christianis militibus in Labaro militari adorari fecit: Pro
serenissimo, potentissimo, piissimoq. Rege, Apostolicae & Catholicae
antiquae Fidei Defensore & Propugnatore. Contra Laico-cardinalis
Bellarmini mendacem, blasphemam & malignam comparationem
serenissimae Regiae Maiestatis cum Iuliano Apostata. Ad excel-
lentissimum, benignissimum, piissimumq. Principem Henricum, Dei
gratia Walliae Principem, &c. Per Ioannem Gordonium Scotobritannum,
sacrae Theologiae Doctorem, & Decanum Ecclesiae Cathedralis
Salisburiensis in Anglo-Britannia. 1612   (STC 12055)

301. *Antitortor Bellarminianus Joannes Gordonius Scotus Pseudodecanus et*
Capellanus Calvinisticus, nuper in Germaniam hirsuto et hispido Capillo
delatus, nunc sine pectine quidem, sed tamen satis eleganter tonsus ac
pexus, et jucundi spectaculi ergo ad Serenissimum Magnae Britanniae
Regem Jacobum remissus. 1611

f) *Cross-Channel Controversies*

Bellarmine now became involved in another, though related, controversy
over the temporal power of the Pope – to be dealt with in the next section.
So his defence against the attacks of Andrewes was taken up by other Jesuit
theologians, particularly Martin Van der Beeck (or Becanus) and Jean
l'Heureux (or Eudaemon-Joannes). The former of these was the more
prolific; and he conducted single-handed a voluminous controversy with four

English divines who now stepped in on behalf of Andrewes, now Bishop of Ely. Becanus had already been engaged in controversy with Gabriel Powell on the subject of Antichrist (to be dealt with later); and he now added his own refutation of James' *Apologia* and 'Praefatio Monitoria' in 1610. He was in turn opposed by the Dean of Lichfield, William Tooker, who published his *Duellum Sive Singulare Certamen* in 1611. To this Becanus responded with a *Duellum Martini Becani* in 1612.

302. *Serenissimi Iacobi Angliae Regis Apologiae, & monitoriae Praefationis ad Imperatorem, Reges & Principes, Refutatio. Authore Martino Becano Societatis Iesu Theologo.* 1610

303. *Duellum Sive Singulare Certamen cum Martino Becano Iesuita, futiliter refutante Apologiam et monitoriam praefationem ad Imperatorem, Reges et principes, et quaedam orthodoxa dogmata. Serenissimi ac pientissimi Iacobi Regis magnae Britanniae. Auctore Guilielmo Tooker, sacrae Theologiae professore, ac Decano Ecclesiae Lichefeldensis.* 1611   (STC 24119)

304. *Duellum Martini Becani, Societatis Iesu Theologi, cum Guilielmo Tooker, Anglicanae Theologiae Professore, & Decano Ecclesiae Lichefeldensis. De Primatu Regis Angliae.* 1612

Becanus next undertook the refutation of Andrewes' *Tortura Torti*. His work, entitled *Refutatio*, was published in Latin in 1610, and in the same year it was translated into English, as *The Confutation*, by John Wilson. In the following year Andrewes was defended by two Anglican divines, Robert Burhill with his *Pro Tortura Torti* and Richard Thomson with his *Elenchus Refutationis*.

305. *Refutatio Torturae Torti Seu Contra Sacellanum Regis Angliae, quod causam sui Regis negligenter egerit. Authore R. P. Becano, Societatis Iesu Theologo.* 1610

306. *The Confutation of Tortura Torti: or, Against the King of Englandes Chaplaine: for that he hath negligently defended his Kinges Cause. By the R. F. Martinus Becanus, of the Society of Iesus: and Professour in Devinity. Translated out of Latin into English by W. I. P.* 1610 (STC 1699, AR 77, ERL 16)

307. *Pro Tortura Torti, Contra Martinum Becanum Iesuitam, Responsio Roberti Burhilli Angli.* 1611   (STC 4118)

308. *Elenchus Refutationis Torturae Torti. Pro Reverendissimo in Christo*

*Patre Domino Episcopo Eliense, Adversus Martinum Becanum Iesuitam.
Authore Richardo Thomsonio Cantabrigiensi.* 1611   (STC 24032)

In 1612 Becanus returned to the attack with a general survey of the
inconsistencies in his opponents' books, entitled *Dissidium Anglicanum.* He
particularly showed how they disagreed with one another on the important
question of the royal supremacy in ecclesiastical affairs. This book was also
translated by John Wilson in the same year, under the title of *The English
Iarre.*

309. *Dissidium Anglicanum De Primatu Regis, Cum Brevi Praefatione ad
    Catholicos in Anglia degentes. Authore Martino Becano Societatis Iesu
    Theologo & Professore ordinario.* 1612

    (The English divines he examines are Andrewes, Tooker, Thomson, and
    Burhill. He also adds a fifth from the continent, Henricus Salcol-
    brigiensis (rendered into English as Henry Salclebridge), who had
    published a *Refutatio Examinis Becani.*)

310. *The English Iarre. or Disagreement amongst the Ministers of great
    Brittaine, concerning the Kinges Supremacy. Written in Latin by the
    Reverend Father, F. Martinus Becanus of the Society of Iesus, and
    Professour in Divinity. And translated into English by I. W. P.* 1612
    (STC 1702, AR 80, ERL 62)

This work of his, touching as it did on such a delicate matter, at once
provoked replies from two English divines. Robert Burhill dealt with it in an
Appendix to his *De Potestate Regia,* which he had written in answer to the
Parallelus of Eudaemon-Joannes (to be shortly considered) in 1613. Richard
Harris devoted a whole book, *Concordia Anglicana,* to its refutation in the
same year. Then, because Becanus' work had been turned into English,
Harris was commanded to do the same with his book. But before he could
publish his translation, entitled *The English Concord,* in 1614, he found
himself faced with Becanus' refutation of his Latin original, under the title
of *Examen Concordiae Anglicanae.* This, he explained in his Dedication to
the King, 'forced me to annex my Reply, and Refutation of his Examen, in
the Interim, in English also, because the other are in English'.

311. *Appendix, ubi auctoris ante biennium edita Responsio, ad Martini
    Becani Refutationem (quam vocat) Torturae Torti, defenditur adversus
    ea quae hactenus ab eodem Becano, vel in Dissidio suo Anglicano, vel
    alibi carpi potuerunt.*

    (Appendix to *De Potestate Regia,* 1613: see 322)

312. *Concordia Anglicana De Primatu Ecclesiae Regio; Adversus Becanum*

De Dissidio Anglicano, Authore Ricardo Harris, SS. Theologiae Professore. 1612   (STC 12814)

313. *The English Concord, In Answer to Becane's English Iarre: Together with a Reply to Becan's Examen of the English Concord. By Richard Harris, Dr. in Divinitie.* 1614   (STC 12815)

314. *Examen Concordiae Anglicanae. De Primatu Ecclesiae Regio. Authore R. P. Martino Becano Societatis Iesu Theologo ac Professore ordinario.* 1613

The indefatigable Becanus immediately went on in 1613 to defend Bellarmine against Andrewes' *Responsio ad Apologiam* of 1610. The result was one of his best known works, the *Controversia Anglicana* – which was, however, never translated into English. It was at once condemned by the theological faculty of the Sorbonne in Paris, which strongly favoured Gallican ideas against the Jesuits. It also prompted an anonymous author styling himself 'Novus Homo', and often identified as Marc'Antonio de Dominis, the wayward Archbishop of Spalata in Dalmatia, to pen a *Supplicatio ad Imperatorem*, appealing for a General Council to be convened against Pope Paul V through the mediation of King James. This 'so strange a Booke', as its publisher called it, was translated into English several years later by William Crashaw, under the title of *The New Man*.

315. *Controversia Anglicana De Potestate Pontificis et Regis; Recognita et aucta. Contra Lancelottum, Sacellanum Regis Angliae, qui se Episcopum Eliensem vocat. Ubi etiam defenditur Illustrissimus Cardinalis Bellarminus, &c. Autore R. P. Martino Becano, Societatis Iesu Theologo & Professore Ordinario.* 1613

316. *Summa Actorum Facultatis Theologiae Parisiensis contra Librum inscriptum, Controversia Anglicana de Potestate Regis & Pontificis &c. Auctore Martino Becano Societatis Iesu.* 1613   (STC 19205)

317. *Supplicatio Ad Imperatorem, Reges, Principes, super causis generalis Concilii convocandi contra Paulum Quintum. Et Summa Actorum facultatis Parisiensis contra librum inscriptum, Controversia Anglicana de potestate Regis & Pontificis &c. Auctore Martino Becano societatis Iesu. Quibus adiicitur annotatio de iis quae Becanus Iesuita in editione eiusdem Controversiae Anglicanae recognita, & Romano Pontifici dicata, expunxit.* 1613

(The Preface bears the signature, 'Novus Homo'.)

318. *The New Man or, A Supplication from an unknowne Person, a Roman*

> *Catholike unto Iames, the Monarch of Great Brittaine, and from him to*
> *the Emperour, Kings, and Princes of the Christian World. Touching The*
> *causes and reasons that will argue a necessity of a Generall Councell to*
> *be forthwith assembled against him that now usurps the papall Chaire*
> *under the name of Paul the fifth, Wherein are discovered more of the*
> *secret Iniquities of that Chaire and Court, then hitherto their friends*
> *feared, or their very adversaries did suspect. Translated into English by*
> *William Crashaw, Batchelour in Divinity, according to the Latine Copy,*
> *sent from Rome into England.* 1622   (STC 1705)

It was finally Robert Burhill who undertook the task of refuting the
Controversia Anglicana. In the same year, 1613, he brought out his *Assertio
Pro iure Regio*, which strangely passed without further reply from Becanus.

319. *Contra Martini Becani, Iesuitae Moguntini, Controversiam Anglicanam*
   auctam & recognitam. Assertio Pro iure Regio, Proque Revdi Episcopi
   Eliensis Responsione ad Apologiam Bellarmini. Auctore Roberto
   Burhillo Anglo. 1613   (STC 4116)

Another refutation of Andrewes' *Tortura Torti* came from the pen of
another Jesuit theologian, Andreas Eudaemon-Joannes (or Jean l'Heureux),
in 1611. This was entitled *Parallelus Torti ac Tortoris eius.* It also provoked
two Anglican replies: first was the *Increpatio* of the Archbishop's chaplain,
Samuel Collins, in 1612. In the following year came the above-mentioned *De
Potestate Regia* of Robert Burhill.

320. *Parallelus Torti ac Tortoris eius L. Cicestrensis: Sive Responsio ad*
   Torturam Torti pro Illustrmo Card. Bellarmino. Auctore R. P. Andrea
   Eudaemon-Ioanne Cydonio e Societate Iesu. 1611

321. *Increpatio Andreae Eudaemono-Iohannis Iesuitae, de infami Parallelo,*
   et, Renovata Assertio Torturae Torti, Pro Clarissimo Domino atque
   Antistite Eliensi. Auctore Samuele Collino, Etonensi, Sacrae Theologiae
   Doctore. Reverendissimo Patri, ac Domino, D. Archiepiscopo
   Cantuariensi, a Sacris. 1612   (STC 5563)

322. *De Potestate Regia, et Usurpatione Papali, Pro Tortura Torti, Contra*
   Parallelum Andreae Eudaemonioannis Cydonii Iesuitae, Responsio
   Roberti Burhilli Angli. 1613   (STC 4117)

An even more eminent Jesuit theologian, the Spaniard Francis Suarez, had
also been requested by the Pope to assist Bellarmine in the task of refuting
the *Apologia* of King James and the 'Praefatio Monitoria'. He now published
his massive *Defensio Fidei Catholicae* in 1613, in six books and four hundred
and forty-eight folio pages.

323. *Defensio Fidei Catholicae Adversus Anglicanae sectae errores, Cum Responsione ad Apologiam pro Iuramento Fidelitatis, & Praefationem monitoriam Serenissimi Iacobi Angliae Regis. Authore P. D. Francisco Suario Granatensi e Societate Iesu Sacrae Theologiae in celebri Conimbricensi Academia Primario Professore. Ad serenissimos totius Christiani Orbis Catholicos Reges, ac Principes.* 1613

(The contents of this work are as follows:

I. Quantum Anglicana secta a fide Catholica dissideat.
II. De peculiaribus erroribus in materia fidei Catholicae, quos rex Angliae profitetur.
III. De Summi Pontificis supra temporales reges excellentia et potestate.
IV. De Immunitate Ecclesiastica, seu exemtione clericorum a iurisdictione temporalium Principum.
V. De Antichristo, cuius nomen, et personam per calumniam, et iniuriam falso Protestantes Pontifici attribuunt.
VI. De Iuramento Fidelitatis Regis Angliae.)

This book was shortly after banned by a decree of the Parlement of Paris in 1614. At the same time it was attacked by the English Benedictine priest, Thomas Preston, writing under the pseudonym of Roger Widdrington, in an Appendix to his *Disputatio Theologica* of 1613 — in which he had taken on the leading theologians of the age, Bellarmine, Gretser, Lessius and Becanus, on this subject of the Oath. This Appendix, to be precise, first appeared in English form at the end of his English translation, entitled *A Theologicall Disputation*, which came out in the same year. In its Latin form it appeared separately in 1616, as *Appendix ad Disputationem Theologicam*, together with the formula of the Oath of Allegiance and the Latin text of the Parlement decree.

324. [= 343] *Disputatio Theologica de Iuramento Fidelitatis Sanctissimo Patri Paulo Papae Quinto Dedicata In qua Potissima omnia Argumenta, quae a Card. Bellarmino, Iacobo Gretzero, Leonardo Lessio, Martino Becano, aliisq. nonnullis contra recens Fidelitatis Iuramentum ex Decreto Regis, & Parliamenti, in Anglia stabilitum hactenus facta sunt, syncere, dilucide, & accurate examinantur, a Rogero Widdringtono Catholico Anglo.* 1613   (STC 25602, AR 667, ERL 359)

(This book properly belongs to the next controversy, in which Bellarmine was involved with the Scottish Catholic theologian, William Barclay. Preston took up Barclay's defence on the latter's death in 1608.)

325. [= 344] *A Theologicall Disputation concerning the Oath of Allegiance,*

dedicated to the most Holy Father Pope Paul the fifth. Wherein all the
principall arguments which have hitherto beene brought by Cardinall
Bellarmine, Jacobus Gretser, Leonard Lessius, Martin Becanus, and
divers others, against the new Oath of Allegiance, lately established in
England by Act of Parliament, are sincerely, perspicuously, and exactly
examined. By Roger Widdrington, an English Catholike. Translated out
of Latin into English by the Author himselfe, whereunto hee hath also
added An Appendix, wherein all the arguments, which that most learned
Divine Franciscus Suarez, hath lately brought for the Popes power to
depose Princes, and against the aforesaid Oath of Allegiance, are
sincerely rehearsed, and answered. 1613   (STC 25603, AR 676)

326. *Appendix ad Disputationem Theologicam de Iuramento Fidelitatis. In
quo Omnia Argumenta, quae a Francisco Suarez celeberrimo Societatis
Iesu Theologo pro potestate Papali Principes deponendi, & contra
recens Fidelitatis Iuramentum allata sunt, dilucide examinantur. A
Rogero Widdringtono Catholico Anglo.* 1616   (STC 25604, AR 663,
ERL 51)

(Appended are:

Forma Iuramenti Fidelitatis lege Regia in Anglia stabiliti.

Decretum Curiae Parliamenti . . . Jun. 27, 1614.)

Among the Anglicans it was the Regius professor of divinity at Oxford,
Robert Abbot, whose lectures *De Suprema Potestate Regia* were directed as
well against Bellarmine as Suarez. They were published posthumously in
1619, though delivered before he was promoted to the see of Salisbury in
1615. Also from England, in 1620, came the *De Republica Ecclesiastica* of
the renegade Archbishop of Spalata, Marc'Antonio de Dominis, who devoted
considerable space in the second volume of his book to a refutation of
Suarez. (There will be more of his brief sojourn in England in the next
chapter.)

327. *De Suprema Potestate Regia Exercitationes habitae in Academia
Oxoniensi, Contra Rob. Bellarminum, & Francisc. Suarez. Auctore
Rob. Abbot ibidem tunc Professore Regio, nuper Sarisburiensi
Episcopo.* 1619   (STC 47)

(In the case of Bellarmine, the lectures were chiefly aimed at his treatise
De Romano Pontifice.)

328. [= 640] *De Republica Ecclesiastica Pars Secunda: Continens Libros
quintum, et sextum. Cum Appendicibus in sexto capite quinti libri. In
quibus Appendicibus Refellitur opus imperfectum D. Cardinalis Perronii,
in ea Parte in qua agitur De sanctissima Eucharistia. Additur in fine post*

sextum Librum Responsio ad magnam partem Defensionis Fidei P. Francisci Suarez. Autore Marco Antonio de Dominis Archiepiscopo Spalatensi. 1620   (London; STC 6995)

(The first volume of this work was published in London in 1617 (STC 6994), with a promise of ten books in three volumes; but only the first two volumes appeared. It will be considered later, in another context.)

g) *Bellarmine v. Barclay*

When he left his fellow Jesuits to deal with the writings of Andrewes, Bellarmine was involved in a similar controversy with the Scottish Catholic theologian, William Barclay, over the nature and extent of the Pope's temporal power. The latter had indeed died at Angers in France in 1608; but a Latin treatise of his, *De Potestate Papae,* which he had left incomplete at the time of his death, was published by his son John in London the following year, after having been revised and edited by Archbishop Bancroft before being sent to the printer. An English translation, *Of the Authoritie of the Pope*, appeared in 1611, and went into two editions that year. While still engaged in controversy with King James, Bellarmine was persuaded to undertake the refutation of this Latin treatise, which was regarded as all the more serious as it came from the pen of an eminent Catholic theologian. He therefore brought out his *Tractatus De Potestate Summi Pontificis* in 1610, as a mature restatement of his theory of the Pope's indirect power over temporal rulers. This work was never translated into English; but an English Jesuit, Anthony Hoskins, made 'a Recapitulation of the whole worke' in view of its relevance to 'the lately enacted Oath of Allegiance, proposed to the Catholikes of England', and this was published in 1611.

329. *De Potestate Papae: An & quatenus in Reges & Principes seculares ius & imperium habeat: Guil. Barclaii I. C. Liber posthumus.* 1609
(STC 1408, AR 69, ERL 136)

330. *Guil. Barclaii J. C. Liber posthumus: Of the Authoritie of the Pope: whether, and how farre forth, he hath power and authoritie over Temporall Kings and Princes.* 1611   (STC 1409)

(Another edition of this book was bound with T. Higgon's *Sermon* and R. Sheldon's *Certain General Reasons* in 1611, as all contributing to the same policy of the State. In the title the words 'Liber posthumus' were replaced at the end.)

331. *Tractatus De Potestate Summi Pontificis in Rebus Temporalibus, Adversus Gulielmum Barclaium: Auctore Roberto S. R. E. Card. Bellarmino.* 1610

332. *A Briefe and Cleare Declaration of Sundry Pointes Absolutely dislyked in the lately enacted Oath of Allegiance, proposed to the Catholikes of England. Togeather With a Recapitulation of the whole worke newly written by a learned Devine, concerning the same Subiect. By H. I.* 1611 (STC 13840, AR 405, ERL 149)

This academic treatise of Bellarmine met with a particularly violent response in France, coming as it did in the aftermath of Henry IV's assassination by Ravaillac in 1610 – when the Jesuits were accused by their enemies of complicity in the crime. The book was condemned by the Parlement of Paris in a special decree, or *arrêt*, which was soon published in Latin under the title of *Commonefactio*. An alarm was also sounded by an anonymous French author, calling himself 'la statue de Memnon', subsequently identified as the lawyer E. Le Jay, in a book entitled *Le tocsin au Roy*. This was immediately translated into English and published in 1611 as *The Tocsin, or Watch-bell*, together with a translation of the Parlement decree.

333. *Commonefactio et Postulationes Regiorum Cognitorum, necnon Arrestum Curiae Parlamenti Parisiensis die 26. Novembr. 1610 latum Adversus librum inscriptum Tractatus de Potestate Summi Pontificis in rebus Temporalibus adversus Gulielmum Barclaium, autore Roberto S. R. E. Cardinali Bellarmino, excusum Romae anno 1610. Accessit Edictum Philippi III Hispaniarum Regis adversus Tractatum de Monarchia Siciliae Caesaris S. R. E. Cardinalis Baronii.* 1611

334. *An Extract of the Registers of the Court of Parliament of Paris: Against the book intitled, Tractatus de Potestate summi Pontificis in temporalibus, adversus Guilielmum Barclaium, auctore Roberto Sanctae Ecclesiae Romanae Cardinali Bellarmino.* 1611 (STC 1845)

(This is really an Appendix to 336.)

335. *Le tocsin au Roy, a la Royne régente, mère du Roy, aux princes du sang, a tous les parlemens, magistrats, officiers et subjects de la couronne de France, contre le livre de la Puissance temporelle du pape mis n'aguères en lumière par le cardinal Bellarmin. Par la statue de Memnon.* 1610

336. *The Tocsin, or Watch-bell: Sent to the King, Queene Regent, Princes of blood, to all the Parlaments, Magistrates, Officers, and loyall Subiects of France. Against the booke of the Popes temporall power, not long since set forth by Cardinall Bellarmine Iesuite. By Memnons Statue. With the permission of the best Genie of Fraunce. And done into English by I. R.* 1611 (STC 1845)

Fuller refutations followed in Latin, in the same year – and from the pens of English Catholics. First, John Barclay defended his father's ideas in his *Ioannis Barclaii Pietas*. Then, the Benedictine priest, Thomas Preston, began his long controversy on this subject with Bellarmine and other Jesuit theologians under the name of Roger Widdrington. His first contribution was somewhat confusingly entitled *Apologia Cardinalis Bellarmini*; and in it he notes that Bellarmine's book against Barclay is in everyone's hands.

337. *Ioannis Barclaii Pietas, sive Publicae pro Regibus, ac Principibus, et Privatae pro Guilielmo Barclaio Parente Vindiciae*. 1611

338. *Apologia Cardinalis Bellarmini pro Iure Principum. Adversus ipsius rationes pro auctoritate Papali Principes Saeculares in ordine ad bonum spirituale deponendi. Authore Rogero Widdringtono Catholico Anglo.* 1611   (STC 25596, AR 661, ERL 309)

Of these two books it was the latter which drew the first and strongest replies. The first was by Bellarmine himself, entitled *Examen ad librum falso inscriptum* and dated 1612 at Rome; but he judged it wiser not to publish it as such, and handed it instead to a Dutch theologian, Adolf Schulcken, who presented it in an altered form under his own name as *Apologia Adolphi Schulckenii*. Another reply came from a professor at Douai, Edward Weston, under the title *Iuris Pontificii Sanctuarium*, which appeared – with the *Apologia* – in 1613. Subsequently, Barclay also received a reply from the Jesuit Eudaemon-Joannes in 1617, in the form of an *Epistola Monitoria.*

339. *Apologia Adolphi Schulckenii Geldriensis, SS. Theologiae apud Ubios Doctoris, et Professoris, atque ad D. Martini Pastoris, Pro Illustrissimo Domino D. Roberto Bellarmino S. R. E. Card. De Potestate Romani Pont. Temporali. Adversus librum falso inscriptum, Apologia Card. Bellarmini pro Iure Principum, &c. Auctore Rogero Widdringtono Catholico Anglo.* 1613

(The author recognizes the identity of Preston beneath the pseudonym of Roger Widdrington.)

340. *Iuris Pontificii Sanctuarium. Defensum ac propugnatum contra Rogerii Widdringtoni in Apologia & Responso Apologetico Impietatem. Authore Odouardo Westono Londinensi S. Theol. Doctore, & in Collegio Anglicano Duaci Professore.* 1613

341. *R. P. Andreae Eudaemon-Ioannis Cydonii e Societate Iesu Epistola monitoria, ad Ioannem Barclaium Guillelmi filium, de libro ab eo pro Patre suo contra Illustrissimum Dominum D. Robertum Bellarminum S. R. E. Card. scripto.* 1617

In reply to his critics Preston defended his book, while maintaining his pseudonym of Widdrington, in two more publications. Already in 1612 he had to deal with the Letter of an unidentified theologian, and so he brought out his *Responsio Apologetica* in that year. Then in 1613 he dealt simultaneously with the objections of Adolphus Schulckenius – 'si ipse libri eius nomine evulgati solus Author sit' – and Edward Weston in the above-mentioned *Disputatio Theologica*. In the same *Disputation*, which he also translated into English and published in the same year, he dealt with the arguments of many other Jesuit theologians against the Oath of Allegiance. In an Appendix he added the 'Praefatio ad Lectorem' (fifty-five pages) which he had omitted from his previous *Responsio Apologetica*.

342. *Rogeri Widdringtoni Catholici Angli Responsio Apologetica. ad Libellum cuiusdam Doctoris Theologi, qui eius pro iure Principum Apologiam tanquam fidei Catholicae aperte repugnantem, atque Ethnicismum sapientem, falso, indocte, & seditiose criminatur.* 1612 (STC 25597, AR 674, ERL 161)

343. [= 324] *Disputatio Theologica de Iuramento Fidelitatis Sanctissimo Patri Paulo Papae Quinto Dedicata In qua Potissima omnia Argumenta, quae a Card. Bellarmino, Iacobo Gretzero, Leonardo Lessio, Martino Becano, aliisq; nonnullis contra recens Fidelitatis Iuramentum ex Decreto Regis, & Parliamenti, in Anglia stabilitum hactenus facta sunt, syncere, dilucide, & accurate examinantur. a Rogero Widdringtono Catholico Anglo.* 1613   (STC 25602, AR 667, ERL 359)

(In the Appendix is added the Preface to 342:

'Rogeri Widdringtoni Catholici Angli Apologeticae Responsionis ad Libellum cuiusdam Doctoris Theologi Praefatio ad Lectorem.')

344. [= 325] *A Theologicall Disputation concerning the Oath of Allegiance, dedicated to the most Holy Father Pope Paul the fifth. Wherein all the principall arguments which have hitherto beene brought by Cardinall Bellarmine, Jacobus Gretser, Leonard Lessius, Martin Becanus, and divers others, against the new Oath of Allegiance, lately established in England by Act of Parliament, are sincerely, perspicuously, and exactly examined. By Roger Widdrington, an English Catholike. Translated out of Latin into English by the Author himselfe, whereunto hee hath also added An Appendix, wherein all the arguments, which that most learned Divine Franciscus Suarez, hath lately brought for the Popes power to depose Princes, and against the aforesaid Oath of Allegiance, are sincerely rehearsed, and answered.* 1613   (STC 25603, AR 676)

(The Latin Preface to 342 is thus rendered into English:

'The Preface of the Apologeticall Answere of Roger Widdrington an English Catholike to a little pamphlet of a certaine Doctor of Divinity.')

The other Appendix against Suarez' *Defensio Fidei Catholicae* (323) here first appeared in English, and was published in Latin three years later in 1616 as *Appendix ad Disputationem Theologicam* (326).

Meanwhile, the Belgian Jesuit theologian, Leonard Lessius, also joined in the controversy with Preston. He, too, had written a *Defensio Potestatis summi Pontificis* in 1611 against William Barclay, as well as George Blackwell, though his book was suppressed soon after printing. Still, it was this against which Preston had directed some of his arguments in his *Responsio Apologetica* in 1612. Accordingly, Lessius now published a *Discussio Decreti* concerning the power of the Church in temporal matters against Preston's *Responsio*, under the pseudonym of William Singleton. After an interval of five years, Preston at last came to deal with Lessius's book in his *Discussio Discussionis Decreti*, which he published in 1618. In it he also dealt with the *Oration* of Cardinal Perron of 1615, which belongs to another, related controversy involving King James once again (see 436–7).

345. *Defensio Potestatis summi Pontificis adversus librum regis magnae Britanniae, Guilielmi Barclaii Scoti, et M. Georgii Blacuelli, authore Leonardo Lessio Societatis Iesu sacrae Theologiae Professore.* 1611

346. *Discussio Decreti Magni Concilii Lateranensis et quarundam rationum annexarum, de potestate Ecclesiae in temporalibus, et incommoda diversae sententiae: autore Guil. Singletono.* 1613

347. *Discussio Discussionis Decreti Magni Concilii Lateranensis, adversus Leonardum Lessium Societatis Iesu Theologum nomine Guilhelmi Singletoni personatum. In qua omnia argumenta, quae idemmet Lessius pro Papali potestate Principes deponendi ex Iure Canonico, & decretis Conciliorum, atque Pontificum, aliisque incommodis adducit, dilucide examinantur, & refutantur. Et quaedam egregia Illustrissimi Cardinalis Perronii artificia perspicue deteguntur & refelluntur, A Rogero Widdringtono Catholico Anglo.* 1618   (STC 25601, AR 666, ERL 292)

Yet another reply to Preston's *Responsio Apologetica*, this time in English, came from the pen of the President of Douai, Matthew Kellison. In 1617 he published his controversial book of *The Prelate and the Prince* under the initials I. E. Preston responded in 1620 with his *New-Yeares Gift for English Catholikes* under the reversed initials E. I., claiming that he had 'out of Roger Widdringtons expresse doctrine and grounds collected this little Treatise'. A Latin translation, entitled *Strena Catholica*, also came out that year. In the following year Kellison brought out a second edition of his book, 'newlie revewed and augmented', with a Preface to the Reader explaining the circumstances of this edition and the addition of fresh material here and there in answer to Preston's objections. Also in 1621 Preston published *An Adioynder* to his *New-Yeares Gift* by way of supplement to his arguments, in the form of 'A Letter to R. P.'

348. *The Right and Iurisdiction of the Prelate and the Prince. Or, A Treatise of Ecclesiasticall and Regall authoritie. Compyled by I. E. Student in Divinitie for the ful Instruction and appeacement of the consciences of English Catholikes, concerning the late Oath of pretended Allegeance. Togeather with a cleere & Ample declaration of every clause thereof.* 1617   (STC 14910, AR 427)

(The second edition of 1621 adds the words, 'newlie revewed and augmented by the Authoure', to the above title (STC 14911, AR 428, ERL 208).)

349. *A New-Yeares Gift for English Catholikes, a A Briefe and cleare Explication of the New Oath of Allegiance. By E. I. Student in Divinitie; For a more full Instruction, and appeasement of the consciences of English Catholikes, concerning the said Oath, then hath beene given them by I. E. Student in Divinitie, who compiled the Treatise of the Prelate and the Prince.* 1620   (STC 14049, AR 670, ERL 130)

(The following documents are contained in the text:

A Copie of the new oath of Allegiance, devided into eight Branches as it is in this Treatise explayned. A Copie of the Protestation, which thirteene Reverend Priests made of their Allegiance to Queene Elizabeth, by a publike Instrument the last day of Ianuary 1602. in the last yeere of her Maiesties Reigne. (1603) A Copie of Master Iohn Colletons Petition . . . wherein hee confirmeth his former Protestation (1610)

At the end are given the two decrees of the Parlement of Paris, condemning the books of Bellarmine against Barclay and of Suarez against the *Apology* and *Premonition*.)

350. *An Adioynder to the late Catholike New-Yeares Gift, Or Explication of the Oath of Allegeance. Wherein Certaine principall difficulties, obiected by a very learned Roman-Catholike, against the sayd New-yeares Gift, and Explication of the Oath, are very clearely explained. Published by E. I. the Author of the New-yeares Gift.* 1620 (STC 14050, AR 660, ERL 378)

(The identity of the 'very learned Roman-Catholike' is concealed under the initials, M. B.)

351. *Strena Catholica, seu Explicatio brevis, et dilucida novi Fidelitatis Juramenti. Ab E. J. Sac. Theol. Studioso composita (Ad conscientias Catholicorum Anglorum plenius cira idem Juramentum instruendas et serenandas, quam fuerint instructae ab I. E. Sacrae Theologiae Studioso qui Tractatum Anglicum de Ecclesiastica et Regia potestate compilavit.* 1620   (Not in STC, AR 675)

Meanwhile, on 16 March 1614, two of Preston's books, his *Apologia pro Iure Principum* and *Disputatio Theologica*, had been placed on the Index of Prohibited Books by order of Pope Paul V. Preston responded by publishing *A Copy of the Decree*, along with a defence or 'purgation' of himself – first in Latin, then in English – in 1614. To the English translation he appended 'An Admonition to the Reader' concerning *The Reply of T. F.* (or Thomas Fitzherbert), which had just come out with another English translation of the Index decree (cf. 371). After waiting in vain for a response from Rome, Preston renewed his appeal to the Pope in the form of a longer *Supplicatio*, which was published (in Latin) in 1616, together with a lengthy Appendix against the accusations of Bellarmine as Adolphus Schulckenius. It was, however, promptly placed on the Index. In the same year he brought out a self-defence in English by way of reply to Thomas Fitzherbert and Cardinal Bellarmine, under the title of *A Cleare, Sincere and Modest Confutation*, which also has its place in the following controversy. Later in 1620 he returned to his appeal with an *Appellatio* turning from the Cardinals of the Holy Office to the Pope himself, on behalf not only of himself, but also of his Benedictine supporter, Thomas Green – but with no better result. On the accession of Pope Gregory XV in 1621 he renewed his appeal in a *Humillima Supplicatio*, and then relapsed into silence.

352. *Exemplar Decreti: In quo duo Libri Rogeri Widdringtoni, Catholici Angli condemnantur, & Authori ut se purget praeceptum imponitur atq; Epistolae. Quam idem Ro. Widdringtonus, ad Sanctissimum Dominum Paulum Quintum Pontificem Max. pro se purgando transmisit.* 1614   (AR 669)

353. *A Copy of the Decree: Wherein Two Bookes of Roger Widdrington an English Catholick are condemned, and the Author commanded to purge himselfe: And A Copy of the Purgation which the same Roger Widdrington sent to his Holinesse Pope Paul the fift. Translated out of Latine into English by the Author, whereunto he hath also adioined an Admonition to the Reader concerning the Reply of T. F. &c. and the condemnation of Fa: Suarez booke by a Decree of the Parliament of Paris.* 1614   (STC 25606, AR 665, ERL 337)

354. *Roger Widdringtoni, Catholici Angli ad Sanctissimum Dominum Paulum Quintum, Pontificem Max. humillima Supplicatio, cui*

Adiungitur Appendix, in quo plurimae calumniae cum insigni fraude, & maledicentia coniunctae, quas Adolphus Schulckenius Doctor Theologus eidem Widdringtono ad eum haeresews accusandum falso, summamque per iniuriam imposuit, perspicue deteguntur, et Idem Schulckenius in ius vocatur, atque in manifestae calumniae iudicium a Widdringtono adducitur. 1616   (STC 25605, AR 673, ERL 65)

(The running title is: *Supplicatio ad Paulum V. Pont. Max.* The appendix has the following title:

Appendix ad Supplicationem praecedentem. In quo Plurimae calumniae cum insigni fraude, & maledicentia coniunctae, quas Adolphus Schulckenius Doctor Theologus Rogero Widdringtono ad eum haereseos accusandum falso, summamque per iniuriam imposuit, clare ac perspicue deteguntur. Et Idem Schulckenius in manifestae calumniae iudicium a Widdringtono adducitur.)

355. [= 372] *A cleare, Sincere, and Modest Confutation of the unsound, fraudulent, and intemperate Reply of T. F. who is known to be Mr. Thomas Fitzherbert now an English Iesuite. Wherein also are confuted the chiefest obiections which D. Schulckenius, who is commonly said to be Card. Bellarmine, hath made against Widdringtons Apologie for the right, or Soveraigntie of temporall Princes. By Roger Widdrington an English Catholike.* 1616   (STC 25598, AR 664, ERL 223)

356. *Appellatio qua Reverendi Patres, Thomas Prestonus, & Thomas Greenaeus Angli Benedictini ac Sacrae Theologiae Professores, ab Illmis Dominis Cardinalibus ad Indicem deputatis ad Romanum, Summumq; Pontificem immediate provocarunt.* 1620   (Not in STC, AR 677, ERL 354)

357. *Reverendorum Patrum D. Thomae Prestoni Congregationis Cassinensis, & Fr. Thomae Greenaei Congregationis Hispanicae Ordinis S. Benedicti Religiosorum, & Sacrae Theologiae Professorum, Ad Sanctissimum ac Beatissimum Patrem Gregorium Decimum quintum, Pontificem Maximum, Sanctamq Sedem Apostolicam, Humillima Supplicatio.* 1621   (Not in STC, AR 678, ERL 354)

Other Anglican opponents of Bellarmine's theory of the Pope's temporal power were George Carleton, later Bishop of Llandaff, and John Buckeridge, Bishop of Rochester. The former criticized Bellarmine in more general terms in his *Iurisdiction Regall, Episcopall, Papall,* in 1610; while the latter dealt more specifically with the *De Potestate Papae* in 1614. Subsequently, when Bellarmine brought out his minor work *De Officio Principis Christiani* in 1619, Thomas Morton, then Bishop of Coventry and Lichfield, responded a year later with his *Causa Regia.* Lastly, in 1621 Richard Crakanthorpe brought out a criticism of 'the Popes temporall Monarchie' entitled *The Defence of Constantine.*

358. *Iurisdiction Regall, Episcopall, Papall, Wherein is declared How the Pope hath intruded Upon the Iurisdiction of Temporall Princes, and of the Church. The intrusion is discovered, and the peculiar and distinct Iurisdiction to each properly belonging, recovered. Written by George Carleton.* 1610 (STC 4637)

(The author refers mainly to Bellarmine's treatise *De Romano Pontifice* in the first volume of his *De Controversiis*, which had first appeared in 1586 but continued to come out in new editions almost every other year.)

359. *De Potestate Papae in Rebus Temporalibus, sive in Regibus Deponendis usurpata; Adversus Robertum Cardinalem Bellarminum, Libri duo. In quibus respondetur Authoribus, Scripturis, Rationibus, Exemplis, contra Gulielmum Barclaium allatis. Necnon sex, vel verius quinque exemplis: quibus, morte praeventus, non responderat G. B. Authore Ioanne Episcopo Roffensi.* 1614 (STC 4002)

360. *De Officio Principis Christiani Libri tres. Auctore Roberto Bellarmino S. R. E. Card. E Societate Iesu. Ad Sereniss. Principem, Wladislaum Sigismundi III Poloniae & Sueciae Regis filium. Quibus accessit Admonitio Ad Episcopum Theanensem Nepotem suum, De necessariis Episcopo ad salutem suam in tuto ponendam.* 1619

361. *Causa Regia, sive De Authoritate et Dignitate Principum Christianorum, Dissertatio; Adversus Rob. Cardinalis Bellarmini Tractatum, De officio Principis Christiani inscriptum, edita. Authore Reverendo Patre Thoma Mortono Coventriensi & Lichfeldensi Episcopo.* 1620 (STC 18178)

362. *The Defence of Constantine: With a Treatise of the Popes temporall Monarchie. Wherein, besides divers passages, touching other Counsels, both Generall and Provinciall, the second Roman Synod, under Silvester, is declared to be a meere Fiction and Forgery. By Richard Crakanthorp, Doctor of Divinity.* 1621 (STC 5974)

h) *The English Controversy*

While the major controversy over the *Apologia* of King James was being conducted in Latin, a parallel controversy was also being conducted in English. This began when Persons in 1608 brought out his *Iudgment of a Catholicke English-man* on the *Triplici nodo, triplex cuneus*, before James had declared his royal authorship. Persons, who maintained his own anonymity, professed to find in that book the hand of Thomas Morton, with whom he was then waging his other controversy over conspiracy and equivocation. The King, however, when he brought out the second edition of his *Apologie* with the 'Premonition', recognized the identity of the *Catholicke Englishman* as the 'perverse Pamphleter Parsons'. The fuller answer to the Jesuit he left to his Anglican divines: the Archdeacon of Ely, Robert Tynley, who preached a *Sermon* at Paul's Cross on 5 November 1608, against 'that lewde English Libell, written by a Prophane Fugitive'; and the Bishop of Lincoln, William Barlow, who penned a more elaborate *Answer* in the following year.

363. *The Iudgment of a Catholicke English-man, living in banishment for his Religion: Written to his private friend in England. Concerning A late Booke set forth, and entituled: Triplici nodo, triplex cuneus, Or, An Apologie for the Oath of Allegiance. Against two Breves of Pope Paulus V. to the Catholickes of England; & a Letter of Cardinall Bellarmine to M. George Blackwell Arch-priest. Wherin, the said Oath is shewed to be unlawfull to the Catholicke Conscience; for so much, as it conteyneth sundry clauses repugnant to his Religion.* 1608
    (STC 19408, AR 630, ERL 82)

364. [= 540] *Two Learned Sermons. The one, of the mischievous subtiltie, and barbarous crueltie, the other of the false Doctrines, and refined Haeresies of the Romish Synagogue. Preached, the one at Paules Crosse the 5. of November, 1608. The other at the Spittle the 17. of Aprill. 1609. In the first, are examined divers passages of that lewde English Libell, written by a Prophane Fugitive, against the Apologie for the Oath of Allegeance. In the seconde, are answered many of the arguments published by Rob. Chambers Priest, concerning Popish Miracles; and Dedicated (forsooth) to the Kings most excellent Maiestie. By Robert Tynley, Doctor of Divinitie, and Archdeacon of Ely.* 1609   (STC 24472)

(The second sermon deals with Chambers' book on *Miracles*, translated from the French of P. Numan in 1606 — to be dealt with in the next chapter (538–9).

365. *An Answer To A Catholicke English-man (so by himselfe entituled) who, without a Name, passed his Censure upon the Apology, made by the Right High and mightie Prince Iames by the Grace of God King of Great Brittaine, France, and Ireland &c. for the Oath of Allegiance; which censure is heere examined and refuted. By the Bishop of Lincoln.* 1609 (STC 1446)

Overlooking Tynley's sermon, Persons set about composing a *Discussion* of Barlow's *Answer*. But death intervened in 1610, before he could bring his work to completion. This task was undertaken by his friend and colleague,

Thomas Fitzherbert, who brought out the book in 1612, with a Confutatory Preface by the Jesuit Edward Coffin. Persons also had a hand in the *Dutifull and Respective Considerations* on the King's 'Praefatio Monitoria', which appeared in 1609; though it was presented as the work of Humphrey Leech, who, after being an Anglican minister, became a convert to Rome in 1608 and subsequently a Jesuit priest.

366. *A Discussion of the Answere of M. William Barlow, D. of Divinity, to the Booke intituled: The Iudgment of a Catholicke Englishman living in banishment for his Religion &c. concerning The Apology of the new Oath of Allegiance. Written By the R. Father, F. Robert Persons of the Society of Iesus. Wherunto since the said Fathers death, is annexed a generall Preface, laying open the Insufficiency, Rayling, Lying, and other Misdemeanour of M. Barlow in his writing.* 1612   (STC 19409, AR 628, ERL 227)

367. *Dutifull and Respective Considerations upon foure severall heads of Proofe and Triall in matters of Religion. Proposed by the High and Mighty Prince, Iames King of Great Britayne, France, and Ireland &c. in his late Booke of Premonition to all Christian Princes, for clearing his Royall Person from the imputation of Heresy. By a late Minister & Preacher in England.* 1609   (STC 15362 = 19404, AR 449, ERL 74)

(There used to be a manuscript of this book in Persons' handwriting at the English College, Rome. But the attribution to Leech is recognized by P. Alegambe, *Bibliotheca Scriptorum Societatis Iesu* (1643).)

Fitzherbert went on to publish *A Supplement to the Discussion* in 1613 under his own name. Besides further criticism of Barlow, he also attacked John Donne's *Pseudo-Martyr*, which had been published in 1610 to persuade Catholics 'to take the Oath of Allegeance'. Then to his Supplement he added *An Adioynder* against Andrewes' *Answer* to Bellarmine's *Apology*, considering that this book of Andrewes 'hath not yet byn answered by any in our tongue'.

368. *Pseudo-Martyr. Wherein out of certaine Propositions and Gradations, This Conclusion is evicted. That those which are of the Romane Religion in this Kingdome, may and ought to take the Oath of Allegeance.* 1610   (STC 7084)

369. *A Supplement to the Discussion of M. D. Barlowes Answere To the Iudgment of a Catholike Englishman &c. interrupted by the death of the Author F. Robert Persons of the Society of Iesus. Wherein Many foule Absurdities, Ignorances, and Falsities are discovered in M. D. Barlow. And by the way is briefly censured M. Iohn Dunnes Booke, intituled Pseudo-martyr. Also An Adioynder, contayning a Confutation*

of certaine Absurdities, Falsities, and Follies uttered by M. D.
Andrewes in his Answere to Cardinall Bellarmines Apology, concerning
certaine points incident to matters treated in this Supplement.
Togeather with the Censure of the whole Worke. By F. T. 1613
(STC 11021, AR 318, ERL 228)

(The *Adioynder* has a separate title-page, and it may be treated as a
separate item, as follows:)

370. *An Adioynder to the Supplement of Father Robert Persons his
Discussion of M. Doctor Barlowes Answere &c. Contayning A
Discovery, and Confutation of very many foule Absurdityes, Falsities,
and Lyes in M. D. Andrewes his Latin Booke intituled, Responsio ad
Apologiam Cardinalis Bellarmini &c. An Answere to the Apology of
Card. Bellarmine. Written by F. T. Authour of the Supplement, to
iustify certaine places, and authorities alleaged, as well by him in the
said Supplement, as by the Cardinall in his Apology, and pretended to
be answered by M. D. Andrewes. Also An Appendix touching a Register
alleaged by M. Franc. Mason for the lawfull Ordayning of Protestant
Bishops in Q. Elizabeths Raigne. 1613* (STC 11022, AR 309,
ERL 238)

(Reference is made in the Appendix to Francis Mason's book, *Of the
Consecration of the Bishops* (1613), which belongs to another
controversy in the next chapter (577).)

These books of Fitzherbert provoked two separate controversies: one with
the Catholic priest, Thomas Preston (or Roger Widdrington); the other with
the Anglican minister, Samuel Collins. In the first place, when he came to
publish his *Theological Disputation* in 1613 (325), Preston describes in the
Preface how he received 'an English booke printed but lately, and entituled,
A Supplement to the discourse of Master Doctor Barlowes Answere, &c.
composed by F. T.' He therefore added a criticism of the first two chapters
of this *Supplement* in particular. This led Fitzherbert (who had meanwhile
joined the Society of Jesus at the ripe age of sixty-one) to bring out *The
Reply of T. F.* – reversing his previous initials. He also added a copy of the
decree of the Index prohibiting the *Disputatio Theologica* and the *Apologia*
of Widdrington. In reply, Preston published a *Confutation* in 1616, adding
an answer to the arguments of Bellarmine as Adolphus Schulckenius against
his *Apologia* of 1611 (338–9). This was followed by his *Last Reioynder* in
1619, in which he adapted much of his *Discussio Discussionis* of 1618 (347)
in an English form.

371. *The Reply of T. F. in defence Of the two first Chapters of his
Supplement to the Discussion &c. impugned By one falsely naming
himself Roger Widdrington, in a Latin Booke intituled, Disputatio*

*Theologica de Iuramento Fidelitatis. Also a Copy of a Decree lately
made, & published by the expresse Commaundement of his Holynes,
for the condemnation, & prohibition of the aforesayd Disputatio
Theologica, & of a former Booke of the same Authour, intituled,
Apologia Cardinalis Bellarmini &c.* 1614   (STC 11023, AR 315,
ERL 160)

372. [= 355] *A Cleare, Sincere, and Modest Confutation of the unsound,
fraudulent, and intemperate Reply of T. F. who is known to be Mr.
Thomas Fitzherbert now an English Iesuite. Wherein also are confuted
the chiefest obiections which D. Schulckenius, who is commonly said
to be Card. Bellarmine, hath made against Widdringtons Apologie for
the right, or Soveraigntie of temporall Princes. By Roger Widdrington
an English Catholicke.* 1616   (STC 25598, AR 664, ERL 223)

373. *Roger Widdringtons Last Reioynder to Mr. Thomas Fitz-herberts Reply
concerning The Oath of Allegiance, And the Popes power to depose
Princes. Wherein all his arguments, taken from the Lawes of God, in the
old and new Testament, of Nature, of Nations, from the Canon and
Civill Law, and from the Popes Breves, condemning the Oath, and the
Cardinalls Decree, forbidding two of Widdringtons Bookes are
answered: Also many Replies and Instances of Cardinall Bellarmine in
his Schulckenius, and of Leonard Lessius in his Singleton are confuted,
and divers cunning shifts of Cardinall Peron are discovered.* 1619
(STC 25599, AR 671, ERL 280)

As for Samuel Collins, one of the royal chaplains, he dealt with
Fitzherbert's *Adioynder* against Andrewes in his *Epphata to F. T.* in 1617.
Four Years later, Fitzherbert retorted, in a similar vein, with *The Obmutesce
of F. T.* And the rest was silence.

374. *Epphata to F. T. or, The Defence of the Right Reverend Father in God,
the Lord Bishop of Elie, Lord High-Almoner and Privie Counsellour to
the Kings Most Excellent Maiestie. Concerning his Answer to Cardinall
Bellarmines Apologie: Against the slaunderous cavills of a namelesse
Adioynder; entitling his Booke in every page of it, A Discoverie of
many fowle absurdities, falsities, lyes, &c. Wherein these things cheifely
are discussed, (besides many other incident.) 1. The Popes false
Primacie, clayming by Peter. 2. Invocation of Saints, with Worship of
creatures, and Faith in them. 3. The Supremacie of Kings both in
Temporall and Ecclesiasticall matters and causes, over all states and
persons, &c. within their Realmes and Dominions. By Dr. Collins,
chaplaine to His Maiestie.* 1617   (STC 5561)

375. *The Obmutesce of F. T. to the Epphata of D. Collins. or The Reply of*

> *F. T. to D. Collins his defence of my Lord of Winchesters Answere to*
> *Cardinall Bellarmines Apology. In which Reply M. Collins is convinced*
> *of most manifest frauds, falsityes, fooleryes, & lyes. Written by Thomas*
> *Fitzherbert Priest of the Society of Iesus, in defence of his Adioynder*
> *impugned by M. Collins: wherein the Authors name was cyphred with*
> *the two letters F. T. 1621* (STC 11020, AR 314, ERL 188)

(Andrewes had meanwhile been promoted from the See of Ely to that
of Winchester, in 1619.

The references for 'Epphata' and 'Obmutesce' are (respectively) Mark
vii. 34, and i. 25.)

i) *Anglican and Catholic Defences of the Oath*

In addition to all these controversial writings there were many more books,
not only by Anglicans but also by Catholics, and on both sides of the
Channel, in defence of the Oath of Allegiance. On the Anglican side, this was
a common subject of sermons, as we have seen in Tynley's sermon at Paul's
Cross against Persons' *Iudgment of a Catholicke English-man.* Other sermons
defending the Oath, and extolling the divine right of kings, were given by
Richard Crakanthorpe at Paul's Cross in 1609, by Thomas Ireland at York in
1610, and by Sebastian Benefield at Oxford in 1613; and they were all
published soon afterwards. The same subject was dealt with in a book
entitled *Eclogarius* by John Panke, which came out in 1612, discussing 'the
questions of late risen . . . especially now about the oath of allegiance'.

376. *A Sermon at the Solemnizing of the Happie Inauguration of our most*
     gracious and Religious Soveraigne King Iames. Wherein is manifestly
     proved, that the Soveraignty of Kings is immediatly from God, and
     second to no authority on Earth whatsover. Preached at Paules Crosse,
     the 24. of March last. 1608. By Richard Crakanthorpe, Doctor of
     Divinitie. 1609 (STC 5979)

377. *The Oath of Allegeance, Defended by a Sermon preached at a Synode*
     in the Metropoliticall Church of Yorke; By Thomas Ireland, Bachelour in
     Divinitie. 1610 (STC 14267)

378. *A Sermon preached in St. Maries Church in Oxford, March xxiv,*
     MDCII. at the solemnizing of the happy inauguration of our gracious
     Soveraigne King Iames. Wherein is prooved, that Kinges doe hold their
     Kingdomes immediately from God. By Sebastian Benefield D. of
     Divinitie, Fellow of Corpus Christi College. 1613 (STC 1871)

379. *Eclogarius, or Briefe Summe of the Truth of that Title of Supreame*
     Governour, given to his Maiestie in causes Spirituall, and Ecclesiasticall,

from the Kings of Israell, in the old Testament; the Christian
Emperours in the Primitive Church; confirmed by 40 Epistles of Leo
the Bishop of Rome, unto the Emperours, Theodosius, Martianus, and
Leo. Not published before. By Iohn Panke. 1612   (STC 19170)

On the Catholic side, other priests joined Thomas Preston — and George
Blackwell — in defending the Oath, after having taken it themselves. This was
not infrequently a prelude to their submission to the Church of England.
Thus in 1611 Richard Sheldon published *Certain General Reasons* for
accepting the Oath. It was bound with the English translation of William
Barclay's treatise on papal power and Theophilus Higgons' *Sermon* of
recantation, since they all served 'to declare the iustnesse of the Oath of
Allegiance in England' (as the publisher declared in his 'Advertisement'). In
the following year Sheldon, too, preached and published a *Sermon* of
recantation — to be dealt with in the next chapter, along with that of
Higgons. Next came William Warmington, whose *Moderate Defence of the*
Oath in 1612 won him release from prison (where he had been kept since
1608) and a pension from the Bishop of Winchester.

380. *Certain General Reasons, proving the lawfulnesse of the Oath of*
Allegiance, written by R. S. Priest, to his privat Friend. Whereunto is
added the Treatise of that learned man, M. William Barclay, concerning
the temporall power of the Pope. And with these is ioyned the Sermon
of M. Theophilus Higgons, Preached at Pauls Crosse the third of March
last, because it containeth something of like argument. 1611
(STC 22393)

381. *A Moderate Defence of the Oath of Allegiance: Wherein the Author*
proveth the said Oath to be most lawful, notwithstanding the Popes
Breves prohibiting the same; and solveth the chiefest obiections that are
usually made against it; perswading the Catholickes not to resist
soveraigne Authoritie in refusing it. Together with the Oration of
Sixtus 5. in the Consistory at Rome, upon the murther of Henrie 3. the
French King by a Friar. Whereunto also is annexed strange Reports or
newes from Rome. By William Warmington Catholicke Priest, and
Oblate of the holy congregation of S. Ambrose. 1612   (STC 25076,
AR 882, ERL 276)

Of greater weight than these English books of Sheldon and Warmington, who
had after all (like Blackwell) been subjected to moral pressure by the English
authorities, was the Latin treatise of William Barret, *Ius Regis*, which he
published at Basle in 1612. As an Anglican divine at Cambridge, he had led
the reaction there against the teaching of Calvin in the 1590's; and in 1597
he had fled to the continent and become a Catholic. Now, influenced by the
attitude of Blackwell and the book of William Barclay, he came out in
defence of the King against the Pope.

382. *Ius Regis, Sive De Absoluto & independenti Secularium Principum dominio & obsequio eis debito. Adversus fictam Iuris Subditorum praeexistentiam aut populi in principatum meram cessionem: praecipue contra Papalem in Reges & Principes Secularem potestatem Libri tres. In quibus Summo Pontifici Ius non esse Principes deponere aut civiliter plectere Autoritate sacra, Historica & Forensi. Probat Guil. Barret, Anglus. I. C. Et obiecta diluit.* 1612   (STC 1501, AR 72, ERL 224)

From the other side of the Channel, the Gallican jurist, Edmond Richer, brought out his Latin treatise, *De Ecclesiastica et Politica Potestate*, in 1612. This was translated into English in the same year, as *A Treatise of Ecclesiasticall and Politike Power*, with a Preface 'To the Romish Catholikes of England' appealing to the example not only of Blackwell, Warmington and Sheldon, but also of Widdrington who 'at least was free'.

383. *De Ecclesiastica et Politica Potestate, Liber unus. Ecclesia, est Politia Monarchica, ad finem supernaturalem instituta: regimine aristocratico, quod omnium optimum & naturae convenientissimum est, temperata a summo animarum Pastore Domino nostro Iesu Christo.* 1612

(In an Appendix is added a decree of the Sorbonne:

Decreta Sacrae Facultatis Theologiae Parisiensis, De Potestate Ecclesiastica, & Primatu Romani Pontificis, contra Sectarios huius seculi.)

384. *A Treatise of Ecclesiasticall and Politike power. Shewing, the Church is a Monarchicall government, ordained to a supernaturall and spirituall end, tempered with an aristocraticall order, (which is the best of all and most conformable to nature) by the great Pastor of soules Iesus Christ. Faithfully translated out of the Latin originall, of late publikely printed and allowed in Paris. Now set foorth for a further warrant and encouragement to the Romish Catholikes of England, for theyr taking of the Oath of Allegiance; seeing so many others of their owne profession in other Countries doe deny the Popes infalibility in iudgement and temporal power over Princes, directly against the doctrine of Iesuits. To the Prince.* 1612   (STC 21024)

On the Huguenot side in France, King James found a faithful champion of his ideas in the eminent divine, Pierre Du Moulin (Molinaeus). There it was a Dominican theologian, Nicolas Coeffeteau, who stood out in opposition to the *Apologie* and 'Premonition' of James with his *Responce a l'Advertissement* in 1610. In reply, Du Moulin brought out his *Defense de la Foy Catholique* in the same year, with a Dedication to King James, and it was immediately translated into English by John Digby, Earl of Bristol, as *A Defence of the Catholicke Faith*. A third part of this work was published

separately as *Accomplissement des Propheties,* and translated into English by
John Heath in 1613 as *The Accomplishment of the Prophecies.* Finally, Du
Moulin published a Latin treatise, *De Monarchia Temporali Pontificis
Romani,* in 1614, to defend King James against the objections and
arguments of Bellarmine and Coeffeteau. This was published in London, but
not translated into English.

385. *Responce a l'Advertissement, adressé par le Serenissime Roy de la
grande Bretagne, Iacques I. à tous les Princes & Potentats de la
Chrestienté. Par F. N. Coeffeteau Docteur en Theologie, de l'Ordre des
Fr. Prescheurs, & Predicateur ordinaire du Roy. 1610*

(This is written in the form of a letter to King James.)

386. *Defense de la Foy Catholique contenue au Livre de Trespuissant &
Serenissime Roy Iaques I. Roy de la grand' Bretagne & d'Irlande.
Contre la Response de F. N. Coeffeteau Docteur en Theologie, &
Vicaire general des Freres Prescheurs. Par Pierre Du Moulin Ministre de
la parole de Dieu en l'Eglise de Paris. 1610*

387. *A Defence of the Catholicke Faith: Contained in the Booke of the most
Mightie, and most Gracious King Iames the first, King of Great
Britaine, France and Ireland, Defender of the Faith. Against the
Answere of N. Coeffeteau, Doctour of Divinitie, and Vicar Generall of
the Dominican Preaching Friars. Written in French, by Pierre Du
Moulin, Minister of the word of God in the Church of Paris. Translated
into English according to his first Coppie, by himselfe reviewed and
corrected. 1610* (STC 7322)

388. *Accomplissement des Propheties. Traitté Où est monstré que les
Propheties de Sainct Paul, & de l'Apocalypse, & de Daniel, touchant les
combats de l'Eglise, sont accomplies. Par Pierre du Moulin, Ministre de
la parole de Dieu en l'Eglise de Paris.* (Edition of 1621)

389. *The Accomplishment of the Prophecies; or the third booke in defense
of the Catholicke faith, contained in the booke of the high & mighty
King Iames I. by the grace of God King of Great Brittaine and Ireland.
Against the allegations of R. Bellarmine; and F. N. Coeffeteau & other
Doctors of the Romish Church: By Peter Du Moulin Minister of the
word of God in the Church of Paris. Translated out of French by I.
Heath, Fellow of New College in Oxford. 1613* (STC 7306)

390. *Petri Molinaei De Monarchia Temporali Pontificis Romani Liber, Quo
Imperatoris, Regum, & Principum jura adversus usurpationes Papae
defenduntur: Et docetur quibus artibus Papa ab humili statu ad tantae*

> *potentiae culmen ascenderit: & liber Serenissimi ac Potentissimi Regis*
> *Iacobi ab adversariorum obiectionibus, praecipue vero Roberti*
> *Bellarmini, et Cuffetelli Dominicani, vindicatur.* 1614   (STC 7335)

This may be the place to insert a strange by-product of this long and complicated controversy over the Oath of Allegiance. In 1615 there appeared an anonymous dialogue in Latin, entitled *Deus & Rex*, and published by royal privilege and command, as a vindication of the Oath of Allegiance. At the same time it was brought out in an English translation, *God and the King*. Soon afterwards a royal proclamation was issued, on 8 November, requiring every householder in England and Scotland to buy a copy, that every subject might understand the lawfulness of the Oath of Allegiance. Its authorship was variously attributed to the King himself and to his Archbishop's chaplain, Richard Mocket; but the latter fell into disgrace the very next year on account of another publication already mentioned, *Doctrina, et Politia Ecclesiae Anglicanae* (101), and he died in 1618. The same lesson was further inculcated by the anonymous author of *The doctrine of Subiection to God and the King*, which appeared in 1616 and has been attributed to the Puritan Stephen Egerton. The Catholic response is to be seen partly in Kellison's above-mentioned book on *The Prelate and the Prince*, but chiefly in a skilful Latin parody by the Jesuit, John Floyd, similarly entitled *Deus et Rex*. In the same form of dialogue, but with different speakers, Floyd aimed at discrediting the main Anglican writers in the controversy, Morton, Burhill, Thomson, Tooker and Barlow. His work was soon translated into English by his fellow-Jesuit, Thomas More.

391. *Deus & Rex: Sive Dialogus, quo demonstratur Serenissimum*
     D. nostrum Iacobum Regem immediate sub Deo constitutum in Regnis
     suis, iustissime sibi vendicare quicquid in Iuramento Fidelitatis
     requiritur. Londini, Excusum cum speciali Regiae Maiestatis privilegio
     & mandato. 1615   (STC 14415)

   (The speakers are Theodidactus and Philalethes. The history of Catholic 'plots' against Elizabeth is repeated, with special reference to Allen and Bristow, Persons and Campion.)

392. *God and the King: or, A Dialogue, shewing that our Soveraigne Lord*
     King Iames, being immediate under God within his Dominions, Doth
     rightfully claime whatsoever is required by the Oath of Allegeance.
     1615   (STC 14419)

393. *By the King. A Proclamation for the confirmation of all Authorized*
     Orders, tending to the Universall publishing and teaching, of a certaine
     Religious Treatise, compiled by Authoritie, and Intituled by the Name
     of 'God, and the King'. 1615   (STC 8531)

394. *The doctrine of Subiection to God and the King. Gathered out of the 5. Commandement fit for all the Kings Subiects to read, wherein they may learne true obedience.* 1616

395. *Deus et Rex Sive Dialogus, in quo agitur de fidelitate Serenissimo Domino nostro Iacobo Regi in regnis suis praestanda; Qua (sublatis controversiis & turbarum suspicionumque causis omnibus) subditi insolubili amoris & obedientiae vinculo Regi suo astringantur.* 1619

(The speakers are Aristobulus and Philanax. The seeds of rebellion are ascribed to the Protestant reformers.)

396. *God and the King. Or A Dialogue Wherein is treated of Allegiance due to our most Gracious Lord, King Iames, within his Dominions. Which (by removing all Controversies, and causes of Dissentions and Suspitions) bindeth Subiects, by an inviolable band of Love & Duty, to their Soveraigne. Translated out of Latin into English.* 1620   (Not in STC, AR 325, ERL 9)

j) *Controversy over Regicide*

The assassination of the French King Henry IV by Francois Ravaillac in 1610 was attributed by their enemies to the Jesuits — as a recurrence of what had happened, or had been about to happen, in England at the time of the Gunpowder Plot in 1605. In particular, a copy of *De Rege et Regis Institutione* by the Jesuit Juan Mariana (1599), in which tyrannicide was defended under certain conditions, was said to have been found in Ravaillac's possession and to have inspired his evil action. This prompted the Sorbonne to pass a decree condemning Mariana's opinion; while the Parlement of Paris ordered his book to be burnt in public. These proceedings were immediately translated into English by J. B. and published in 1610, with a Preamble drawing the connection between these events in France and Garnet's implication in the recent Gunpowder Plot in England, as well as the Jesuit opposition to the Oath of Allegiance. The aim of this publication, *The Copie of a Late Decree*, was explicit: that 'the milder and more moderate sort of Priests, and other Recusants, might be induced not to refuse the said Oath of Allegiance'.

397. *Arrest de la Cour de Parlement, Ensemble la Censure de la Sorbone, contre le livre de Iean Mariana, Intitulé De Rege & Regis institutione. Avec Un avertissement aux bons Francois sur la lettre declaratoire presentee à la Royne Mere du Roy, Regente en France, par le Pere Coton. Avec quelque Stances a la loüange de tres-heureuse memoire Henry le grand Roy de France & de Navarre.* 1610

398. *The Copie of a Late Decree of the Sorbonne at Paris, for the*
condemning of that impious and haereticall opinion, touching the
murthering of Princes; Generally maintained by the Iesuites, And
amongst the rest, of late by Ioannes Mariana, a Spaniard: Together,
with the Arrest of the Parliament, for the confirmation of that Decree,
And the condemning of the said Marianas Booke, to be publiquely
burnt by the Executioner. Taken out of the Register of the Parliament,
and translated into English. 1610   (STC 19204)

The news of the French King's assassination also prompted King James, who
felt himself personally in danger, to issue a royal proclamation on 2 June
1610, enforcing the laws against recusants, banishing all priests and Jesuits
from the realm, and enjoining the Oath of Allegiance to be carefully
administered. Another proclamation followed on 31 May 1611, urging the
due administration of the Oath.

399. *By the King. A Proclamation for the due execution of all former Lawes*
against Recusants, giving them a day to repaire to their owne dwellings,
and not afterwards to come to the Court, or within 10 miles of
London, without speciall Licence; And for disarming of them as the
Law requireth. And withall, that all Priests and Iesuits shall depart the
land by a day, no more to returne into the Realme; And for the
ministring of the Oath of Allegiance according to the Law. 1610
(STC 8447)

400. *By the King. A Proclamation, whereby it is commanded, That the Oath*
of Allegeance be administered according to the Lawes. 1611
(STC 8468)

Against the first of these proclamations two Jesuit writers published
vigorous protests. In 1610 Michael Walpole, using the pseudonym Michael
Christopherson, published *A Briefe Admonition* warning the Catholics
against the recent proclamation and also against J. B.'s pamphlet. He
dedicated his work to the Queen, reputedly a Catholic, to intercede like
Esther of old for her persecuted co-religionists. In the following year, Joseph
Cresswell published *A briefe & moderate Answere* to the proclamation, with
an abstract of the penal laws then in force against Catholics, so as to
emphasize their inhuman cruelty and injustice.

401. *A Briefe Admonition to all English Catholikes, concerning A late*
Proclamation set forth against them. Dedicated to the Queenes most
Excellent Maiesty. Togeather with the Confutation of a Pamphlet,
newly published, concerning a Decree of the Sorbon at Paris &c. And
An Epistle to Doctor King, in the behalfe of the Iesuites. By M. C. P.
1610.   (STC 24992, AR 871, ERL 159)

402. *A Proclamation published under the name of Iames King of Great*
Britanny. With a briefe & moderate Answere therunto. Whereto Are
added the penall Statutes, made in the same Kingdome, against
Catholikes. Togeather With a Letter which sheweth the said Catholikes
piety: And divers Advertisements also, for better understanding of the
whole matter. Translated out of Latin into English. 1611   (STC 8448,
AR 265, ERL 58)

(The abstract has the following title:

An Abstract or briefe summe of the Lawes, that in the former
Proclamation are termed good and wholsome, made by his Maiesty, and
the Parliament of England, against the Catholikes of that Kingdome.

No Latin original seems to have survived.)

Neither of these books prompted any answer from the Anglican side. But the
political situation led to the publication of two Anglican books against
regicide about this time. In 1610 David Owen published his *Herod and Pilate*
reconciled, as well against Puritans as against Papists, though chiefly the
latter. Two years later George Hakewill, who had been active in translating
many of the anti-Jesuit pamphlets current in France, brought out a Latin
treatise against all regicides, entitled *Scutum Regium*.

403. *Herod and Pilate reconciled: or, The Concord of Papist and Puritan*
(Against Scripture, Fathers, Councels, and other Orthodoxall Writers)
for the Coercion, Deposition, and Killing of Kings. Discovered by David
Owen Batchelour of Divinitie, and Chaplaine to the right Honourable
Lord Vicount Hadington. 1610   (STC 18983)

404. *Scutum Regium. id est, adversus omnes Regicidas et Regicidarum*
Patronos, ab initio mundi usque ad interitum Phocae Imp. circa annum
ab Incarnatione Domini 610. Ecclesiae Catholicae consensus
Orthodoxus. In tres Libros divisus, quorum 1. Primus continet
testimonia & exempla Sacrae Scripturae utriusque testamenti.
2. Secundus Ecclesiae Primitivae innocentiam, & erga Principes
obedientiam, sub decem gravissimis persequutionibus. 3. Tertius
Orthodoxorum fidelitatem in Haereticos, & nefarios Imp. ab Imperio
Constantini Magni usque ad exitum Phocae, Authore Georgio Hakewill,
Sacrae Theologiae Doctore e Coll. Exoniensi in Academia Oxon. 1612
(STC 12618)

Meanwhile, a vigorous controversy had arisen in France out of a *Letter*
written by Henry IV's former confessor, Pierre Coton, to the Queen Regent
in defence of his fellow-Jesuits. This was published in French as *Lettre*
Declaratoire, and immediately translated into English by Thomas Owen under
the title, *A Letter of a Catholike Man Beyond the seas*. Both appeared in
1610.

405. *Lettre Declaratoire de la Doctrine des Peres Iesuites Conforme aux decrets du Concile de Constance, adressee à la Royne mere du Roy Regente en France. Par le Pere Coton, de la Compagnie de Iesus, Predicateur ordinaire de sa Maiesté.* 1610

(Mention is made of 'Bellarmin . . . sa responce Apologetique au livre du Roy de la grand Bretagne'.)

406. *A Letter of a Catholike Man Beyond the seas, written to his friend in England: Including Another of Peter Coton Priest, of the Society of Iesus, to the Queene Regent of France. Translated out of French into English. Touching The imputation of the death of Henry the IIII. late K. of France, to the Priests, Iesuites, or Catholicke Doctrine.* 1610 (STC 19000, AR 591, ERL 138)

(The title of Coton's *Letter* is given as follows:

A Letter Declaratory of the Common Doctrine of the Fathers of the Society of Iesus, conforme to the Decrees of the Councell of Constance: Written to the Queene, Mother of the King, Regent in France. By Father Peter Coton of the same Society, his Maiesties ordinary Preacher at Paris.)

In answer to Coton's *Letter* there immediately appeared two anonymous pamphlets; and they were both immediately translated into English, in view of their relevance to the political situation in England. One was a scurrilous work, entitled *The Hellish and horribble Councell*, which only seems to have survived in its English translation. It was also addressed to the Queen Regent, and had as its inner title, 'The Secret and hidden Mysterie, which the Iesuites doe use, when they resolve to have a King murthered'. The other was a more reasoned and damaging document, entitled *Anticoton*, which was translated into English by G. H. (George Hakewill) early in 1611. Assuming the complicity of the Jesuit Garnet in the English Gunpowder Plot, the author pointed out that he had been commended by 'Bellarmine in his second Booke against the King of England', and further defended by 'a Iesuite named Iohn l'Heureux, but disguising his name in an Hyrogliphicall forme'. The English translator also appended a recent 'Supplication of the Universitie of Paris' against a recent Jesuit petition for the reopening of their school in the city, in view of 'their King-killing Doctrine' — in spite of Coton's insistence that Mariana's theory was by no means common to the Jesuit order.

407. *The Hellish and horribble Councell, practiced and used by the Iesuites, (in their private Consultations) when they would have a man to murther a King. According to those damnable instructions, given (by them) to that bloody villaine Francis Ravilliacke, who murdered Henry*

the Fourth, the late French King. Sent to the Queene Regent, in answere of that impudent Pamphlet published by Peter Cotton Iesuite, in defence of the Iesuites, and their doctrine; which also is hereunto annexed. Translated out of French. 1610   (STC 5862)

408. *Anticoton, ou Refutation de la lettre Declaratoire du Pere Coton. Livre ou est prouvé, que les Iesuites sont coulpables, & autheurs du parricide execrable commis en la personne du Roy tres-Chrestien Henry IIII, d'heureuse memoire.* 1610

409. *Anti-Coton, or A Refutation of Cottons Letter Declaratorie: lately directed to the Queene Regent, for the Apologizing of the Iesuites Doctrine, touching the Killing of Kings. A Booke, In which it is proved that the Iesuites are guiltie, and were the Authors of the late execrable Parricide, committed upon the Person of the French King, Henry the Fourth, of happie memorie. To which is added, A Supplication of the Universitie of Paris, for the preventing of the Iesuites opening their Schooles among them: in which their King-killing Doctrine is also notably discovered, and confuted. Both translated out of the French by G. H. Together with the Translators animadversions upon Cottons Letter.* 1611   (STC 5861)

(The supplementary material is as follows:

The Supplication of the Universitie of Paris, for the preventing of the Iesuites opening of their Schooles in Paris. Wherein their King-killing Doctrine is also opened and refuted.
The Translator to the Reader.)

The French Jesuits took this attack very seriously, as endangering their very existence in France. There soon appeared an anonymous *Response Apologetique a l'Anticoton*, published in 1610 by 'un Pere', who was naturally identified as Coton himself. It was immediately translated into Latin by another Jesuit, John Perpezatio, as *Responsio Apologetica,* and into English by Thomas Owen in *The Copie of a Letter sent from Paris.* The Jesuit theologian, Eudaemon-Joannes, also brought out his *Confutatio Anticotoni* in 1611, in close succession to his defence of Garnet the previous year. A testimonial was, moreover, obtained from the King himself, in the form of 'A Proclamation of the most Christian King of France & Navar Lewis the 13. wherby he confirmeth the Society of Iesus in France', dated July 1610. To this was added a similar testimonial by the dead King Henry IV, which he had granted the Jesuits in 1603, and another from the Bishop of Paris, dated 16 June 1610.

410. *Response Apologetique a l'Anticoton et a ceux de la suite. Presentee a la Royne, Mere du Roy, Regente en France. Ou il est monstré, que les*

Autheurs anonymes de ces libelles difamatoires sont attaints des crimes d'Heresie, leze Majesté, Perfidie, Sacrilege, & tres-enorme Imposture. Par un Pere, de la Compagnie de Iesus. 1610

411. *Responsio Apologetica adversus Anticotoni & Sociorum criminationes. Reginae Ludovici XIII. Galliarum Regis parenti per huius aetatem Regnum administranti dedicata. In qua demonstratur famosorum, qui nunc volitant, libellorum authores anonymos reos esse haereseos, perduellionis, perfidiae, sacrilegii, atrocissimaeque imposturae. Scripta primum Gallice ab uno e Patribus Societatis Iesu, ac postmodum Latine transcripta a P. Ioanne Perpezatio Sacerdote eiusdem Societatis. 1611*

412. *The Copie of a Letter sent from Paris to the Reverend Fathers of the Society of Iesus, who live in England. Contayning An Answere to the calumniations of the Anti-Coton against the same Society in generall, and Fa. Coton in particuler. 1611* (STC 18999, AR 590, ERL 143)

413. *Confutatio Anticotoni, Qua Respondetur calumniis, ex occasione caedis Christianissimi Regis Franciae, & sententiae Marianae, ab Anonymo quodam in P. Cottonem & socios eius congestis. Authore R. P. Andrea Eudaemon—Ioanne Cydonio e Societate Iesu. 1611*

414. *Christianissimorum Galliae et Navarrae Regum Henrici IV. et Ludovici XIII. Itemq; Illustrissimi Principis ac Praesulis Parisiensis Henrici Condaei Apologiae. Pro Societate Iesu Calumniis haereticorum oppositae. Accessit damnationis sententia contra Ioan. Ant. Ioalinum libellorum famosorum ex Anticotono propagatorem. 1610*

(Published at Ingolstadt under the care of Fr. James Gretser.)

415. *The Apologies of the most Christian Kinges of France and Navar, Henry IIII and Lewis XIII. As also of the most worthy Bishop of Paris, for the Fathers of the Society of Iesus. Translated out of Latin into English. 1611* (STC 13124, AR 32, ERL 48)

(The titles of the separate items are as follows:

An Answere of the most Christian King of France and Navar, Henry the fourth, to the calumnies obiected to the Society of Iesus, 1603.
A Proclamation of the most Christian King of France & Navar Lewis the 13. wherby he confirmeth the Society of Iesus in France . . . Paris Iuly 1610.
The Testimony of the most Reverend & worthy Bishop of Paris, that he gave of the Society of Iesus against their calumniators . . . the 16 of Iune, 1610.
The Sentence of Condemnation given against Iohn Antony Ioalin (for publishing Anti-Coton).

All this, however, was insufficient to silence the many enemies of the Jesuits, whether among the Huguenots, or in the Sorbonne, or in the Parlement of Paris, who were now united in accusing them of having assassinated their principal patron. The Jesuit *Response Apologetique* to the *Anti-Coton* was criticized by the Huguenot scholar, Isaac Casaubon, in his Letter *Ad Frontonem Ducaeum*, which he published in London in 1611. He was answered the following year by the Jesuit, Eudaemon-Joannes, in the *Responsio ad Epistolam* which gave rise to the above-mentioned *Castigatio cuiusdam Circulatoris* by John Prideaux in 1614.

416. *Isaaci Casauboni ad Frontonem Ducaeum S. J. Theologum Epistola; In qua de Apologia disseritur cummini Iesuitarum nomine ante aliquot menses Lutetiae Parisorum edita.* 1611 (London)   (STC 4742)

417. *R. P. Andreae Eudaemon-Ioannis, Cydonii e Societate Iesu Responsio ad Epistolam Isaaci Casauboni.* 1612

418. [= 283] *Castigatio cuiusdam Circulatoris, qui R. P. Andream Eudaemon-Iohannem Cydonium e Societate Iesu seipsum nuncupat. Opposita ipsius calumniis in Epistolam Isaaci Casauboni ad Frontonem Ducaeum. Per Iohannem Prideaux SS Theologiae Doctorem & Collegii Exoniensis Rectorem.* 1614   (STC 20344)

Next, the Sorbonne passed a formal *Censura* on the Jesuit reply; and this was published with a theological analysis of its contents in 1612. The French divines went on to oppose the petition of the Jesuits for the reopening of their school in Paris; and their 'Supplication' before the court of the Parlement of Paris was presented by the lawyer, Pierre de la Marteliere. This was not only published in French, in 1612, but also immediately translated into English by G. Browne. In his Dedication to the Chief Justice, Sir Thomas Fleming, Browne comments that 'The matter heerein handled is a notable & famous controversie, arising between the ancient and renowned University of Paris, and the new and infamous, yet cunning and powerfull sect of the Iesuits'. A strong criticism, as well of this *Plaidoyé* of de la Marteliere as of the *Anticoton*, followed from the pen of the Jesuit provincial, Louis Richeome in 1613.

419. *Censura Sacrae Facultatis Theologiae Parisiensis, contra doctrinam de Regum parricidiis, quae continetur in libro, cui titulus Responsio ad Anticotonum. Item Analysis sive tractatus super praecedentem censuram, a quibusdam eiusdem sacrae Facultatis Theologiae Parisiensis.* 1612

420. *The Supplication of the Universitie of Paris, for the preventing of the*

Iesuites opening their Schooles in Paris. Wherein their King-killing Doctrine is also opened and refuted.

(From the Appendix to the English translation of the *Anticoton* by G. H., 1611 – cf. 409.)

421. *Plaidoyé de M^e. Pierre de la Marteliere, Advocat en la Cour, fait en Parlement, assisté de M^e^s. Antoine Loisel, Denis Boutillier, Omer Tallon anciens Advocats, les grand Chambre, Tournelle, & de l'Edict assemblees les dixseptiesme & dixneufiesme Decembre, mil six cens unze. Pour le Recteur et Université, de Paris, defendeurs & opposans. Contre les Iesuites demandeurs, & requerans l'entherinement des lettres patentes par eux obtenuës, afin de pouvoir lire & enseigner en ladite Université.* 1612

422. *The Argument of Mr. Peter de la Marteliere Advocate in the Court of Parliament of Paris, made in Parliament, the chambers thereof being assembled. For the Rector and Universitie of Paris, Defendants and Opponents, against the Iesuits Demandants, and requiring the approbation of the Letters Patents which they had obtained, giving them power to reade and to teach publiquely in the aforesaid Universitie. Translated out of the French Copie set forth by publike Authoritie.* 1612   (STC 15140)

(The translation is accompanied by 'An Advertisement to the Reader . . . touching the first institution of the Iesuites, with their beginning, and proceedings in France, and the occasion of this present controversie'.)

423. *Examen Categorique du Libelle Anticoton, auquel est corrigé le plaidoyé de Maistre Pierre de la Marteliere, Advocat au Parlement de Paris, & plusieurs calomniateurs des Peres Iesuites refutez. Et les droicts inviolables de la Majeste & personne des Roys defendus. A Monseigneur de Silleri Chancelier de France, & de Navarre. Par Louis Richeome, Provençal, Religieux de la Compagnie de Iesus. Avec une lettre du mesme, respondant a la plainte de quelques uns de la pretenduë Religion reformée, sur la severité de ses escrits, à leur opinion, contre les Ministres, & calomniateurs, envoyée, à un Gentil-homme de Provence.* 1613

Largely arising out of this French controversy, there now appeared a cluster of anti-Jesuit pamphlets in England – many of them translations from the French. Already before the assassination of Henry IV there had appeared in France an exposure of the 'secret practises' of the Jesuits in 1609, in the form of *Aphorismes* gathered from Jesuit writings and presented out of context; and it was inevitably translated into English within a year. It was, in fact, a ninth edition of a notorious book, and had been occasioned by a Latin refutation, *Aphorismi Doctrinae Calvinistarum*, by Martin Becanus in 1608. Two more translations from the French appeared in the next two years: the one entitled, *A Discoverie of the most secret and subtile practises of the Iesuites*, in 1610; and the other, a verse satire entitled, *The Iesuites Pater Noster*, in 1611. Two other works, which are considered in a separate context, have similar titles and were doubtless occasioned by this controversy: William Crashaw's *The Iesuites Gospel*, in 1610 (545); and Thomas James' *The Iesuites Downefall*, in 1612 (275).

424. *Aphorismes ou Sommaires de la Doctrine des Iesuites, & de quelques autres Docteurs de l'Eglise Romaine. Par lesquels le vray Christianisme est corrompu, la paix publique troublee, & les liens de la societé humaine sont entierement desliez & rompus, Extraicts des escripts, sentences & actes publics des Papes, des Iesuites & autres Docteurs de l'Eglise Romaine: Et traduicts de latin en Francois iaixte la copie imprimee en Allemagne.* 1609

425. *Aphorismes. Or, Certaine selected points of the Doctrine of the Iesuits, with a treatise concerning their secret practises and Close studies. All taken out of the writings, sayings, and publike Acts, of the Iesuits and other Popish Doctors. Printed by permission of the Superiors.* 1609 (STC 14525)

426. *Aphorismi Doctrinae Calvinistarum, ex eorum libris, dictis et factis collecti; cum brevi Responsione ad Aphorismos falso Iesuitis impositos. Per Martinum Becanum Societatis Iesu Theologum.* 1608

427. *A Discoverie of the most secret and subtile practises of the Iesuites. Translated out of French.* 1610   (STC 14528)

(The inner title reads:

A Relation of the most secret desseigns of the Iesuits.)

428. *The Iesuites Pater Noster Given to Philip III King of Spaine for his new yeares gift this present yeare 1611. Together with the Ave Maria. Written first in French; Englished by W. I.* 1611   (STC 14534)

All this is the immediate, rather unsavoury context within which John Donne – under the auspices of Thomas Morton, his patron – made his own contribution to anti-Jesuit literature, with *Ignatius his Conclave*. This he published in 1611, first in Latin and then in his own English translation, in a light, satirical vein after his more serious labours spent in defence of the Oath of Allegiance in *Pseudo-Martyr* (1610).

429. *Conclave Ignati: Sive Eius in Nuperis Inferni Comitiis Inthronisatio. Ubi varia De Iesuitarum Indole, De novo inferno creando, De Ecclesia Lunatica instituenda, per Satyram congesta sunt. Accessit et Apologia pro Iesuitis. Omnia Duobus Angelis Adversariis, qui Consistorio Papali, & Collegio Sorbonae praesident, dedicata.* 1611   (STC 7026)

430. *Ignatius his Conclave: or His Inthronisation in a late Election in Hell: Wherein many things are mingled by way of Satyr; Concerning The Disposition of Iesuits, The Creation of a new Hell, The establishing of a Church in the Moone. There is also added an Apology for Iesuites. All dedicated to the two Adversary Angels, which are the Protectors of the Papall Consistory, and of the Colledge of Sorbon. Translated out of Latine.* 1611   (STC 7027)

k) *The King v. the Cardinal of France*

About this time King James became involved in controversy with yet another cardinal, Jacques Du Perron, the learned Primate of France. At first, it was conducted indirectly between the Cardinal and Casaubon, who had retired to England soon after the assassination of Henry IV and had there been welcomed by James. Du Perron had written a private letter to Casaubon, with whom he was on friendly terms, and had praised the English King as one in whom nothing was wanting 'excepting the only Title of Catholike'. Casaubon naturally showed this letter to James, who expressed his surprise at the Cardinal's words. This prompted Du Perron to write again; and this time his letter was printed in Paris without his permission, in 1612. Shortly afterwards it was translated into English by the Jesuit, Thomas Owen, and published in the same year. Casaubon immediately replied in Latin; and his *Responsio* was likewise translated into English within the year.

431. *Lettre de Monseigneur le Cardinal Du Perron, Envoyée au Sieur Casaubon en Angleterre.* 1612

432. *A Letter written from Paris, by the Lord Cardinall of Peron, to Monsr. Casaubon in England. Translated out of the French corrected Copie, into English.* 1612   (STC 6383, AR 286, ERL 72)

433. *Isaaci Casauboni Ad Epistolam Illustr. et Reverendiss. Cardinalis Perronii, Responsio.* 1612   (STC 4740)

434. *The Answere of Master Isaac Casaubon to the Epistle of the most illustrious, and most reverend Cardinall Peron. Translated out of Latin into English.* 1612.

In the course of his *Answere*, Casaubon touched on the King's faith in the real presence of Christ in the Blessed Sacrament, though not in transubstantiation; and he cited the similar opinion of the Bishop of Ely, Lancelot Andrewes, in his book against Bellarmine. This prompted an anonymous Catholic author, signing himself with the initials R. N., to publish *The Christians Manna*, in which he hailed this declaration as a means of winning Anglican readers from Calvinist theology.

435. *The Christians Manna. or A Treatise of the most Blessed and Reverend Sacrament. Devided into two Tracts. Written by a Catholike Devine, through occasion of Monsieur Casaubon his Epistle to Cardinal Peron expressing therin the Grave and Approved Iudgment of the Kings Maiesty, touching the doctrine of the Reall Presence in the Eucharist.* 1613   (STC 18334, AR 564, ERL 177)

Soon after this brief exchange, Casaubon became preoccupied – according to the King's wishes – with his refutation of the monumental *Annales* by Cardinal Baronius; and he died in 1614. But in the following year Du Perron provoked James to a controversy of a more direct kind, and in a more direct relation to that which had brought James into conflict with the Jesuit Cardinal Bellarmine. For in 1615 a General Assembly was held of the three estates in France; and an Oath of Allegiance, similar to that drawn up in England, was proposed for consideration by the strong Gallican party. It was, however, defeated largely owing to a powerful speech made to the Assembly by Du Perron, who relied on arguments similar to those of Bellarmine and the Jesuit theologians against the English Oath. This speech was published that year in the original French, and translated the following year into English, with a Preface by the Translator emphasizing 'the extreme obligation which al good English Catholikes have to him' and 'the advantage which our cause hath got by his Oration'.

436. *Harangue Faicte de la Part de la Chambre Ecclesiastique, En celle du tiers Estat, sur l'Article du Serment. Par Monseigneur le Cardinal du Perron, Archevesque de Sens, Primat des Gaules & de Germanie, & Grand Aumosnier de France.* 1615

437. *An Oration made on the part of the Lordes Spirituall, In the Chamber of the Third Estate (or Communalty) of France, upon the Oath (pretended of Allegiance) exhibited in the late Generall Assembly of the three Estates of that Kingdome: By the Lord Cardinall of Peron, Arch-bishop of Sens, Primate of Gaule and Germany, Great Almenour of France &c. Translated into English, according to the French Copy, lately printed at Paris, by Antoine Estiene. Whereunto is adioyned a Preface, by the Translatour.* 1616   (STC 6384, AR 287, ERL 366)

At this, James felt his own position directly challenged by Du Perron, in view of the obvious parallel between the two Oaths; and he accordingly published a *Declaration* or *Remonstrance* (as it was variously entitled) 'For the Right of Kings' in 1615. In its original French form, it was polished by Pierre Du Moulin, then residing at the English court, and for his pains he was rewarded with the degree of Doctor of Divinity by the university of Cambridge. The English translation was published first in 1615 in conjunction with another Remonstrance (on a more political affair), and then in 1616 by itself. A Latin translation was also published in 1616.

438. *Declaration du Serenissime Roy Iaques I. Roy de la Grand' Bretagne France et Irlande, Defenseur de la Foy. Pour le Droit des Rois & independance de leurs Couronnes, Contre la Harangue De L'Illustrissime Cardinal du Perron prononcee en la chambre du tiers Estat le XV de Ianvier 1615.* 1615   (STC 14367)

439. *Remonstrances made by the Kings Maiesties Ambassadour, unto the French King and the Queene his Mother, Iune last past, 1615. Concerning the marriages with Spaine; As also certayne Diabolicall opinions maintayned by Cardinall Perron, about the deposing and murthering of Kings. Together with the French Kings Letter to the Prince of Conde, Dated the 26 of Iuly last. 1615. and the Prince his Answere thereunto. Translated according to the French Copie.* 1615 (STC 9237)

(The second Remonstrance is entitled:

A Declaration made by his Maiesties Ambassadour of Great Brittaine unto the French King, and the Queene his Mother, concerning an Oration made by the Cardinall of Perron, in the late generall Assembly of the Estates at Paris.)

440. *A Remonstrance of the most Gratious King Iames I. King of Great Britaine, France, and Ireland, Defender of the Faith, &c. For the Right of Kings, and the independance of their Crownes. Against an Oration of the most Illustrious Card. of Perron, pronounced in the Chamber of the third Estate. Ian. 15. 1615. Translated out of his Maiesties French Copie.* 1616   (STC 14369)

(In the 1619 edition the translator is identified on the title-page as 'R. B. Pastor of the Church at Ashele in the Countie of Norfolke'.)

441. *Serenissimi Iacobi, Magnae Britanniae, Franciae, et Hiberniae Regis, Fidei Defensoris, Declaratio Pro Iure Regio, Sceptrorumque immunitate. Adversus illustriss. Cardinalis Perronii Orationem, in Comitiis Franciae generalibus ad Ordinem plebeium Parisiis habitam. 18 Cal. Feb. 1615.* 1616   (STC 14368)

The Cardinal now returned to Casaubon's *Responsio* of 1612, in which he recognized the thought of the King himself. Devoting his time to this task, he at length brought out a *Replique a la Response* in some 1120 pages, which he published in 1620. The King entrusted its reply to Bishop Andrewes, who, however, limited his attention to two chapters of the book, in the form of *Stricturae* (in English) which remained unpublished at his death in 1626. They were subsequently published in 1629 as two items of his *Opuscula quaedam posthuma*.

442. *Replique a la Response du Serenissime Roy de la Grand Bretagne. Par l'Illustrissime et Reverendissime Cardinal du Perron, Archevesque de Sens, Primat des Gauls & de Germanie, & grand Aumosnier de France.* 1620

443. *Reverendi in Christo Patris, Lanceloti, Episcopi Wintoniensis, Opuscula quaedam posthuma.* 1629 (STC 602)

(The two relevant items in this collection are entitled:

Stricturae: Or, A Briefe Answer to the XVIII. Chapter of the first Booke of Cardinall Perron's Reply written in French, to King Iames-his Answer written by Mr. Casaubon in Latine. (STC 625)

An Answer to the XX. Chapter of the Fifth Booke of Cardinall Perron's Reply, written in French, to King Iames – his Answer written by Mr. Casaubon to the Cardinall in Latine.)

l) *Controversy over Antichrist*

Also in connection with the foregoing controversies over allegiance, both in England and in France, there was a noticeable recurrence of mutual accusations regarding Antichrist – though the Protestants were more often than not on the offensive. Treatises on this subject had appeared from the beginning of James' reign, mainly directed against Bellarmine's discussion 'de Summo Pontifice' in the third controversy of Vol. I of his celebrated *Disputationes*, which had first been published in 1586. In 1603 Robert Abbot had brought out his Latin treatise, entitled *Antichristi Demonstratio*, and George Downame, his English *Treatise concerning Antichrist*. In 1605 Gabriel Powell followed them with his scholastic disputations *De Antichristo & eius Ecclesia*, prefacing them with a 'Compellatio Auctoris ad blasphemos Monachos'.

444. *Antichristi Demonstratio, contra Fabulas Pontificias, & ineptam Roberti Bellarmini de Antichristo disputationem. Authore Roberto Abbotto, Oxoniensi, olim a Collegio Baliolensi, sacrae Theologiae professore.* 1603 (STC 43)

445. *A Treatise concerning Antichrist, divided into two bookes, the former,*
proving that the Pope is Antichrist: the latter, maintaining the same
assertion, against all the obiections of Robert Bellarmine, Iesuit and
Cardinall of the Church of Rome. By George Downame, Doctor of
Divinitie, and lately reader of the Divinity Lecture in Paules. 1603
(STC 7120)

446. *Gabrielis Poueli Ordovicis Britanni, Davidis F. Disputationum*
Theologicarum & Scholasticarum de Antichristo & eius Ecclesia, Libri
II. In quibus certissimis Argumentis, clarissimisque Testimoniis
irrefutabiliter demonstratur Papam Romanum Magnum illum esse
Antichristum, & Papanam Ecclesiam ipsissimam Antichristi Synagogam;
Monachorum blasphemae Societatis Examini, Disquisitioni &
Considerationi humiliter submissi. 1605   (STC 20147)

It was partly these English books, but chiefly a work of 'Marpurgensis
quidam Calvinista', that first drew Martin Becanus into the controversies of
this reign with his *Disputatio Theologica de Antichristo Reformato* in 1608.
In an Appendix to this volume he dealt with the question, 'An Romana
Ecclesia defecerit a fide?' It was only this part of his book that received an
English translation in 1612, under the title, *A Defence of the Roman*
Church. Subsequently in 1611, his fellow-Jesuit, Leonard Lessius, published
twin disputations under the title, *De Antichristo et eius Praecursoribus,*
maintaining against the recent 'Praefatio Monitoria' (in which he refused to
recognize the authorship of King James): 1) that the Pope is not Antichrist;
and 2) that heretics are precursors of Antichrist. A third Jesuit, the
Englishman Michael Walpole, writing under the pseudonym of Michael
Christopherson, added his *Treatise of Antichrist,* defending Bellarmine
against Downame in two parts which came out in successive years, 1613 and
1614. He also dealt with the disputations of Abbot and Powell.

447. [= 622] *Disputatio Theologica de Antichristo Reformato. In qua tum*
alii, tum Marpurgensis quidam Calvinista refutatur, qui nuper duplici
Elencho conatus est probare, Papam esse Antichristum. Cum
Appendice, An Romana Ecclesia defecerit a fide? Authore Martino
Becano Societatis Iesu Sacerdote & Theologo. 1608

448. [= 623] *A Defence of the Roman Church. Wherin is treated, Whether*
the said Church of Rome hath fallen in faith, or no? Written in Latin by
the R. F. Martinus Becanus of the Society of Iesus, Professour in
Divinity: And Now translated into English. 1612   (STC 1700, AR 79,
ERL 28)

(The inner and running title reads:

Whether the Church of Rome hath fallen in faith or no?

A second edition was published in 1621, as an appendix to Lessius'
Consultation – to be considered later.)

449. *De Antichristo et eius Praecursoribus Disputatio Apologetica gemina:*
Qua refutatur Praefatio Monitoria falso, ut creditur, adscripta Magnae
Britanniae Regi: Auctore Leonardo Lessio Soc. Iesu S. Theologiae
Professore. 1611

(The work is dedicated to 'Serenissimis Orbis Christiani Principibus', in
imitation of the 'Praefatio Monitoria', in which (Lessius complains)
'Summus Pontifex, omnium Christianorum Pater & Pastor, Antichristus
asseritur'. The contents are divided as follows:
a) *De Antichristo Disputatio. Utrum Papa Romanus sit Antichristus.*
b) *De Antichristi Praecursoribus Disputatio. Utrum haeretici huius*
saeculi . . . sint praecursores Antichristi.)

450. *A Treatise of Antichrist. Conteyning The defence of Cardinall*
Bellarmines Arguments, which invincibly demonstrate, That the Pope is
not Antichrist. Against M. George Downam D. of Divinity, who
impugneth the same. By Michael Christopherson Priest. The First Part.
1613   (STC 24993, AR 872, ERL 220)

(In the twenty-fourth chapter 'the fable of Pope Ioane the Woman is
confuted' – a fable that recurs in the later controversies of this reign.)

451. *A Treatise concerning Antichrist. Conteyning An Answere to the*
Protestant proofes: by which M. George Downam Doctour of Divinity
&c. with no lesse folly then malice, would make men believe, That the
Pope is Antichrist. By Michael Christoferson Priest. The Second Part.
1614   (STC 24994, AR 873, ERL 221)

A fertile source for the Protestant proofs that the Pope was Antichrist was
provided by the Apocalypse, with its identification of Babylon with imperial
Rome. About this time, therefore, there appeared a series of largely Puritan
commentaries on this final book of the New Testament. In 1610 Hugh
Broughton published his *Revelation of the Holy Apocalyps*, in which he
claimed to have turned 'all the Apocalyps against Rome'. In the following
year there appeared a new edition of John Napier's popular *Plaine Discovery*,
which had first been published in Scotland in 1593 and had attracted the
favourable notice of King James. But the most popular of these
commentaries was the Puritan Thomas Brightman's *Revelation of the*
Apocalyps, which came out for the first time in 1611 – with a long
digression at the end of chapter 17, adding his refutation of Bellarmine. A
Latin translation followed in 1612, with the title, *Apocalypsis Apocalypseos*;
and then two more English editions, each with a different title – *A*
Revelation of the Revelation in 1615, and *The Revelation of S. Iohn* in

1616. Of all these commentaries it was only the Latin volume of Brightman which incurred a detailed refutation from the pen of the Jesuit Eudaemon-Joannes, who published his *Castigatio Apocalypsis Apocalypseos* in 1613 in defence of Bellarmine.

452. *A Revelation of the Holy Apocalyps. By Hugh Broughton.* 1610
    (STC 3883)

453. *A Plaine Discovery, of the whole Revelation of S. Iohn: set downe in two treatises: the one searching and proving the true interpretation thereof: The other applying the same paraphrasticallie and Historicallie to the text. Set foorth by Iohn Napeir L. of Marchiston. And now revised, corrected and inlarged by him. With a resolution of certaine doubts, mooved by some well-affected brethren. Whereunto are annexed, certaine Oracles of Sibylla, agreeing With the Revelation and other places of Scripture.* 1611   (STC 18356)

    (Two editions had already appeared in Scotland in 1593 and 1594
    (STC 18354–55))

454. *A Revelation of the Apocalyps, that is, The Apocalyps of S. Iohn illustrated with an Analysis & Scolions: Where the sense is opened by the scripture, & the events of things foretold, shewed by Histories. Hereunto is prefixed a generall View: and at the end of the 17. Chapter, is inserted a Refutation of R. Bellarmine touching Antichrist, in his 3. Book of the B. of Rome. By Thomas Brightman.* 1611   (STC 3754)

455. *Apocalypsis Apocalypseos, id est, Apocalypsis D. Iohannis. Praefigitur Synopsis universalis: & Refutatio Rob. Bellarmini de Antichristo libro tertio de Romano Pontifice, ad finem capitis decimi septimi inseritur. Per Thomam Brigtmannum Anglum.* 1612

    (The digression against Bellarmine is entitled:

    Refutatio Antichristi quem describit Bellarminus, & argumentis pro viribus confirmat lib. 3. de Romano Pontifice.)

456. *A Revelation of the Revelation, that is, The Revelation of St. John opened clearly with a logicall Resolution and Exposition. Wherein the sense is cleared out of the scripture, the event also of thinges foretold is Discussed out of the Church-Historyes. By Thomas Brightman.* 1615
    (STC 3755))

457. *The Revelation of S. Iohn illustrated with an Analysis & Scholions. Wherein the Sence is opened by the Scripture, & the event of things fore-told, showed by Histories. The third Edition Corrected &*

amended, With supply of many things formerly left out. By Thomas Brightman. 1616   (STC 3756)

(The inner title and page heading remains: *A Revelation of the Apocalyps*. The digression in chapter 17 is headed:

'The confuting of that counterfait Antichrist, Whom Bellarmine describeth, and laboureth to prove by arguments with all his might. Booke 3. touching the Pope of Rome'.)

458. *R. P. Andreae Eudaemon-Ioannis Cydonii e Societate Iesu, Castigatio Apocalypsis Apocalypseos Thomae Brightmanni Angli.* 1613

(In 'Auctor Lectori' the author relates how he turned to this task immediately on completing his refutation of Andrewes' *Tortura Torti*.)

This repeated emphasis by Protestant writers on the identification of the Pope as Antichrist was not now only against the Catholic writers, led by Bellarmine, but also against an enemy in their own midst — those of Arminian tendencies who were increasingly reluctant to make this identification. Long before Richard Montague came out openly with this opinion, in his above-mentioned *Gagg for the new Gospell?* (138) in 1624, such members of the Calvinist party in the Church of England as Joseph Hall and John Prideaux were expressing their misgivings. In a sermon on *Pharisaisme and Christianity*, preached at Paul's Cross in 1608, Hall complains how

'Our yong students (the hope of posteritie) newly crept out of the shell of Philosophie, spend their first houres in the great Doctours of Popish controversies; Bellarmine is next to Aristotle; yea our very ungrounded Artizans, yong Gentlemen, fraile Women, buie, read, traverse promiscuously the dangerous Writings of our subtilest Iesuites.'

Similarly, in another sermon, entitled *Ephesus Backsliding*, preached at Oxford in 1614, Prideaux has the following lament:

'Is this a time to make a doubt, whether the Pope be Antichrist or no, seeing his hornes and markes are so apparantly discovered? And must we now fall back to be catechized by Lumbard, and Aquinas; as though our own mens doctrine . . . were not conclusive, and acute enough?

459. *Pharisaisme and Christianity: Compared and set forth in a Sermon at Pauls Crosse, May 1. 1608. By I. H. Upon Matth. 5. 20.* 1608 (STC 12699)

460. *Ephesus Backsliding considered and applyed to these times, in a*

> *Sermon preached at Oxford, in S. Maries, the tenth of Iuly, being the*
> *Act Sunday. 1614. By Iohn Prideaux, Doctor of Divinity, and Rector*
> *of Exeter College.* 1614   (STC 20352)

Two later books may be added to the list of Antichristian literature in the reign of James. Yet another *Key of Knowledge* to open the mysteries of the Apocalypse was offered by the Puritan Richard Bernard in 1617, with special reference to 'these obstinate Recusants' and 'disloyall Ignatian Locusts'. For his interpretation he relied on such authors as Napier, Broughton and Brightman, as well as 'His Maiesties Meditations'. Downame, whom he does not mention (perhaps because that divine had since defected to the Episcopal party, and had been given a bishopric in Ireland), also brought out in 1620 a further elaboration of his former theory, this time in Latin, under the title, *Papa Antichristus*, to defend King James against the criticism of Lessius. He also refers to the confutation by Michael Christopherson, but dismisses it as not worth the labour of refuting.

461. *A Key of Knowledge For the opening of the secret mysteries of St*
    Iohns mysticall Revelation. By Ric: Bernard, preacher of Gods word, at
    Batcombe in Somersetshire. 1617   (STC 1955)

462. *Papa Antichristus, sive Diatriba de Antichristo, cuius duae partes: Prior,*
    ΚΑΤΑΣΚΕΥΗ, qua Orthodoxa Serenissimi Regis Iacobi, de Antichristo
    sententia demonstratur: Posterior, ΑΝΑΣΚΕΥΗ, qua Leonardi Lessii
    sedecim Demonstrationes, monitoriae Regis Praefationi oppositae,
    refutantur. Auctore Reverendo in Christo Patre, Georgio Dounamo
    Episcopo Derensi. 1620   (STC 7119)

CHAPTER 4

Catholic v. Anglican

a) *Kellison v. Sutcliffe*

From the beginning of James' reign the Catholics did not limit their attention to appeals for toleration, but went on to present arguments for their doctrinal position against that of the Protestants. During the first few years they dedicated many of these 'apologies' to the new King, appealing to him for a relaxation of the severe penal laws, while at the same time expressing the hope that their reasons might convince him of the truth of the Catholic religion. The first of such works to appear, *A Survey of the New Religion*, came from the pen of an eminent professor at the English College, Douai, Matthew Kellison. This was first published in 1603, with a dedication to King James, and again in a 'newly augmented' form in 1605 (ERL 333).

463. *A Survey of the New Religion, detecting many grosse absurdities which it implieth. Set forth by Matthew Kellison, Doctor and Professor of Divinitie. Divided into eight bookes.* 1603   (STC 14912, AR 429)

Two Anglican answers appeared in 1606, each of them associated with the name of Matthew Sutcliffe, who was busy at the same time refuting Catholic appeals for toleration, as well as Persons' *Treatise of Three Conversions*. One of these answers was published anonymously, but with Sutcliffe's name attached to the Dedication, under the title of *The Examination and Confutation of A certaine scurrilous treatise*. The other was *An Abridgement Or Survey of Poperie*, which had Sutcliffe's name on the title-page. In it he refers to the above-mentioned work as already undertaken but not yet brought to completion by 'a man both learned, grave and eminent in this Church of England'. Here he is presumably speaking of himself.

464. *The Examination and Confutation of A certaine scurrilous treatise entituled, The Survey of the newe Religion, Published by Matthew Kellison, in disgrace of true religion professed in the Church of England.* 1606   (STC 23464)

465. *An Abridgement Or Survey of Poperie, Conteining a compendious declaration of the grounds, doctrines, beginnings, proceedings, impieties, falsities, contradictions, absurdities, fooleries, and other manifold abuses of that religion, which the Pope and his complices doe now mainteine, and wherewith they have corrupted and deformed the true Christian faith, Opposed unto Matthew Kellisons Survey of the new Religion, as he calleth it, and unto all his malicious invectives and lies, By Matthew Suttcliffe.* 1606   (STC 23448)

To the former of these books, which he attributed to 'one Matthew Sotcliff, who calleth himselfe Dean of Exeter', Kellison replied two years later, with a glance at 'other his bookes against the booke of the three conversions'. This time his *Reply* elicited no response from Sutcliffe, who was then busy with plans for his abortive College of Controversy at Chelsea. Kellison went on to develop his criticisms along similar lines in a Latin treatise, entitled *Examen Reformationis Novae*, which appeared many years later in 1616.

466. *A reply to Sotcliffes Answer to the Survey of the new Religion, in which his insufficient answers, and manifold follies are discovered, wherwith the Adversarie was charged: most partes of the Catholike Doctrine explicated, and al is averred, and confirmed: and almost al pointes of the new faith of Ingland disproved. Set forth by Matthew Kellison Doctor of Divinitie, and Professor of the same in the Universitie of Rhemes.* 1608   (STC 14909, AR 426, ERL 330)

467. [= 582] *Examen Reformationis Novae Praesertim Calvinianae in quo synagoga et doctrina Calvini, sicut et reliquorum huius temporis novatorum, tota fere ex suis principiis refutatur. Authore Matthaeo Kellisono Sacrae Theol. Doctore Ac Collegii Anglorum Duaceni Praeside.* 1616

A postscript to this brief controversy appeared in 1618, when John Pickford, a seminary priest, published his *Safegarde from Ship-wracke*. In his Dedication he confessed he had been converted to the Catholic faith by a reading of Kellison's *Survey*, though at first he had utterly rejected it with contempt.

468. *The Safegarde from Ship-wracke, or Heavens Haven. Compiled by I. P. Priest.* 1618   (STC 19073, AR 647, ERL 271)

(The inner title has the following addition:

The Safegarde from Ship-wracke, or Heavens Haven. Wich is not to be attained with out the Shippe of S. Peter: to wit, The unitie of the

*auncient Catholike Church, whose faith therefore through all ages, as in
a glasse is heere presented unto you.)*

b) *Bishop v. Abbot*

After Kellison another of the Douai professors, William Bishop, who had
been prominently involved in the appeal of the secular priests to Rome,
brought out a similar apology in 1604. This he wrote against William Perkins'
Reformed Catholicke, which had first appeared in 1598 with a second
edition in 1604. In his answer, *A Reformation of a Catholike Deformed*,
Bishop recognized his opponent's work as 'more Schollerlike, then the
Protestants use to do ordinarily' and therefore all the more apt 'to deceive
the simple'. He also added a Dedication to King James, appealing to him to
support the Catholic cause for his mother's memory and so to become a
second Constantine. For the present, however, he published only the first
part of his book, and did not bring out the second part till 1607.

469. *A Reformed Catholicke; or A Declaration shewing how neere we may
come to the present Church of Rome in sundrie points of Religion; and
wherein we must for ever depart from them: with an Advertisement to
all favourers of the Romane religion, shewing that the said religion is
against the Catholike principles and grounds of the Catechisme.* 1598
(STC 19736)

(A second edition appeared in 1604, followed by two others in 1611
and 1619 (STC 19737–9).)

470. *A Reformation of a Catholicke Deformed: by M. W. Perkins. Wherein
the chiefe controversies in religion, are methodically, and learnedly
handled. Made by D.B.P. The Former Part.* 1604   (STC 3096,
AR 115).

471. *The Second Part of the Reformation of a Catholike Deformed by
Master W. Perkins.* 1607   (STC 3097, AR 117)

(An Appendix follows, with new pagination, and the title: *An
Answere unto M. Perkins Advertisement.*)

Before Bishop could bring out his *Second Part*, two Anglican ministers
had published their several replies. The first was Anthony Wotton's *Answere
to a popish Pamphlet*, which came out in 1605. This was primarily an answer
to Thomas Wright's *Certaine Articles or Forcible Reasons*, which had been
published in 1600 (in two editions) and again in 1605; but in his Preface
Wotton noted that his *Answere* to Wright might also 'serve as part of an
answere, to divers points lately set out against Maister Perkins reformed

Catholick: till a more particular refutation thereof be ready'. This refutation he produced in the following year under under the title, *A Defence of M. Perkins Booke*.

472. *Certaine Articles or Forcible Reasons. Discovering the palpable absurdities, and most notorious and intricate errors of the Protestants Religion*. 1600   (STC 23618, AR 920, ERL 301)

   (The thrid edition of 1605 was falsely dated 1600. Already before Wotton's *Answere* it had been refuted twice before the end of Elizabeth's reign: by William Barlow in his *Defence* of 1601, and by Edward Bulkley in his *Apologie* of 1602.)

473. *An Answere to a popish Pamphlet, of late newly forbished, and the second time Printed, Entituled: Certaine articles, or forcible reasons discovering the palpable absurdities, and most notorious errors of the Protestants religion. By Anthony Wotton*. 1605   (STC 26002)

474. *A Defence of M. Perkins Booke, called A Reformed Catholicke: Against the cavils of a Popish writer, one D. B. P. or W. B. in his deformed Reformation. By Antony Wotton*. 1606   (STC 26004)

A weightier reply was published in 1606 by Robert Abbot, the elder brother of George Abbot, future Archbishop of Canterbury. The latter was then engaged on another controversy with Thomas Hill, against whose *Quartron of Reasons* (1600) he brought out a severe reply in 1604. The elder now joined his younger brother in a controversy which eventually led to his promotion to the See of Salisbury in 1615. His first contribution was entitled *A Defence of the Reformed Catholicke*, and came out in two parts in successive years. In *The First Part* he concentrated on Bishop's 'Epistle Dedicatory to the King'; and in *The Second Part*, published with a second edition of *The First Part* in 1607, he dealt with Bishop's arguments, most of them taken (he observes) 'out of Bellarmine's disputations, who is now become their common oracle, and the chiefe fountaine whereat they all draw'.

475. *A Quartron of Reasons of Catholike Religion, with as many briefe reasons of refusall: By Tho. Hill*. 1600   (STC 13470, AR 400, ERL 98)

   (This was also refuted by Francis Dillingham in 1603, STC 6889.)

476. *The Reasons which Doctour Hill hath brought, for the upholding of Papistry, which is falselie termed the Catholike Religion: Unmasked, and shewed to be very weake, and upon examination most insufficient for that purpose: By George Abbot Doctor of Divinity & Deane of the Cathedrall Church in Winchester. The first part*. 1604   (STC 37)

   (No second part ever appeared.)

477. *A Defence of the Reformed Catholicke of M. W. Perkins, lately deceased, against the bastard Counter-Catholicke of D. Bishop, Seminary Priest. The First Part: For answer to his calumniations generally framed against the same, and against the whole Religion and state of our Church, in his Epistle Dedicatory to the Kings most excellent Maiesty. Wherein is to be seene the audaciousnesse and impudencie of these Romish brokers in their Supplications and Dedications to his Highnesse: their religion is dismasked of that antiquity which they pretend for it: the religion established in our Church by law is iustified to be no other but what was anciently received in the Church, and namely in the ancient Church of Rome. By Robert Abbot Doct. of Divinitie.* 1606 (STC 48)

478. *The Second Part of the Defence of the Reformed Catholicke. Wherein the Religion established in our Church of England (for the points here handled) is apparently iustified by authoritie of Scripture, and testimonie of the auncient Church, against the vaine cavillations collected by Doctor Bishop Seminary Priest, as out of other Popish writers, so specially out of Bellarmine, and published under the name of The marrow and pith of many large volumes, for the oppugning thereof. By Robert Abbot Doctor of Divinitie.* 1607 (STC 48)

Bishop returned to the attack in 1608, with *A Reproofe of M. Doct. Abbots Defence* against Abbot's 'answere to my Epistle unto his Maiesty' — i.e. against *The First Part* of 1606. This was entitled *The First Part* against Abbot's *First Part*; but no second part followed against Abbot's *Second Part*. Nor did Abbot ever publish a reply to Bishop's *Second Part of the Reformation of a Catholike Deformed*. For the time being he merely brought out a provisional reply in the form of a sermon, entitled *The Old Waye*, in 1610 — with an apology for his delay in producing a fuller refutation. This eventually appeared in 1611, similarly entitled *The True Ancient Roman Catholike* — emphasizing a point commonly made by Anglican apologists of this period, against the Catholic claim to antiquity and universality. Even so, he was able to proceed no further than one part of Bishop's *Reproofe*, and presented this 'in the mean time'.

479. *A Reproofe of M. Doct. Abbots Defence, of the Catholike Deformed by M. W. Perkins. Wherein His sundry abuses of Gods sacred word, and most manifold mangling, misaplying, and falsifying, the auncient Fathers sentences, be so plainely discovered, even to the eye of every indifferent Reader, that whosoever hath any due care of his owne salvation, can never hereafter give him more credit, in matter of faith and religion. The First Part. Made by W. B. P. and Doct. in divinity.* 1608 (STC 3098, AR 116).

480. *The Old Waye. A Sermon Preached at Oxford, The eight day of Iuly, being the Act Sunday. 1610. By Robert Abbott, Doctor of Divinitie, and Maister of Balioll Colledge. 1610* (STC 53)

481. *The True Ancient Roman Catholike. Being an Apology or Counter-proofe against Doctor Bishops Reproofe of the defence of the Reformed Catholike. The First Part. Wherein the name of Catholikes is vindicated from Popish abuse, and thence is shewed that the faith of the Church of Rome as now it is, is not the Catholike faith, nor the same with the faith commended in the Epistles of St. Peter and St. Paul, and that confirmed by the testimony of the ancient Bishops of Rome, and other Writers of that Church. By Robert Abbot Doctor of Divinity, Master of Balioll Colledge in Oxford. 1611* (STC 54)

This last work was answered by Bishop in *A Disproofe of D. Abbots Counterproofe*, which he published in 1614 while 'prisoner by the gatehouse in Westminster'. In his Preface he complained that Abbot would not consent to a meeting with him 'about the verification of our writings'. Finally, receiving no further answer from Abbot, who had since become Bishop of Salisbury, Bishop put together a final version of his refutation both of Perkins and of Abbot; but this was not published till the end of the reign, in 1625, when the two protagonists were both dead.

482. *A Disproofe of D. Abbots Counterproofe against D. Bishops Reproofe of the defence of M. Perkins reformed Catholike. The First Part. wherin the now Roman Church is maintained to be the true ancient Catholike church, and is cleered from the uniust imputation of Donatisme. where is also briefly handled, whether every Christian can be saved in his owne religion. By W. B. P. and D. in Divinity. 1614* (STC 3094, AR 113)

483. *Maister Perkins reformed Catholique together with maister Robert Abbots defence thereof largely refuted and the same refutation newly reviewed and augmented. By William Bishop Doctor of Sorbonne and late Bishop of Chalcedon. 1625* (STC 3095, AR 114, ERL 385)

Also in connection with this controversy, mention may be made of another, belated answer to Wright's *Articles* (or possibly a MS variant of this work which cannot be precisely identified), Richard Woodcock's *Godly and Learned Answer*, published in 1608. He speaks of its being a year and a half since 'there came to my knowledge a Popish Pamphlet made and scattered abroad, as it seemeth, by some popish seedesman'.

484. *A Godly and Learned Answer, To a lewd and unlearned Pamphlet: Intituled, A few plaine and forcible Reasons for the Catholike Faith,*

against the Religion of the Protestants. By Richard Woodcoke
Batchellor of Divinitie. 1608   (STC 25965)

(The inner title is as follows:

An Answer to a leude and unlearned Pamphlet, sent abroad in writing
by some Popish Corner-creeper.)

c) *Fisher v. Wotton and White*

A related controversy, arising to some extent out of Wright's *Articles* and
also dealing with the identity and nature of the true Church, was first
initiated on a private level by the Jesuit John Percy, or (as he later became
more generally known under his alias) John Fisher. He describes how he was
prevailed upon by his friends to develop his MS notes on this question in the
form of a book, which he published in 1605 under the title *A Treatise of*
Faith and the initials A. D. (for 'A Divine').

485. *A Treatise of Faith, wherin is briefely, and planly shewed, a direct*
     way, by which every man may resolve, and settle his minde, in all
     doubtes, questions, or controversies, concerning matters of Faith. A. D.
     1605   (Not in STC, AR 608).

This *Treatise* was again answered (like so many Catholic books of this
period) by a pair of Anglican divines, Anthony Wotton and John White, who
both published their confutations in the same year, 1608. The former
professed to make *A Trial of the Romish Clergies Title to the Church*; while
the latter, in a more popular style, sought to show his readers *The Way to*
the True Church. White informs us that he first came across the Jesuit
treatise in MS and as such he answered it. It was only after the printing of his
book that he first heard about the printing of this treatise in an enlarged
form in 1605.

486. *A Trial of the Romish Clergies Title to the Church: By way of answer*
     to a Popish Pamphlet written by one A. D. and entituled A Treatise of
     Faith, wherein is briefly and plainly shewed a direct way, by which
     every man may resolve and settle his mind in all doubts, questions and
     controversies, concerning matters of Faith. By Antonie Wotton. In the
     end you have three Tables: one of the texts of Scripture expounded or
     alledged in this booke; another of the Testimonies of ancient and later
     Writers, with a Chronologie of the times in which they lived: a third of
     the chiefe matters contained in the Treatise and Answer. 1608
     (STC 26009)

487. *The Way to the True Church: wherein The principall Motives*
     perswading to Romanisme, and Questions touching the nature and

authority of the Church, and Scriptures, are familiarly disputed, and driven to their issues, where, this day they sticke betweene the Papists and us: Contrived into an Answer to a Popish Discourse, concerning the Rule of Faith, and the marks of the Church. And published to admonish such as decline to Papistrie, of the weake and uncertaine grounds, whereupon they have ventured their soules. Directed to all that seeke for resolution: and especially to his loving countrimen of Lancashire. By Iohn White Minister of Gods word at Eccles. 1608 (STC 25394)

(This book went into four more editions in the reign of James I, in 1610, 1612, 1616 and 1624 (STC 25395—8).)

The Jesuit answer to these two divines took a variety of forms in the ensuing years. There first appeared in 1612 *A Reply made unto Mr. Anthony Wotton and Mr. Iohn White Ministers*, with two important appendices: 'A Catalogue of the Names of some Catholike Professours', and 'A Challenge to Protestants: requiring a Catalogue to be made of some Professours of their fayth, in all ages since Christ'. This was followed by an augmented edition of the *Treatise of Faith* in 1614, with marginal notes indicating the points criticized by Percy's opponents and his answer to them. Thirdly, the *Catalogue of divers visible professors of the Catholike Faith* was published separately in 1614 at the special request of some friends; and it was also bound with the 1614 edition of the *Treatise*. This *Catalogue* was subsequently added to the 1619 edition of Gregory Martin's *Love of the soule* (originally published as *Certen epistles* with his *Treatyse of Christian peregrination* in 1583). Two other Jesuits, Silvester Norris and Anthony Clarke, further expanded the *Catalogue*: the former in his *Appendix to the Antidote* in 1621 (610), the latter in his *Defence of the Honor of God* in 1623 (728). Thereby it became the starting point of an important controversy in the closing years of the reign — as remains to be seen.

488. *A Reply made unto Mr. Anthony Wotton and Mr. Iohn White Ministers. Wherin it is shewed, that they have not sufficiently answered the Treatise of Faith. AND Wherin also the truth of the chief points of the said Treatise is more cleerely declared, and more strongly confirmed. By A. D. Student in Divinity. The First Part.* 1612 (STC 10914, AR 607, ERL 193)

489. *A Treatise of Faith. wherein Is briefly, and plainely shewed, a direct Way, by which every man may resolve, and settle his mind in all Doubts, Questions, & Controversies, concerning matters of Faith. Reviewed corrected, and augmented with marginall notes. By A. D. Student in Divinity.* 1614 (STC 10916, AR 609, ERL 20)

490. *A Catalogue of divers visible professors of the Catholike Faith. Which*

sheweth, that the Roman Church hath byn (as the true Church must be) continually Visible, in all Ages since Christ. Taken out of the Appendix to the Reply of A. D. unto M. Ant. Wotton, and M. Ioh. White Ministers. 1614   (STC 10912, AR 606, see ERL 20)

(The second edition of 1619, bound with Gregory Martin's *The Love of the soule*, is announced in the following title:

The Love of the soule . . . With a new addition of a catalogue of the names of popes and other professors of the ancient Catholike faith; and a challenge to Protestants.   (STC 17506, AR 530, ERL 363)

To all this Wotton made no further response; but White dealt with Percy's *Reply* in *A Defence of the Way to the True Church*, which he published in 1614 — just a year before his death. He attributed the arguments of his opponent, for once, rather to Thomas Stapleton and Gregory of Valencia than to Cardinal Bellarmine.

491. *A Defence of the Way to the True Church against A. D. his Reply. Wherein The Motives leading to Papistry, And Questions, touching the Rule of Faith, The Authoritie of the Church, The Succession of the Truth, And The Beginning of Romish innovations: are handled and fully disputed. By Iohn White Doctor of Divinity, sometime of Gunwell and Caius Coll. in Cambridge.* 1614   (STC 25390)

On the other side, Percy found himself supported by two other priests, one a Jesuit, William Wright, under the initials W. G. (Wright Gulielmus), and the other a former president of Douai, Thomas Worthington, under the initials T. W. P. (Thomas Worthington Priest). They both directed their criticism rather against *The Way* of White than his *Defence of the Way*. In 1614 Wright brought out *A Discovery of Certaine Notorious Shifts,* as a short dialogue 'in earnest of a larger Discourse in refutation of M. Whites Absurdities'. This discourse followed in 1616 under the title of *A Treatise of the Church*. Meanwhile, Worthington published his *Whyte dyed Black* in 1615, with a Preface to the Reader explaining 'the occasion inducing me to wryte it'. Considering 'the worthles esteeme, which we have had of M. Whyte his booke (howsoever his owne followers do magnify it)', he had decided not to answer it; but 'seing in diverse passages of his late second worke, he vaunteth in great exultation, and iolity of words', he has taken up his pen against both, but mainly the first.

492. *A Discovery of Certaine Notorious Shifts, Evasions, and Untruthes uttered by M. Iohn White Minister, (and now made Doctour) In a Booke of his lately set forth, and intituled, A Defence of the Way &c. Wherein It is briefly shewed, that his pretended Company of Visible professors is far inferiour to the Synagogue of the Iewes. And a*

> *Catalogue also is framed and set downe for his Negative and Faithlesse*
> *Church, according to his owne Doctrine, untill himselfe produce a*
> *better. By W. G. Professour in Divinity, in manner of a Dialogue.*
> 1614   (STC 26045, AR 927, ERL 115)

493. *A Treatise of the Church. In which is proved M. Iohn White his Way to*
the true Church, to be indeed no way at all to any Church, true or
false: by demonstrating, that his visible Company of Protestants, is but
a Chymaera of his owne braine. For that there was never yet any one,
eyther Man, Woman, or Child a member of it, in all Antiquity, by the
Confession of the most famous Protestants themselves, that ever were.
Written by W. G. Professour in Divinity: in manner of Dialogue. 1616
(STC 26049, AR 930, ERL 377)

494. *Whyte dyed Black. or A Discovery of many most foule blemishes,*
impostures, and deceiptes, which D. Whyte haith practysed in his book
entituled The way to the true Church. Devyded into 3 sortes
Corruptions or depravations. Lyes. Impertinencies, or absurd
reasoninges. Writen by T. W. P. And Dedicated to the University of
Cambridge. 1615   (STC 26001, AR 919, ERL 354)

The place of John White, who died in 1615, was soon taken by his brother
Francis, who was subsequently made Doctor of Divinity and Dean of
Carlisle. In 1617 he brought out *The Orthodox Faith and Way to the Church*
in answer to T. W. P. — ignoring the criticisms of W. G. Later in 1624 he
published a second, enlarged edition, at the height of his later controversy
with Percy, and added it to the collected *Workes* of his brother (in five
books).

495. *The Orthodox Faith and Way to the Church Explained and iustified: in*
answer to a Popish Treatise, entituled, White died blacke; wherein
T. W. P. in his triple accusation of D. White for impostures, untruths,
and absurd illations, is proved a trifler: And the present controversies
betweene us and the Romanists are more fully delivered and cleared. By
Francis White Bachelour in Divinitie. 1617   (STC 25380)

496. *The Workes of that learned and reverend Divine, Iohn White Doctor in*
Divinitie: Together with a Defence of the Way to the True Church, in
answer to a Popish Treatise written by T. W. P. entituled White died
Blacke. By Francis White Doctor in Divinitie and Deane of Carlile.
1624   (STC 25389)

(The contents of *The Workes* are as follows:

1. *The Way to the True Church* (fifth impression)
2. *The Defence of the Way to the True Church*

3. *Two Sermons* (preached in 1615 and 1613)
4. *The Orthodox Faith and Way to the Church*, by F. White
5. *A Replie* of F. White (to J. Percy in the later controversy — 750)

It may have been on the occasion of the 1614 edition of Percy's *Treatise of Faith* — though no explicit mention is made of it — that George Carleton decided to publish his *Directions to know the True Church* in the following year. At least, it fits into the controversy by reason of its subject-matter. In it he gave an English summary of his Latin treatise, *Consensus Ecclesiae Catholicae contra Tridentinos*, which had come out in 1613, in view (as he explained in his Preface) of 'divers bookes . . . that are written in English to seduce the simple that cannot iudge, insinuating to them faire pretences of a shewe of the Church'.

497. *Consensus Ecclesiae Catholicae contra Tridentinos. Demonstrans unam ac perpetuam doctrinam e sacris Scripturis excerptam, & in Ecclesia Catholica conservatam usque ad Concilium Tridentinum, in gravissimis fidei controversiis, quae sunt De Scripturis sive regula fidei. De Ecclesia. De Fide iustificante. De Gratia. Opus praelectionibus Oxoniensibus inchoatum, deinde auctum, & in publicum editum. Auctore Georgio Carletano, Anglo.* 1613   (STC 4631)

498. *Directions to know the True Church. Written by George Carleton, Doctor of Divinitie.* 1615   (STC 4632)

d) *Woodward v. Bell*

Another controversy of this period, of more amusement than importance, was provoked by the apostate priest, Thomas Bell. Ever since 1593, when he had brought out his *Motives* explaining his recent abjuration of his former faith and priesthood, he had been issuing regular challenges to the Papists; only to be met with resolute silence. In the new reign, however, when he returned to the attack with his *Downefall of Poperie* in 1604, and renewed his challenge 'To all English Iesuits, Seminarie priests, and Iesuited papists', he had his wishes at last fulfilled by two seminary priests. One of them, Philip Woodward, had already supported Persons against Sutcliffe in 1602, publishing *A Detection* under the initials E. O. (which Sutcliffe had recognized as those of 'Philip Woodward alias Owlyglasse'). He now published *The Fore-runner of Bels Downefall* under the initials B. C. — with two editions in 1605. The other, Richard Smith, now made his first appearance in the field of controversy with a more reasoned *Answer to Thomas Bels late Challeng* (under the initials S. R.), which also went into two editions in 1605–6.

499. *Thomas Bels Motives: concerning Romish Faith and Religion.* 1593 and 1605   (STC 1830–31)

500. *The Downefall of Poperie: Proposed by way of a new challenge to all English Iesuits and Iesuited or Italianized Papists: daring them all ioyntly, and every one of them severally, to make answer thereunto if they can, or have any truth on their side; knowing for a truth that otherwise all the world will crie with open mouths, Fie upon them, and their patched hotch-potch religion.* 1604   (STC 1817)

(A second edition was published that year, and a third in 1605 (STC 1818–19).)

501. *The Fore-runner of Bels Downefall, Wherin, is breifely answered his bragging offer of disputation, and insolent late challenge; the particularities of the confutation of his bookes, shortly by goddes grace to be published, are mentioned: with a breife answere, to his crakinge and calumnious confutinge of Papistes by Papistes them selves: and lastly a taste. Given of his rare pretended sinceritye, with som few examples.* 1605   (STC 19407 – under Parsons; AR 908, see ERL 322)

502. *An Answer to Thomas Bels late Challeng named by him The Downfal of Popery Wherin al his arguments are answered, his manifold untruths, slaunders, ignorance, contradictions, and corruption of Scripture, & Fathers discovered and disproved: With one table of the Articles and Chapters, and an other of the more markable things conteyned in this booke. What controversies be here handled is declared in the next page. By S. R. Babylon is surprised, Bel is confounded.* 1605   (STC 22809, AR 771, ERL 315)

Before either of these replies came to his attention, Bell issued in 1605 yet another challenge to Rome, under the title, *The Woefull crie of Rome,* as a 'second challenge to all favorites of that Romish faction'. He also brought out a second edition of his *Motives,* 'newly corrected and inlarged by the Author' – though the only noticeable alteration was the addition of these words to the title-page! Then, on his receipt of Woodward's book, he immediately published his reply, *The Popes Funerall,* early in the following year – under the mistaken impression that his adversary was none other than 'Robert Parsons, the trayterous Iesuite'. He went on to add 'A Fresh Larum or New Challenge', as an appendix. Soon after, Smith's book came to his attention; and he responded with *The Iesuites Antepast* in 1608, once more identifying his adversary as Robert Parsons.

503. *The Woefull crie of Rome. Containing a defiance to popery. With Thomas Bells second challenge to all favorites of that Romish faction.*

Succinctly comprehending much variety of matter, full of honest recreation, and very profitable and expedient for all sorts of people: but especially for all simply seduced Papists. 1605   (STC 1833)

(The inner title reads:

Thomas Bels defiance to Poperie, with a second challenge.)

504. *The Popes Funerall. Containing a plaine, succinct, and pithy reply, to a pretensed answere of a shamelesse and foolish Libell, intituled, The Forerunner of Bels downfall. Which is nothing else indeede, (as the indifferent Reader shall perceive by the due peruse thereof,) but an evident manifestation of his owne folly; with the utter confusion of Poperie, and all popish vassals throughout the Christian world.* 1606 (STC 1825)

(The appendix is entitled as follows:

A Fresh Larum or New Challenge, to all English Iesuites and Iesuited Papists in the universall World, tagge and ragge none at all excepted, whosoever shall appeare in the shape of a man.

A second edition was published in the same year, and bound with Bell's other book against the Puritans, *The Regiment of the Church*, in which he noticed the appearance of the second edition of *The Fore-runner*. The title is somewhat altered, as follows:

The Popes Funerall, Containing an exact and pithy reply, to a pretended answere of a shamelesse and foolish Libell, called, The Forerunner of Bells downfall. With a fresh Larum, or a third Challenge to all Iesuites, whatsoever and wheresoever in the universall world, none excepted, that shall appeare in the shape of a man. Together with his Treatise, called, The Regiment of the Church. 1606   (STC 1826)

505. *The Iesuites Antepast, Conteining, A Reply against a pretensed aunswere to the Downe-fall of Poperie, lately published by a masked Iesuite Robert Parsons by name, though he hide himselfe covertly under the letters of S. R. which may fitly be interpreted (A Sawcy Rebell.).* 1608   (STC 1824)

Smith now left the further prosecution of this controversy in the hands of Woodward, who answered *The Popes Funerall* in 1607 with *The Dolefull Knell, of Thomas Bell*. He also made a passing allusion, which is echoed in his title, to 'another booke called by hym, the Wofull crye of Rome'. In response to Bell's repeated challenges, he reminded his opponent of the many fruitless petitions made by the Catholics for a public conference such as that which had been held before the King of France in 1600, between Du Perron, then Bishop of Evreux, and the Huguenot leader, the Sieur du

Plessis-Mornay. Of bibliographical interest is his account of the four most popular anti-Papist authors of the time: Josias Nichols, with his *Abrahams Faith* (1602); Oliver Ormerod, with his *Picture of a Papist* (1606); Andrew Willet, with his *Synopsis Papismi* (1600, in a third enlarged edition) and *Tetrastylon Papismi* (1599, also in a third enlarged edition); and Matthew Sutcliffe, with his *New Challenge* (1600) and *Survey of Poperie* (1606).

506. *The Dolefull Knell, of Thomas Bell. That is A full and sounde answer, to his Pamphlet, Intituled. The Popes Funeral. Which he published, against a Treatise of myne, called. The Fore-runner of Bels Downefal. Wherein his manifest untruthes, grosse corruptions, cunning slightes, vaine cavils, immodest railing, insolent challenging, and idle excursions, be noted, examined, and refuted. By B. C. Student in Divinitye. Divided into two bookes, and severall chapters: according to Bels method. The particular contents whereof, are to be founde in the end of this booke. Bel with Golias . . . B. C. with David.* 1607
(STC 19403, AR 907, ERL 253)

Strangely enough, Bell never responded to this *Dolefull Knell*, but proceeded in 1608 to pen another general attack on the Church of Rome, entitled *The Tryall of the New Religion* – with implicit reference to Kellison's *Survey of the New Religion* (1603), then under attack from Sutcliffe. For at that time each side was seeking to cast the imputation of novelty on the other. Woodward again undertook the refutation of his book, and brought out *Bels Trial Examined* in the same year. He also dealt with two other Anglican works: Thomas Rogers' *The Faith, Doctrine, and religion . . . of England*, which had appeared in 1607 mainly against the Puritans (54); and Thomas Udall's *Brief Viewe of the weake Grounds of Poperie*, which had come out in 1606 and has its place in the next controversy to be considered (521).

507. *The Tryall of the New Religion. Contayning a plaine Demonstration, that the late Faith and Doctrine of the Church of Rome, is indeede the New Religion. By Thomas Bell.* 1608 (STC 1832)

508. *Bels Trial Examined that is A refutation of his late Treatise, intituled. The Triall of the Newe Religion. By B. C. Student in divinitie. Wherein his many & grosse untruthes, with divers contradictions are discovered: Together with an examination of the principal partes of that vaine Pamphlet: and the antiquitie and veritie of sundry Catholike articles, which he calleth rotten ragges of the newe religion, are defended against the newe Rag-master of Rascal. In the Preface likewise, a short viewe of one Thomas Rogers untruthes is sett downe, taken out of his booke called. The faith doctrine and religion, professed and protected in the realme of England, &c. with a short memorandum for T. U. otherwise called Th.Udal.* 1608 (Not in STC, AR 905, ERL 247)

After publishing yet another general attack on the Roman Church in his *Christian Dialogue* of 1609, Bell turned his attention to his adversary in his last book, entitled *The Catholique Triumph*, which came out in 1610, the year of his death. Many years later, in 1628, there appeared one more book with his name in initials and the characteristic title, *The Fall of Papistry*, as a belated echo of his endless refrain.

509. *A Christian Dialogue, betweene Theophilus a deformed Catholike in Rome, and Remigius a reformed Catholike in the Church of England. Conteining. A plaine and succinct resolution, of sundry very intricate and important points of religion, which doe mightily assaile the weake consciences of the vulgar sort of people; penned for the solace of all true hearted English subiects, and for the utter confusion of all seditious Iesuites and Iesuited Popelings in England or elsewhere, so long as they shall persist inordinately in their novelties, heresies, errours, and most grosse and palpable superstitions.* 1609   (STC 1816)

510. *The Catholique Triumph: Conteyning, A Reply to the pretensed Answere of B. C. (a masked Iesuite) lately published against the Tryall of the New Religion. Wherein is evidently prooved, that Poperie and the Doctrine now professed in the Romish Church, is the New Religion: And that the Fayth which the Church of England now mayntaineth, is the ancient Romane Religion.* 1610   (STC 1815)

511. *The Fall of Papistry, and the weake foundation thereof plainely Showed: by way of Articles. With a Challenge to all English Iesuites, and Iesuited, or Italianiz'd Papists: daring them all joyntly, and every one of them severally, to make answer thereunto; if they can, or have any Truth on their side: Knowing for a Truth, that otherwise, all the world will cry with open mouths, Fie upon them and their patched hotch-potch Religion. By T. B.* 1628   (STC 1820)

(This is little more than a rehash of *The Downefall of Poperie*, with which the controversy began.)

e) Brereley v. Morton

About this time there appeared a relatively new method of controversy: that of refuting one's opponent out of his own mouth or the mouths of his supporters. This was to some extent used by Bell, in what Woodward called his 'calumnious confutinge of Papistes by Papistes them selves' (*The Fore-runner*). It was, however, a seminary priest, writing under the pseudonym of John Brereley, who first made extensive use of this method in his *Apologie of the Romane Church* in 1604. (He has been identified as the seminary priest, Lawrence Anderton; but this is not certain.) Here he proposed to establish the Roman claims 'by testimonies of the learned Protestants themselves', with a Preface to the Parliament then in session. His book created something of a sensation at the time of its publication; and it was frequently praised and imitated by subsequent Catholic apologists. On the Anglican side, it was Thomas Morton who chiefly used the same method and turned it against the Catholics in his *Apologia Catholica*, which was published in Latin the following year. In his Dedication to Archibishop Bancroft, he described his book as 'ex nostris Adversariis Religionis nostrae defensio'.

512. *The Apologie of the Romane Church, devided into three severall Tractes whereof 1. The first, Concerneth the Antiquitie and continuence of the Catholike Romane Religion ever since the Apostles time. 2. The second That the Protestantes Religion was not so much as in being, at or before Luthers first appearing. 3. The thirde That Catholickes are no lesse Loyall and dutifull to their Soveraigne, then Protestantes. All which are undertaken and proved by testimonies of the learned Protestantes themselves.* 1604   (STC 3604, AR 131)

513. *Apologia Catholica ex meris Iesuitarum Contradictionibus conflata, in qua Paradoxa, Haereses, Blasphemiae, Scelera, quae a Pontificiis obijci Protestantibus solent, ex ipsorum Pontificiorum testimoniis diluuntur omnia. Eius Libri duo De Notis Ecclesiae. Autore Thoma Mortono Sacrae Theologiae Baccalaureo, & quondam in celeberrima Academia Cantabrigiensi Collegii Iohannis Evangelistae, Socio.* 1605   (STC 18174)

(An 'editio castigatior' was brought out in 1606 (STC 18175).)

A second stage in this implicit controversy came in 1608, when Brereley brought out a revised and enlarged version of his *Apology*, which he renamed *The Protestants Apologie for the Roman Church*. In place of his former 'Preface to the Parliament', he had a 'Preface to the Christian Reader, Catholicke or Protestant' and a Dedication 'To the Kinges most excellent Maiesty'. He also appended an 'Advertisement to him that shall answere this Treatise', referring to Morton, who had recently undertaken in the Dedication of his *Preamble Unto an Incounter with P.R.* (1608) to elaborate an answer to 'the misconceived Catholicke Apology'. This answer, as distinct from Morton's previous work in Latin, appeared in 1609 under the title of *A Catholike Appeale for Protestants*. It was also dedicated to King James.

514. *The Protestants Apologie for the Roman Church. Devided into three severall Tractes. Wherof The first Concerneth the Antiquity & Continuance of the Roman Church & Religion, ever since the Apostles times. 1. That the Protestants Religion was not so much as in being, at, or before Luthers first appearing. The second 2. That the Marks of the*

true Church are apperteyning to the Roman, and wholy wanting to the
severall Churches, begun by Luther & Calvin. The third That Catholicks
are no lesse loyall, and dutifull to their Soveraigne, than Protestants. All
which is undertaken, & proved by testimonies of the learned
Protestants themselves. With A Conclusion to the Reverend Iudges, and
other the grave and learned Sages of the Law. By Iohn Brereley Priest.
1608   (STC 3605, AR 133, ERL 75)

515. *A Catholike Appeale for Protestants, Out of the confessions of the
Romane Doctors; particularly answering the mis-named Catholike
Apologie for the Romane faith, out of the Protestants: Manifesting the
Antiquitie of our Religion, and satisfying all scrupulous Obiections
which have bene urged against it. Written by Th. Morton Doctor of
Divinitie. 1609   (STC 18176)*

The example of John Brereley was followed by another Catholic author,
who remained anonymous but is generally identified as the seminary priest,
Richard Broughton. In 1607 he brought out *The First Part of Protestant
Proofes, for Catholikes Religion and Recusancy*, limiting his field of
reference to contemporary Anglican divines. Thus he frequently quotes from
the recent writings of Matthew Sutcliffe, John Dove, Richard Field, Andrew
Willet, Anthony Wotton, William Middleton, Thomas Bilson and William
Covell — the last two of whom he commends as 'two of your best writers'.
Also included was 'The Table or Argument of the second part'; but the
second part never appeared. Instead, after a long interval of time there came
out two books of a similar nature, and with similar titles, from what was
apparently the same pen. In 1615 the anonymous *Protestants
Demonstrations, for Catholiks Recusance* was published, with a Dedication
to King James. It became involved in a controversy, to be mentioned below,
over the Anglican episcopal succession. Then in 1617 the equally anonymous
English Protestants Recantation came out in specific answer to Morton's
Catholike Appeale. A significant indication of common authorship is that
the range of Protestant authors cited in all three books remains more or less
the same, though two of them appeared so much later than the first.

516. *The First Part of Protestant Proofes, for Catholikes Religion and
Recusancy. Taken only from the writings, of such Protestant Doctors
and Divines of England, as have beene published in the raigne of his
Maiesty over this Kingdome. 1607   (STC 20448, AR 160, ERL 100)*

(The volume ends with 'The Table or Argument of the second part, of
Protestant proofes, for Catholikes religion, and recusancy'.)

517. *Protestants Demonstrations, for Catholiks Recusance. All taken from
such English Protestant Bishops, Doctors, Ministers, parlaments, lawes,*

decrees, and proceedings, as have beene printed, published, or allowed
among them in England; since the cominge of our king Iames into this
kingdome: and for the most parte within the first six or seven yeares
thereof. And evidentlie provinge by their owne writings, that english
Catholiks may not under damnable syn, communicate with English
Protestants, in their Service, Sermons, or matters of Religion: and so
convincinge by themselves, their Religion to be most damnable, &
among other things, their ministery to bee voide, false & usurped.
1615   (STC 20450, AR 168, ERL 155)

518. *A Booke Intituled: The English Protestants Recantation, in matters of
Religion. Wherein is demonstratively proved, by the writings of the
principall, and best learned English Protestant Bishops, and Doctors,
and Rules of their Religion, published allowed, or subscribed unto, by
them, since the comminge of our King Iames into England: That not
onely all generall grounds of Divinitie, are against them: But in every
particular cheife Question, betweene Catholicks & them, they are in
errour, by their owne Iudgments: Divided accordingly, into two parts:
whereof the first entreateth of those generall Grounds: The other of
such particular Controversies. Whereby will also manifestely appear the
vanitie of D. Mortons Protest. Bishop of Chester his booke called
Appeale, or Answeare to the Catholicke Authour of the booke
entituled: The Protestants Apologie.* 1617   (STC 10414, AR 153,
ERL 26)

Another work of the same nature published about this time by another
seminary priest, Edward Mayhew, was *A Treatise of the Groundes of the Old
and Newe Religion*, which appeared in 1608. He likewise notes that even by
the profession of the chief Protestant writers 'our religion and faith is true,
theirs false'. His main attention is devoted to the recent treatise of Richard
Field, *Of the Church*, which had been published in 1606 to refute the
reasons of Bellarmine and Stapleton against the Anglican doctrine on the
nature of the Church. In his title he seems to be glancing at Thomas Udall's
Brief Viewe of the weake Grounds of Poperie, which had also come out in
1606 and had been criticized by Woodward in his Preface to *Bels Trial
Examined* in 1608; but he makes no mention of it in his text. In an
Appendix he also touched on a third book which had appeared in 1606, and
which has already been mentioned in another context, William Crashaw's
denunciation of *Romish Forgeries and Falsifications*.

519. [= 273] *A Treatise of the Groundes of the Old and Newe Religion.
Devided into two parts. Whereunto is added an Appendix, containing a
briefe Confutation of William Crashaw his first Tome of Romish
forgeries and falsifications.* 1608   (STC 24247, AR 493, ERL 124)

(The Second Part, 'that they have neither true faith, nor religion', is given new pagination.)

520. *Of the Church, Five Bookes, By Richard Feild, Doctor of Divinitie.* 1606   (STC 10856)

(Only the first four books were published in 1606. The fifth book, with an Appendix for self-defence, was not added till 1610.)

521. *A Briefe Viewe of the weake Grounds of Popery; As it was propounded to D. Norrice, Priest, by T. U. Gent: and returned without answere.* 1606   (Not in STC)

(The MS of this book was originally submitted to the Jesuit, Fr. Norris, who returned it without comment. The author procured the approval of Matthew Sutcliffe and Anthony Wotton for the publication of his book, which is in the form of a dialogue between a Protestant and a Papist.)

522. [= 271] *Romish Forgeries and Falsifications: Together with Catholike Restitutions. The first Booke of the first Tome . . .* 1606   (STC 6014)

In response to both Broughton and Mayhew, as well as to Theophilus Higgons (to be considered later), Richard Field added a special Appendix to *The Fifth Booke of the Church,* which came out in 1610. As for Mayhew's criticism of Crashaw, it was taken up and answered by Thomas James in his *Treatise of the Corruptions* in 1611. Here he identifies 'the Unknowne Author' as 'one May, a Priest', whom he generously recognizes as 'a man (to give my Adversarie his due praise) neither immodest nor unlearned'. Another answer to Broughton came in an Appendix by Andrew Willet to his *Loidoromastix* of 1607 against Richard Parkes. Richard Crakanthorpe also undertook to refute Broughton's book; but his MS, entitled *Popish Falsifications,* was apparently never published, though Anthony Wood mentions it in his *Athenae Oxonienses* as still preserved at Oxford.

523. [= 558] *The Fifth Booke of the Church. Together with an Appendix, containing a defense of such partes and passages of the former Bookes, as have bene either excepted against, or wrested, to the maintenance of Romish errours. By Richard Field, Doctour of Divinity.* 1610 (STC 10856)

(The Appendix, with new pagination, has three parts:

The First Part, Containing a discovery of the vanitie of such silly exceptions, as have beene taken against the former foure bookes, by one Theophilus Higgons. The second part, concerning the Author of the Treatise of the grounds of the Old and New religion, and such

> *exceptions as have beene taken by him against the former Bookes. The*
> *Third Part, conteining a briefe examination of such pretended Proofes*
> *for Romish Religion and Recusancy, as are produced and violently*
> *wrested by a late Pamphleter out of the former Bookes.)*

524. [= 274] *A Treatise of the Corruptions of Scripture, Councels, and*
     Fathers, by the Prelats, Pastors, and Pillars of the Church of Rome . . .
     1611   (STC 14462)

525. *Further advertisements to the Reader, containing a briefe answere to a*
     certaine Popish pamphlet, intituled, The first part of Protestant
     proofes. &c. 1607   (STC 25639)

     (Appendix to Andrew Willet's |*Loidoromastix* (76))

526. *Popish Falsifications. Or, an answer to a treatise of a Popish Recusant,*
     intit. The first part of Protestant proofs for Catholicks Religion and
     Recusancy . . . (MS)

     (Mentioned in *Athenae Oxonienses*, I, 418.)

This may be the place to mention other Protestant attacks made about
this time against the Papists, though they remained unanswered by the latter
save as means of showing up the self-contradictions among their opponents.

In 1604, the Puritan Samuel Hieron published *An Answer to a Popish*
Ryme, echoing the earlier *Answere to a Romish Rime* of John Rhodes
which had appeared two years before.

527. *An Answere to a Popish Ryme, lately scattered abroad in the West*
     Parts, and much relyed upon by some simply-seduced. By Samuel
     Hieron, Minister of the Word of God, at Modbury in Devon. 1604
     (STC 13388)

A couple of years later, many more anti-Papist books were published in the
aftermath of the Gunpowder Plot. A work which was never refuted by the
Catholics, but to which Broughton made frequent reference, was William
Middleton's *Papisto-Mastix*. This is presented in its inner title as 'A Briefe
Answere to a Popish Dialogue between two Gentlemen: the one a Papist, the
other a Protestant'; but the Dialogue in question does not appear to have
survived. Another popular anti-Papist work of this year was the *Picture of a*
Papist by Oliver Ormerod, which he offered as a companion to his previous
Picture of a Puritane of 1605 (42). It was (as we have seen) briefly dealt with
by Woodward in his *Dolefull Knell* in 1607 (506). Also in 1606 John
Swinnerton brought out *A Christian Love-Letter*, as an attempt to convert
the Papists through shame for 'the late discovered Treasons'. This idea was
first suggested by a desire to refute Hill's *Quartron of Reasons* (1600), till he
found the book already refuted by Francis Dillingham.

528. *Papisto-Mastix, Or The Protestants Religion defended. Shewing briefely when the great compound heresie of Poperie first sprange; how it grew peece by peece till Antichrist was disclosed; how it hath been consumed by the breath of Gods mouth: and when it shall be cut downe and withered. By William Middleton Bachelor of Divinitie, and Minister of Hardwicke in Cambridge-shire.* 1606   (STC 17913)

529. *The Picture of a Papist: or A Relation of the damnable heresies, detestable qualities, and diabolicall practises of sundry hereticks in former ages, and of the papists in this age. Wherein is plainly shewed, that there is scarse any heresie which the auncient Church knew, and withal condemned to the pit of hell, which the Romish Church hath not raked up againe, and propounded to the world with new Varnish and fresh Colours. Together with a discourse of the late treason, and of the late execution of some of the Traitors: wherin is shewed the haynousnesse of their crime, and the lawfulnesse of their punishment. Written to stop the mouthes of those, that complaine of rigour, and scandalize the state of cruelty, in their iust severitie. Whereunto is annexed a certain treatise, intituled Pagano-Papismus: wherein is proved by irrefragable demonstrations, that Papisme is flat Paganisme: and that the Papists doe resemble the very Pagans, in above sevenscore severall things.* 1606   (STC 18850)

(This book is in the form of a Dialogue between a Minister and a Recusant, as is also the treatise, which is entitled: 'Pagano-Papismus: or, A Discovery of Popish Paganisme'.)

530. *A Christian Love-Letter: Sent particularly to K. T. a Gentle-woman mis-styled a Catholicke, but generallie intended to all of the Romish Religion, to labour their conversion to the true faith of Christ Iesus.* 1606   (STC 23558)

In 1608 John Panke published his *Fal of Babel* 'against the Papists of this, and former ages', but without attacking any writer in particular, though he glances at the growing tendency of Catholic apologists to produce 'catalogues of professors'. In the following year Joseph Hall published his *Peace of Rome* (in an ironical sense), along with *A Serious Disswasive from Poperie*, addressed 'To W. D. Revolted'. In his Dedication to Prince Henry he proposes (like Morton) to offer 'not so much any fight of ours against them of Rome, as theirs against themselves, and therein for us'. Also in 1609 one R. M., calling himself 'an unlearned Protestant', came out first with *Sixe Demaunds* made to the Papists, and secondly with *A Profitable Dialogue* for a perverted Papist.

531. *The Fal of Babel. By the confusion of tongues, directly proving against*

the Papists of this, and former ages; that a view of their writings, and bookes being taken, it cannot be discerned by any man living, what they would say, or how be understoode, in the question of the sacrifice of the Masse, the Reall presence or transubstantiation; but in explaning their mindes, they fall upon such termes, as the Protestants use and allow. Further In the question of the Popes supremacy is shewed, how they abuse an authority of the auncient father St. Cyprian, A Canon of the 1 Niceene counsell, And the Ecclesiasticall historie of Socrates, and Sozomen. And lastly is set downe a briefe of the succession of Popes in the sea of Rome for these 1600. yeeres togither; what diversity there is in their accompt, what heresies, schismes, and intrusions there hath bin in that sea, delivered in opposition against their tables, wherewith now adaies they are very busie; and other things discovered against them. By Iohn Panke 1608 (STC 19171)

532. *The Peace of Rome. Proclaimed to All the world, by her famous Cardinall Bellarmine, and the no lesse famous Casuist Navarre. Whereof the one acknowledgeth, and numbers up above three hundred differences of Opinion, maintained in the Popish Church. The other confesses neere threescore differences amongst their own Doctors in one onely point of their Religion. Gathered faithfully out of their writings in their own words, and divided into four Bookes, and those into severall Decads. Whereto is prefixed a serious Disswasive from Poperie. By J. H. 1609* (STC 12696)

533. *Six Demaunds (from an unlearned Protestant, to a learned Papist,) so forcible against all obstinate Papists, that not any of them are able to reply, without absurd Equivocation. Also an invincible Argument, to prove the Church of Rome to erre, with an infallible note whereby to know the Spirit of Truth, and the spirit of Error. 1609* (STC 6574)

534. *A Profitable Dialogue for a perverted Papist, or A little Labour of a Layman, tending to the profit of a perverted Papist: namely, by laying open unto him his owne errour, in beleeving that the Church of Rome cannot erre. Composed in Dialogue maner, as it were betweene a simple Lay man, and certaine grave Divines, and published onely for the benefit of the Lay Papist. Written by R. M. Gent. and Student in Divinity. 1609* (STC 17149)

(In 'The Authour to the learned Reader', he speaks of 'my Sixe demaunds to the learned Papists'. He also glances at 'our late Minister (but now an Apostata) Theophilus Higgons'.)

In 1610 John Dove, who had published his *Perswasion to the English Recusants* in 1602, followed it up with *An Advertisement to the English*

Seminaries, and Iesuites – presumably in support of the royal proclamations of that year (399, 400). It was now his duty, he declared in his Introduction, 'to speake somewhat to them also which sit in the chaire of Moses'. In the next year Thomas Sanderson spoke out against *Romanizing Recusants, and Dissembling Catholicks*, in answer to a pamphlet by the seminary priest, Ralph Buckland, entitled *An Embassage from Heaven*.

535. *An Advertisement to the English Seminaries, and Iesuites: Shewing their loose kind of writing, and negligent handling the cause of Religion, in the whole course of their workes. By Iohn Dove Doctor in Divinity.* 1610   (STC 7077)

536. *Of Romanizing Recusants, and Dissembling Catholicks. A Countermaund of a counterfeit Embassage. Or, An Answere to the posthume Pamphlet of Ralfe Buckland sometime a Popish Priest, secretly printed and published after his death about a yeare agoe.* 1611   (STC 21711)

(The Dedication is signed Th. Sanderson.)

537. *An Embassage from Heaven. Wherein our Lord and Saviour Christ Iesus giveth to understand, his iust indignation against al such, as being Catholikely minded, dare yeelde their presence to the rites and publike praier, of the malignant Church. By Raphe Buckland Priest.* [c. 1610] (STC 4007, AR 180, ERL 298)

(The book opens with 'An Epistle to al Schismatikes'.)

f) *Miracles and Martyrs*

A particular controversy that appeared about this time between Catholic and Anglican writers was one concerning miracles. Whereas the latter maintained that the age of miracles had long since ceased with the apostles or soon after, the former appealed to the continuance of miracles in their midst as one of the four marks of the true Church. A contemporary case of miracles, said to have been worked through the intercession of the Virgin Mary at her shrine of Montaigu in Brabant, aroused considerable interest both in the Low Countries and in England as well – and no small controversy. An authoritative account of the miracles was drawn up and published by the city clerk of Brussels, Philip Numan, in 1604 – first in Flemish, and then in French translation under the title, *Histoire des Miracles*. These two versions had each appeared in three editions by the year 1606, when an English translation by the seminary priest, Robert Chambers, was also published with the title, *Miracles lately wrought by the Intercession of the Glorious Virgin Marie*. In his lengthy Dedication to King James the translator spoke of these 'straunge, and wunderfull things which lately have happened in these Netherlands . . . where at all the world here standeth so much amazed and astonished'. A Spanish translation also appeared in 1606.

538. *Histoire des Miracles advenuz n'agueres a l'intercession de la Glorieuse Vierge Marie, au lieu dit Mont-aigu, prez de Sichen, au Duché de Brabant. Mise en lumiere, & tirée hors des actes, instrumens publicqz, & informations sur ce princes, Par authorité de Monseigneur l'Archevecque de Malines.* 1604

(The name of the author appeared on the title-page of the third edition of 1606, with the following additions:

Par M. Philippe Numan Greffier de la Ville de Bruxelles. Par charge & authorité de Monseigneur l'Archevesque de Malines. Troisiesme Edition, augmentee de Divers miracles jusques oires non imprimées.)

539. *Miracles lately wrought by the intercession of the glorious Virgin Marie, at Mont-aigu, nere unto Sichem in Brabant. Gathered out of the publick instruments, and informations taken thereof. By authoritie of the Lord Archbishop of Maclin. Translated out of the French copie into English by M. Robert Chambers Priest, and confessor of the English Religious Dames in the Citie of Bruxelles.* 1606 (STC 18746, AR 578, ERL 241)

Three years later, this work was strongly criticized by Robert Tynley, in a sermon preached on 17 April 1609, which was published in the same year with his above-mentioned sermon against Persons' *Iudgment of a Catholicke English-man* of 1608 (363).

540. [= 364] *Two Learned Sermons. The one, of the mischievous subtiltie, and barbarous crueltie, the other of the false Doctrines, and refined Haeresies of the Romish Synagogue. Preached, the one at Paules Crosse the 5. of November, 1608. The other at the Spittle the 17. of Aprill. 1609. In the first, are examined divers passages of that lewde English Libell, written by a Prophane Fugitive, against the Apologie for the Oath of Allegeance. In the seconde, are answered many of the arguments published by Rob. Chambers Priest, concerning Popish Miracles; and Dedicated (forsooth) to the Kinges most excellent Maiestie. By Robert Tynley, Doctor of Divinitie, and Archdeacon of Ely.* 1609 (STC 24472)

Meanwhile, the Catholic humanist, Justus Lipsius, had entered the controversy with a couple of books in Latin on this subject. The first, published in 1604, was devoted to another shrine of the Virgin Mary at Halle, to the south of Brussels, and entitled *Diva Virgo Hallensis*. The second, published in the following year, was a similar work on the shrine of Montaigu, under the similar title *Diva Sichemiensis sive Aspricollis*. The former book was immediately attacked by two Calvinist ministers in the Low Countries: Albert van Oosterwijck, who translated it into Dutch in 1605 with sarcastic annotations, under the title, *I. Lipsii heylige maghet van Halle*; and Peter Denaise (Denaisius), who published an anonymous dialogue against it in the same year, entitled *Dissertatio De Idolo Hallensi* – first in Latin, then in Flemish. The other book, which criticized what Numan described as 'A certaine pamphlet in flemmish . . . by some pernicious Calvinist of Holland against the honour donne to the Moother of God at Mountaigue', was in turn subjected to the criticism of the Scots divine, George Thomson, who devoted his Latin treatise, *Vindex Veritatis*, to this and another book by Lipsius on Fate.

541. *I. Lipsi Diva Virgo Hallensis. Beneficia eius & Miracula fide atque ordine descripta.* 1604

542. *Iusti Lipsi Diva Sichemiensis sive Aspricollis: Nova eius Beneficia & Admiranda.* 1605

543. *Vindex Veritatis. Adversus Iustum Lipsium Libri duo. Prior insanam eius religionem politicam, fatuam nefariamque de Fato, sceleratissimam de Fraude doctrinam refellit. Posterior ψευδοπαρθενου Sichemiensis, idest, Idoli Aspricollis, & Deae ligneae miracula convellit. Uterque Lipsium ab orco Gentilismum revocasse docet. Auctore Georgio Thomsono Andreo-politano Scoto-Britanno.* 1606 (STC 24031)

Lipsius, who died in 1606, was defended not only by Philip Numan, but also by the Belgian Jesuit, Charles Scribani (Scribanius). In 1605 the latter brought out the first edition of his famous *Amphitheatrum Honoris*, in answer to various Calvinist calumnies against the Society of Jesus; and he devoted the eighth chapter of Book III to this subject, 'Calvinistarum in Divam Hallensem dentes retusi'. It was precisely against his defence of Lipsius, and a poem of his 'Ad Divam Hallensem & Puerum Iesum', that the Puritan preacher William Crashaw was prompted to publish his *Iesuites Gospel* in 1610. In an introduction Crashaw describes 'the Occasion of this Iesuiticall Blasphemye', noting how Lipsius, having 'at last set up his rest in Poperye', has written two books in honour of the Virgin, and how Scribanius has come 'to defend their friend Lipsius, and his legend of our Ladye of Hall', besides making a poem 'to our Ladye of Hall and the Child Iesus'. He also speaks slightingly of 'Iustus Lipsius his history of our Lady of Sichem, or of our Ladies picture, of the craggy-rocke or sharpe hill, and of her new miracles and benefites'. This work and a *Sermon* which Crashaw had published two years before, in 1608, were together confuted by the Jesuit,

John Floyd (under the initials I. R.), in 1612 in his *Overthrow of the Protestants Pulpit-Babels*.

544. *Clari Bonarscii Amphitheatrum Honoris in quo Calvinistarum in Societatem Iesu criminationes iugulatae.* 1605

   (Crashaw quotes from the second edition of 1606.)

545. *The Iesuites Gospel by W. Crashawe, B. of Divinity and Preacher at the Temple.* 1610   (STC 6016)

   (The second edition of 1621 has the altered title:

   The Iesuites Gospell: Written by themselves. Discovered and published by W. Crashaw, B. of Divinity, and preacher at White-chappell. The second Impression Corrected and enlarged by the Author.   (STC 6017)

546. [= 172] *The Sermon preached at the Crosse, Feb. xiiij. 1607. By W. Crashawe, Batchelour of Divinitie, and preacher at the Temple; Iustified by the Authour, both against Papist, and Brownist, to be the truth: Wherein, this point is principally followed −, that the religion of Rome, as now it stands established, is worse then ever it was.* 1608
   (STC 6027)

   (Crashaw particularly criticizes 'The XX. Wounds found to be in the body of the present Romish religion', in partial response to 'Wright, in his Articles' and 'Kellison in his Survaies'.
   On p. 26 he also turns to attack the Brownists, posing four questions, which were answered by Henry Ainsworth in his *Counterpoyson* of 1608; cf. 172, 176.)

547. *The Overthrow of the Protestants Pulpit-Babels, convincing their Preachers of Lying and Rayling, to make the Church of Rome seeme mysticall Babell. Particularly confuting W. Crashawes Sermon at the Crosse, printed as the patterne to iustify the rest. With a Preface to the Gentlemen of the Innes of Court, shewing what use may be made of this Treatise. Togeather with a discovery of M. Crashawes spirit: and an Answere to his Iesuites Ghospell. By I. R. Student in Divinity.* 1612
   (STC 11111, AR 326, ERL 149)

   This book of Floyd's now led to a strange controversy between him and Sir Edward Hoby. The latter undertook the defence of Crashaw on account of 'certaine passages, in a short letter of mine, which some few yeares since, past from my pen to the presse'. This had been his *Letter to Mr. T. H.* (Theophilus Higgons), which he had published in 1609, and against which Floyd had presumed to write − as will be seen later (cf. 556). Hoby\brought out his book in 1613, and entitled it *A Counter-snarle For Ishmael*

Rabshacheh, referring the initials I. R. to the railing Assyrian of II Kings xviii. Floyd at once replied (in the same year) with his *Purgatories Triumph over Hell*, reminding his adversary of the ill fame of both Crashaw's *Sermon* and *Iesuits Gospell* even in the Parliament. This provoked Hoby to bring out his *Curry-Combe for a Coxe-combe* in 1615, in the form of a racy dialogue between the Mayor, the Minister and Nick Groome of Queenborough, and one 'Iabal Rachil Libeller' (from iv. 20 Genesis)

548. *A Counter-snarle For Ishmael Rabshacheh, A Cecropidan Lycaonite. By Sr. Edward Hoby, Knight, one of the Gentlemen of his Maiesties Privie-Chamber.* 1613   (STC 13539)

(The author speaks of his adversary as 'this falsefiing Cecropidan', from Ovid *Met.* book xiv; and as 'this roaring Lycaonite', from book i.)

549. *Purgatories Triumph over Hell, Maugre The barking of Cerberus in Syr Edward Hobyes Counter-snarle. Described in a Letter to the sayd Knight, from I. R. Authour of the Answere unto the Protestants Pulpit-Babels.* 1613   (STC 11114, AR 329, ERL 143)

550. *A Curry-Combe for a Coxe-combe. Or Purgatories Knell. In answer of a lewd Libell fornicated by Iabal Rachil against Sir Edw. Hobies Counter-snarle: Entituled Purgatories triumph over Hell. Digested in forme of a Dialogue by Nick-groome of the Hobie-Stable Reginoburgi.* 1615   (STC 13540)

(At the end is an 'Appendix de Iesuitica Batrachologia in Ministrorum Britannomachia', by Hoby's secretary, Anthony Tunstall, against the Jesuit Henry FitzSimon's *Britannomachia Ministrorum*, 1614 (576))

A related theme to that of miracles about this time was that of martyrs; as both were regarded by Catholic writers as reinforcing their claim to the 'mark' of sanctity. Thus in 1608 another seminary priest, John Wilson, published *The English Martyrologe* in the form of a calendar of all the British saints, adding yet another catalogue of those who had suffered martyrdom for the faith since the reign of Henry VIII. This prompted an anonymous Protestant writer to publish a 'counter-poyse' in 1611 entitled *The Fierie Tryall of Gods Saints*, with an appendix corresponding to that of Wilson, based on John Foxe's calendar of the Marian martyrs.

551. *The English Martyrologe conteyning a summary of the lives of the glorious and renowned Saintes of the three Kingdomes, England, Scotland, and Ireland. Collected and distributed into Moneths, after the forme of a Calendar, according to every Saintes festivity. Wherunto is annexed in the end a Catalogue of those, who have suffered death in*

*England for defence of the Catholicke Cause, since King Henry the 8.
his breach with the Sea Apostolicke, unto this day. By a Catholicke
Priest.* 1608   (STC 25771, AR 889, ERL 232)

(Earlier catalogues of this kind had been included in Sanders'
De Origine ac Progressu Schismatis Anglicani (1585) and
in Bridgewater's enlarged edition of *Concertatio Ecclesiae
Catholicae in Anglia* (1589))

552. *The Fierie Tryall of Gods Saints; (These suffered for the witnes of
Iesus, and for the word of God, (under Queene Mary,) who did not
worship the Beast, nor his Image, nor had taken his marke upon their
foreheads, or on their hands, or on their Garments, and these live and
raigne with Christ: Revel. 20.4.) As a counter-poyse to I. W. Priest his
English Martyrologe. And the Detestable Ends of Popish Traytors:
(These are of Sathans Synagogue, calling themselves Iewes (or
Catholiques) but lie and are not: These worshipped the beast saying,
who is like unto the Beast? who is able to warre with him. Revel. 13.4.
and these shall drink of the wine of Gods wrath, and shall be tormented
with fire and brimstone before the holy Angells, and before the Saints,
because they worshipped the Beast and his Image. Rev. 4.10 & 11.) Set
downe in a comparative Collection of both their sufferings. Herewith
also the Concurrence and agreement of the raignes of the Kings of
England and Scotland, since the first yeare of Q. Mary, till this present,
the like before not extant.* 1611   (STC 24269)

(The appendix is entitled:

*A Briefe Collection of such Martyrs as within the (lesse than six yeares)
Bloudy Raigne of Queene Mary were burned in England for the
profession of the Gospell of Christ Iesus. Opposed to the following
English-Romish Martyrologe of I. W. Priest.*)

In 1614 there appeared a more particular hagiographical presentation of
The Life and Death of Mr. Edmund Geninges Priest, by his brother, John
Gennings. It was accompanied with an appendix on 'the Life and Death of
M. Swithune Welles', who had suffered with Edmund Gennings in 1591. This
in turn was criticized by the apostate priest, Richard Sheldon, in the
appendix to his *Survey of the Miracles of the Church of Rome*. The main
criticism of Sheldon was directed against Floyd's *Purgatories Triumph;* but
he added two appendices, one against 'certaine Popish miraculous visions',
and the other more particularly against 'a late pamphlet' on this 'Pseudo-
Martyr'.

553. *The Life and Death of Mr. Edmund Geninges Priest, Crowned with
Martyrdome at London, the 10 day of November, in the years MDXCI.*
1614   (STC 11728, AR 358, ERL 69)

(The appendix is entitled:

A Briefe Relation by way of Appendix, Concerning the Life and Death of M. Swithune Welles Gentleman, companion and fellow-Martyr to the foresayd M. Edmund Geninges Priest.)

554. *A Survey of the Miracles of the Church of Rome, proving them to be Antichristian. Wherein are examined and refuted the six fundamentall Reasons of Iohn Flood Ignatian, published by him in defence of Popish Miracles. By Richard Sheldon Catholike Priest, and sometimes in the Church of Rome Mr. Floods Colleague.* 1616 (STC 22399)

('The two appendices are respectively entitled:

An Appendix touching the vanity of certaine Popish miraculous visions which are usually brought by Papists for defence of their Religion.

A second Addition, shewing the vanity of a late pamphlet, in which the life and death of one Edmund Gennings Pseudo-Martyr, is gloriously set downe.)

g) *Convertite Controversies*

From 1609 onwards there were a number of conversions on either side, from Anglican to Catholic and *vice versa*, which led to a number of scattered controversies. They were in some cases connected with each other and with the foregoing controversies, in other cases quite independent and unique. The first to be noticed was in both directions, first from Anglican to Catholic, and then back to Anglican. In 1609 one Theophilus Higgons, after having been an Anglican minister, decided to embrace the Catholic faith and published his reasons for doing so in a book entitled, *The First Motive of T. H.* Here he dealt chiefly with the questions of Purgatory and Prayers for the dead, against the arguments of Richard Field (in his treatise *Of the Church*, 1606) and of Thomas Morton (in his *Apologia Catholica*, 1605). Also in an Appendix, entitled *Try Before You Trust*, he renewed his attack on Field and Morton, adding a further criticism of the latter's *Full Satisfaction* (1606). Inevitably, both Morton and Field soon came out with rebuttals of Higgons' arguments. The former devoted *A Direct Answer* in 1609 to particular points raised by Higgons in his Appendix, referring to him as 'a Motioner' who has followed the 'Moderator' (Broughton) and the 'Mitigator' (Persons). The latter dealt with the main part of Higgons' book in a long section of his Appendix to *The Fifth Booke of the Church* in 1610; but he was persuaded to withdraw it from print for a time, to keep the way open for Higgons' return to the Church of England (cf. Foley VII 1014).

555. *The First Motive of T. H. Maister of Arts, and lately Minister, to suspect the integrity of his Religion: Which was Detection of Falsehood*

in D. Humfrey, D. Field, & other learned Protestants, touching the question of Purgatory, and Prayer for the dead. With his particular considerations perswading him to embrace the Catholick doctrine in theis and other points. An Appendix intituled, Try before you trust. Wherein some notable untruths of D. Field and D. Morton are discovered. 1609   (STC 13454, AR 397, ERL 72)

(The D. Humfrey mentioned here is the Elizabethan divine, Laurence Humphrey, Regius professor of divinity at Oxford and President of Magdalen College. Higgons discusses his *Iesuitismi Pars Secunda* (1584), where he deals with the fifth reason of Campion's *Rationes Decem* (1580).

The Appendix may be treated as a separate item, seeing that it has a new title-page and separate pagination.)

556. *Try Before You Trust. or An Admonition Unto the credulous, and seduced Protestants, to examine the fidelity of their Writers, and particularly of two principall Doctours; viz. D. Field, & D. Morton. A Detection of their falsehood in some matters of great importance: and a discovery of sondry vanities in the new Gospell according to Luther, Zvingl. and others. By T. H. Maister of Arts, and lately Minister. Added by way of Appendix unto his First Motive.* 1609.   (cf. 555)

557. *A Direct Answer unto the Scandalous Exceptions, which Theophilus Higgons hath lately objected against D. Morton. In the which there is principally discussed, Two of the most notorious Obiections used by the Romanists, viz. 1. M. Luthers conference with the divell, and 2. The sence of the Article of Christ his descension into hell.* 1609 (STC 18181)

(The first point, about Luther, was chiefly urged by Persons in his *Defence of the Censure* (1582), which first led Francis Walshingham towards the Catholic position.)

558. [= 523] *The Fifth Booke of the Church. Together with an Appendix containing a defense of such partes and passages of the former Bookes, as have bene either excepted against, or wrested, to the maintenance of Romish errours. By Richard Field, Doctour of Divinity.* 1610 (STC 10856)

(The Appendix is divided into three parts. The other two, against Mayhew and Broughton, have already been mentioned. The first part, against Higgons, is entitled:

The First Part, Containing a discovery of the vanitie of such silly exceptions, as have beene taken against the former foure bookes, by one Theophilus Higgons.)

It was at this point that Sir Edward Hoby joined in against Higgons with his *Letter to Mr. T. H.* in 1609, at the special request of the latter's father, Robert Higgons, whose letter is given in an appendix. This was immediately answered in the same year in *The Apology of Theophilus Higgons*. Here the former minister mentions the fact that he was reconciled to the Church of Rome by the Jesuit John Floyd; and it was this that led to the controversy between Hoby and Floyd considered above (548–50). In the conclusion of his *Apology* Higgons promised that the residue 'shall come foorth, in due time, accompanied with a Reply unto D. Mortons Answere'. But he never fulfilled this promise, as shortly afterwards he recanted and made his submission to the Church of England. This he performed publicly in a *Sermon*, which he preached at Paul's Cross and subsequently published in 1611.

559. *A Letter to Mr. T. H. Late Minister: Now Fugitive: From Sir Edward Hoby Knight. In Answere of his first Motive.* 1609 (STC 13541)

(The Letter of Robert Higgons is introduced by an advertisement from 'The Printer to the Reader':

'As I had neere ended the Printing of the two former Letters, I received a third from Sir Edward Hoby (the originall now remaining with himselfe) directed unto him from the father of the said T. H.'

The first Letter mentioned in this advertisement is the Dedicatory Epistle by Sir Edward 'To all Romish collapsed Ladies of Great Britanie', prefaced to the main *Letter*.)

560. *The Apology of Theophilus Higgons lately Minister, now Catholique. Wherein The Letter of Sir Edw. Hoby Knight, directed unto the sayd T. H. in answere of his First Motive, is modestly examined and clearely refuted.* 1609   (STC 13452, AR 396, ERL 57)

561. *A Sermon preached at Pauls Crosse the third of March, 1610. By Theophilus Higgons. In testimony of his heartie reunion with the Church of England, and humble submission thereunto. Published by command.* 1611   (STC 13456)

A friend of Higgons who went over to Rome about the same time (as mentioned in *The Apology*), but with firmer resolution, was Humphrey Leech. He had become involved in a disputation at Oxford, when he defended the traditional teaching of the Fathers 'concerning Evangelicall Counsayles' against two Anglican divines, Leonard Hutton and Sebastian Benefield. For this reason he was forced out of the university; and soon afterwards he made his way across the seas and was admitted not only into the Church of Rome, but also to the priesthood, and eventually into the Society of Jesus. In the same year, 1609, he published his motives for taking this step in *A Triumph of Truth*, including his 'sermon preached in defence of the Evangelicall Counsayles' and '12 Motives, which perswaded me to embrace the Catholicke Religion'.

562. *A Triumph of Truth. or Declaration of the Doctrine concerning*
   Evangelicall Counsayles; lately delivered in Oxford by Humfrey Leech
   M. of Arts, & Minister. With Relation of sondry occurrents, and
   particularly of D. King, the Vicechancellour, his exorbitant proceedings
   against the sayd H. L. upon his constant propugnation thereof. Also
   The peculiar Motives, ensuing thereupon, which perswaded him to
   renounce the faction of hereticall Congregations & to embrace the unity
   of the Catholique Church. 1609   (STC 15363, AR 450, ERL 169)

By way of answer to Leech's book, Benefield published his Oxford lectures in Latin the following year, under the title of *Doctrinae Christianae Sex Capita* – with one 'De Consiliis Evangelicis' as the second chapter. He also added an Appendix, particularly directed against Leech and his arguments. Also in 1610 another Oxford divine, Daniel Price, published an English refutation of Leech's motives, entitled *The Defence of Truth*.

563. *Doctrinae Christianae Sex Capita, totidem praelectionibus in Schola*
   Theologica Oxoniae pro forma habitis discussa, & disceptata. Accessit
   appendix ad caput secundum, de Consiliis Evangelicis, in qua ad omnes
   SS. Patrum autoritates, ab Humphredo Leechio pro iisdem asserendis
   respondetur. Autore Sebastiano Benefield, SS. Theologiae D. Collegii
   Corporis Christi Socio. 1610   (STC 1867)

564. *The Defence of Truth against a booke falsely called The Triumph of*
   Truth sent over from Arras A.D. 1609. by Humfrey Leech late Minister.
   Which booke in all particulars is answered, and the adioining Motives of
   his revolt confuted: by Daniell Price, of Exeter Colledge in Oxford,
   Chaplaine in ordinary to the most high and mighty, the Prince of Wales.
   1610   (STC 20292)

Yet another publication by a convert to Rome appeared in 1609 under the title, *A Search made into Matters of Religion*, by Francis Walsingham. This is of special interest, as in the course of his conversion the author made one of the most complete surveys of the religious controversies in England over the preceding half-century. His doubts were first aroused by a perusal of Persons' *Defence of the Censure* against William Charke (1582); and he went on to read the leading Anglican controversialists from Jewel onwards, with the Catholic replies. He also discussed in some detail such contemporary controversialists as Thomas Bell, Andrew Willet, Thomas Rogers, and above all Matthew Sutcliffe. After his conversion he entered the Society of Jesus; and he was greatly assisted by Persons in his task of composition. After a second edition of his book in 1615, he is said to have written *Some reasons for embracing the Catholic faith* in 1618; but no copy seems to have survived.

565. *A Search made into Matters of Religion, by Francis Walsingham Deacon of the Protestants Church, before his change to the Catholicke. Wherein Is related, how first he fell into his doubts: And how for finall resolution therof he repayred unto his Maiesty, who remitted him to the L. of Canterbury that now is, and he to other learned men. And what the issue was of all those Conferences. And how after this againe he betooke himselfe to the reading of Protestant and Catholicke Authors for better finding out the truth: As also for discerning where, & on what side true or false dealing was to be found: and what the successe of this Search hath beene. Dedicated to the Kings most Excellent Maiesty.* 1609   (STC 25002, AR 875, ERL 286)

A few years later there appeared an even more eminent convert to Rome from among the Anglican ministry in Benjamin Carier, a Cambridge divine and one of the King's chaplains. He attributed his conversion to the study of 'the church historie, and of the Ancient fathers which had no Interest in ether side'; and he, too, wrote *A Treatise* of his motives, addressing it 'to the King his most excellent Majestie' about the year 1614 – which was also the year of his death. This was followed in 1615 by *A Copy of a Letter*, which he had written from beyond the seas 'to some particular friends in England'. Both works were confuted by George Hakewill in 1616, the former in the main argument of his *Answere to a Treatise*, the latter in an Appendix.

566. *A Treatise Written by Mr. Doctour Carier, wherein he layeth downe sundry learned and pithy considerations, by which he was moved, to forsake the protestant Congregation, and to betake hym self to the Catholicke Apostolicke Roman Church: agreeing verbatim wyth the written copye, addressed by the sayd Doctour to the King his most excellent Majestie.* 1614?   (STC 4623, AR 207, ERL 366)

(A third edition of 1632 is entitled:

A Carrier to a King. Or Doctour Carier (Chaplayne to K. Iames of happy memory) his Motives of renouncing the Protestant Religion, & imbracing the Cath. Roman. Directed to the sayd K. Maiesty. 1632 (STC 4625, AR 210)

567. *A Copy of a Letter, written by M. Doctor Carier beyond Seas, to some particular friends in England. Whereunto are added certaine collections found in his Closet, made by him (as is thought) of the miserable ends of such as have impugned the Catholike Church. To which Also is annexed a briefe exhortation to persevere constantly in the said Catholike Church,*

what opposition soever may occurre, and the danger of living out of the
same; And lastly, a few examples of the admirable prosperity, of such
as have defended the Catholike Church. 1615   (STC 4621, AR 206,
ERL 91)

568. *An Answere to a Treatise Written by Dr. Carier, By way of Letter to his
Maiestie: Wherein he layeth downe sundry politike considerations; By
which hee pretendeth himself was moved. And endevoureth to move
others to be reconciled to the Church of Rome, and imbrace that
Religion, which he calleth Catholike. By George Hakewill, Doctour of
Divinity, And Chapleine to the Prince his Highnesse.* 1616   (STC 12610)

(The Appendix contains the following items:

*An Answere to the Materiall Points of a second Letter of Dr. Cariers
written also from Leige, to his friends heere in England.
A brief Answere to the other collections annexed to the Doctors last
Letter.)*

Another convert to Rome, James Wadsworth, published his *Contrition of
a Protestant Preacher* in 1615 in the form, not of an apology for his
conversion to Rome or a criticism of the Anglican position, but of a personal
meditation on the psalm *Miserere*. So it provoked no Protestant answer.

569. *The Contrition of a Protestant Preacher, converted to be a Catholique
Scholler. Conteyning Certayne Meditations upon the Fourth
Penitentiall Psalme, Miserere. Composed by Iames Waddesworth,
Bachlour of Divinity in the University of Cambridge, & late Parson of
Cotton, and of Great-Thorneham in the County of Suffolke. Who went
into Spaine with the Kinges Maiesties first Embassadour-Legier, as his
Chaplayne: Where by the great Goodnes of Almighty God, he was fully
converted to the Catholique Faith.* 1615   (Not in STC, AR 870,
ERL 150)

On the other hand, there were several defections from the Church of
Rome besides that of Theophilus Higgons, some of them in connection with
the controversy over the Oath of Allegiance. The most notable of the latter
was that of Richard Sheldon who, after publishing his *Certain General
Reasons* in support of the Oath in 1611 (380), renounced the Roman
Church in the following year. Like Theophilus Higgons, he had to preach a
Sermon of recantation, which was soon published in 1612, together with a
further book of *Motives* – in which he admitted that 'all English Ignatians,
and most English priests at this present in England, and elsewhere, are such
violent enemies against the Oath of allegeance'.

570. *The First Sermon of R. Sheldon Priest, after his Conversion from the*

Romish Church: Preached before an honourable Assembly at S. Martins in the Field, upon Passion Sunday, &c. Published by Authoritie. 1612 (STC 22395)

571. *The Motives of Richard Sheldon Pr. for his iust, voluntary, and free renouncing of Communion with the Bishop of Rome, Paul the 5. and his Church. Published by Authority.* 1612 (STC 22397)

Even more notable was the defection of the Archbishop of Spalato in Dalmatia, Marc'Antonio de Dominis, on his arrival in London in 1616 — after having quarrelled with the Pope, Paul V. But he occasioned a whole controversy of his own, which will be dealt with later.

h) *The Mass and the Ministry*

Another controversy about this time, over the Catholic Mass and the Anglican ministry, involved another Jesuit convert from Protestantism, Henry FitzSimon. It all began in 1600 with a dispute he held, while a prisoner in Dublin Castle, with the Dean of St. Patrick's Cathedral, John Rider. The latter was the first to publish his side of the argument in 1602, under the title of *A Friendly Caveat to Irelands Catholickes*. This he apparently followed up with another book, no longer extant, entitled *Tarte tearmes*. It was not till 1608 that FitzSimon was free to present his position, in the form of *A Catholike Confutation of M. Iohn Riders Clayme of Antiquitie*. To this he added *A Replie to M. Riders Rescript*, giving his personal reasons for renouncing the Protestant religion. He went on to publish in 1611 a *Iustification and Exposition of the Divine Sacrifice of the Masse*, with further arguments against Rider's position — as well as particular commendations of 'the booke of M. Walsingham' and 'the late booke of M. Leach'.

572. *A Friendly Caveat to Irelands Catholickes, concerning the daungerous Dreame of Christs corporall (yet invisible) presence in the Sacrament of the Lords Supper. Grounded upon a Letter pretended to be sent by some well-minded Catholickes: who doubted, and therefore desired satisfaction in certaine points of religion. With the aunswere and prooffes of the Romane Catholicke Priests, to satisfie and confirme them in the same. Perused and allowed for Apostolicall and Catholicke, by the subscription of maister Henry Fitzsimon Iesuit, now prisoner in the Castle of Dublin. With a true, diligent, and charitable examination of the same prooffes: wherein the Catholickes may see this new Romane doctrine to bee neither Apostolicall nor Catholicke, but cleane contrarie to the old Romane religion, and therefore to bee shunned of all true auncient Romane Catholickes, unlesse they will be new Romish heretikes. By Iohn Rider Deane of Saint Patrickes Dublin.* 1602 (STC 21031)

573. *A Catholike Confutation of M. Iohn Riders Clayme of Antiquitie; and a Caulming Comfort against his Caveat. In which is demonstrated, by assurances, even of Protestants, that al Antiquitie, for al pointes of Religion in controversie, is repugnant to Protestancie. Secondly, that Protestancie is repugnant particularlie to al articles of Beleefe. Thirdly, that Puritan plots are pernitious to Religion, and State. And lastly, a replye to M. Riders Rescript; with a Discoverie of Puritan partialitie in his behalfe. By Henry Fitzimon Of Dublin in Irland, of the Societie of Iesus, Priest.* 1608   (STC 11025, AR 319, ERL 182)

(It is only here that we learn of 'a second booke against me, full of venimous rayling, which he calleth Tarte tearmes'. Similarly, 'M. Riders Rescript' is only known from the Appendix to this book, which may be treated as a separate item, as it has a new title-page with separate pagination.)

574. *A Replie to M. Riders Rescript. And a Discoverie of Puritan Partialitie in his behalfe. Together with. A briefe narration why this Author himselfe, renounced Protestancie. With sundrie important reasons, tendered by him to the temperate Reader. Also. An Answere to sundrie Complaintive letters of afflicted Catholicques. Declaring the severitie, of divers late Proclamations; As, of the speedie banishment of al Priestes; Of death to them and their receivers, if any remayned; Of the oathe of Alleigance; Ransacking of Purseuvants; And of utter ruine, to any professing Catholique Religion. And Finallie; A friendlie Advertisement to M. Iohn Rider himselfe.* 1608   (STC 11025, AR 319, ERL 182)

575. *The Iustification and Exposition of the Divine Sacrifice of the Masse, and of al Rites and Ceremonies therto belonging devided into two bookes. In the first booke Controversies and Difficulties, and Devotion belonging to the Masse, are discussed in general. In the second the first Masse in the Missal is iustified, and expounded, for al and everie parcel therof.* 1611   (STC 11026, AR 320, ERL 108)

(The second book is given a new title-page, but with continuing pagination. There is no difference in the wording of the title from that given above.)

A final work from the pen of Henry FitzSimon appeared in 1614, in the form of a Latin treatise of the divisions among the Anglican clergy on the subject of their own ministry (akin to Becanus' recent *Dissidium Anglicanum* of 1612), with the title *Britannomachia Ministrorum*. In a Dedication to the Jesuit General, Father Claude Aquaviva, the author traced the origins and development of his controversy with Rider and others on the real presence. The book elicited a response from Hoby's secretary, Anthony Tunstall, in his

'Appendix de Iesuitica Batrachologia' to Hoby's *Curry-combe* (550), and from Francis Mason, in his *Vindiciae Ecclesiae Anglicanae* (588).

576. *Brittannomachia Ministrorum, in plerisque et fidei fundamentis, et fidei articulis dissidentium. Authore P. Henrico FitzSimon, Dublinensi Iberno, Soc. Iesu, in Provincia Belgica.* 1614

The last-mentioned work was further drawn into another controversy, which now arose out of Francis Mason's important treatise *Of the Consecration of the Bishops in the Church of England* in 1613. This treatise was written at the request of the Archbishop of Canterbury, George Abbot, both against Catholic accusations of invalidity and to defend the divine right of bishops against the Puritans. For his thesis Mason drew largely on material provided by Francis Godwin in his earlier *Catalogue of the Bishops of England*, which had first been published in 1601 and was now republished in 1615 in a second edition. The same thesis, claiming apostolic succession for the Anglican bishops, was again put forward in Latin that year (1613) by the learned James Ussher, in his treatise *De Christianarum Ecclesiarum . . . continua successione.*

577. *Of the Consecration of the Bishops in the Church of England: With their Succession, Jurisdiction, and other things incident to their calling: as also Of the Ordination of Priests and Deacons. Five Bookes: Wherein they are cleared from the slanders and odious imputations of Bellarmine, Sanders, Bristow, Harding, Allen, Stapleton, Parsons, Kellison, Eudemon, Becanus, And other Romanists: And iustified to containe nothing contrary to the Scriptures, Councels, Fathers, or approved examples of Primitive Antiquitie. By Francis Mason, Batchelour of Divinitie, and sometimes Fellow of Merton Colledge in Oxeford.* 1613   (STC 17597)

(The important Book III is entitled:

Of the Bishops consecrated in the Raigne of Q. Elizabeth, and of our gracious Soveraigne King Iames.

The crucial chapter of this book was Chapter 4: 'Of the Consecration of the most reverend father, Archbishop Parker', with excerpts from the 'Authenticall records' (*Ex Registro Matth. Park.* tom. i).)

578. *A Catalogue of the Bishops of England, since the first planting of Christian religion in this Island, together with a briefe History of their lives and memorable actions, so neere as can be gathered out of antiquitie. By F. G. Subdeane of Exceter.* 1601   (STC 11937)

The second edition of 1615 (STC 11938) was brought out to support Mason's thesis, which was further emphasized in the altered title of the third edition in 1625: *The succession of the bishops of England* (STC 11939).)

579. *Gravissimae Quaestionis, De Christianarum Ecclesiarum, in Occidentis praesertim partibus, Ab Apostolicis Temporibus ad nostram usque aetatem, continua successione & statu, Historica Explicatio. Authore Jacobo Usserio, Sae Theologiae in Dublinensi Academia, apud Hibernos, Professore.* 1613   (STC 24551)

Mason's thesis naturally provoked considerable opposition from the Catholic side, though no book was devoted entirely to its refutation. Within a year of its appearance no fewer than two Catholic authors had dealt with its claim. In his *Adioynder to the Supplement* (370) Thomas Fitzherbert devoted an Appendix to the 'Register alleaged by M. Franc. Mason', and challenged the Archbishop to produce this Register for inspection by a number of Catholic divines. Accordingly, Abbot invited four Catholic priests, then in prison in London, to his palace at Lambeth for the inspection; but he failed to meet their conditions (cf. Foley VII 1048). In his *Purgatories Triumph* (549) Floyd also criticized Mason, whom he accused of having hatched a cockatrice 'in his Consecration of your Bishops' with his 'secret, concealed, and questionable Registers'. The President of Douai, Matthew Kellison, had apparently been the first, in his *Reply to Sotcliffes Answer* in 1608, to bring up the story of Parker's consecration as bishop at the Nag's Head in Cheapside; and it was to some extent against this that Mason had reacted in his book. So it was natural for Kellison to return to the charge in his Latin work, *Examen Reformationis Novae*, of 1616.

580. *An Appendix touching a Register alleaged by M. Franc. Mason for the lawfull Ordayning of Protestant Bishops in Q. Elizabeths Raigne.*

(From Thomas Fitzherbert's *Adioynder*, 1613 (370).)

581. *That S. Gregory the Pretended greatest Patron of Purgatory, by the Monkes he sent, first Converted the English Nation unto Christianity, the now Catholike Romane Faith. Where also the Falshood of other Ministers, namly of M. White, and M. Mason about this poynt are refuted.*

(Chapter 6 of John Floyd's *Purgatories Triumph over Hell*, 1613 (549). M. White is John White, author of *The Way to the True Church*, 1608, with a second edition in 1612 (487).)

582. [= 467] *Examen Reformationis Novae Praesertim Calvinianae in quo synagoga et doctrina Calvini, sicut et reliquorum huius temporis novatorum, tota fere ex suis principiis refutatur. Authore Matthaeo Kellisono Sacrae Theol. Doctore Ac Collegii Anglorum Duaceni Praeside.* 1616

Also in 1616 there appeared two more substantial criticisms of Mason, though neither of them were devoted to him alone. In his anonymous *Demonstration* Richard Broughton attacked 'the late book, intituled, of the consecration of the Bishops, of the churche of England', and indicated that the way to Mason's thesis had been prepared by the sermons of Bancroft and Barlow, and the treatises of Field and Sutcliffe (against Kellison). Another secular priest, Anthony Champney, added his criticism of Mason, along with Field and the French du Plessis Mornay, in his *Treatise of the Vocation of Bishops*. This appeared two years later in his own Latin translation, as *De Vocatione Ministrorum Tractatus*. Subsequently in 1621 the Jesuit Silvester Norris devoted a chapter to Mason in his *Guide of Faith*, being the Third Part of his voluminous *Antidote*. He spoke slightingly of the 'new Attorneyes' of the Anglican Church, who now 'lay clayme to the pedegree of our Bishops' in order to justify their ministry. As for Ussher, a challenge came in 1615 from the pen of his aged uncle, Richard Stanihurst, in what George Hakewill (writing against Benjamin Carier) called 'his flourish to a future combate with his Nephew'. This was also in Latin, in the form of a *Brevis Praemunitio Pro futura concertatione*; but it went no further, as Stanihurst died in 1618.

583. *A Demonstration: by English Protestant pretended Bishops, and Ministers, and by the cheife growndes of their Religion, against these their owne pretended Bishops, and Mynistery: demonstratively proveinge, by their owne Religion, pillers and principles thereof, published, received, or allowed in their Congregation, since the comeing of our kinge Iames, into England. That they have neither true and lawfull Bishop, Preist, Minister, or any of Cleargie function, nor none but laymen, amongst them. Written by a Catholicke Preist.* 1616 (STC 10403, AR 155, ERL 94)

(The author enumerates Bancroft, Barlow, Field and Sutcliffe among those who 'have claimed their calling to bee, de iure divino, by the law of God', and thus laid the foundations for Mason's thesis.)

584. *A Treatise of the Vocation of Bishops, and other Ecclesiasticall Ministers. Proving the Ministers of the Pretended Reformed Churches in generall, to have no calling: against Monsieur du Plessis, and Mr. Doctour Field: And in particuler the pretended Bishops in England, to be no true Bishops. Against Mr. Mason. By Anth. Champ. P. and D. of Sorbonne.* 1616   (STC 4960, AR 233, ERL 219)

(The first two books mentioned here are: *Traicte de l'Eglise* by Philippe du Plessis-Mornay (1578), translated into English by John Field in 1579 as *A Treatise of the Church*; and Richard Field's *Of the Church* (1606–10) (520, 523).)

585. *Anthonii Champnaei Angli, Sacrae Facultatis Parisiensis Doctoris
Sorbonici, De Vocatione Ministrorum Tractatus. Quo universos cuiusvis
praetensae reformationis Ministros omni penitus legitima vocatione
destitui contra Plessaeum & Fieldeum. Quo etiam praesentes Angliae
Superintendentes, qui sedes Episcopales invaserunt, non esse veros
Episcopos, contra Masonem & Godwinum clare ostenditur. Unde
tandem apud Reformistas nullam esse Ecclesiam, nullam fidem, nullum
denique salutis medium manifeste deducitur.* 1618

586. [= 609] *The Guide of Faith. Or, A Third Part of the Antidote against
the Pestiferous Writings of all English Sectaries. And in particuler,
agaynst D. Bilson, D. Fulke, D. Reynoldes, D. Whitaker, D. Field,
D. Sparkes, D. White and M. Mason, the chiefe upholders, some of Protestancy, and some of Puritanisme. Wherein the Truth, and perpetuall
Visible Succession of the Catholique Roman Church, is cleerly demonstrated. By S. N. Doctour of Divinity.* 1621   (STC 18659, AR 574,
ERL 210)

(Chapter XX is particularly directed against Mason:

'In which Apostolicall succession is declared to be an apparent note of the
true Church: Agaynst Mayster Francis Mason.')

587. *Richardi Stanihursti Hiberni Dublinensis Brevis Praemunitio Pro
futura concertatione cum Iacobo Usserio Hiberno Dublinensi. Qui in
sua historica explicatione conatur probare, Pontificem Romanum
(legitimum Christi, in terris, Vicarium) verum & germanum esse
Antichristum.* 1615

Against these and other Catholic critics Mason brought out an enlarged
second edition of his work in Latin translation, in 1625, under the title,
Vindiciae Ecclesiae Anglicanae. By that time this controversy had expanded
into a considerably larger one, with the King himself as an interested
onlooker and participator.

588. *Vindiciae Ecclesiae Anglicanae; sive De Legitimo Eiusdem Ministerio, id
est, De Episcoporum Successione, Consecratione, Electione, &
Confirmatione: item, De Presbyterorum, & Diaconorum Ordinatione,
Libri V. In quibus Ecclesia Anglicana a Bellarmini, Sanderi, Bristoi,
Hardingi, Alani, Stapletoni, Parsonii, Kellisoni, Eudaemonis, Becani,
aliorumque Romanistarum calumniis, & contumeliis vindicatur. Editio
secunda, priori Anglicana longe auctior, & emendatior. Cui inter alia
accesserunt ad Fitzherberti Presbyteri, Fitz-Simonis Iesuitae, D.
Kellisoni, Champnaei Sorbonistae, Fluddi, & nescio cuius Anonymi
Exceptiones suis quaeque locis intertextae Responsiones. Opus ex
Idiomate Anglicano traductum, & locupletatum ab ipso Authore Franc.
Masono, in S. Theologia Bacchal. Archidiacono Norfolc. Et Socio
Colleg. Mertonensis apud Oxonienses.* 1625   (STC 17598)

i) *Manuals of Controversies*

During the middle years of the reign the Catholics were particularly prolific in bringing out manuals of controversy, which dealt rather with the main theological issues than with any specific Protestant authors. So for the most part they remained unnoticed and unrefuted by the Protestants. The first of such English manuals was Richard Smith's *Prudentiall Ballance of Religion*, whose first part came out in 1609 together with 'A Cathalogue of the cheefe Protestant writers'. The second part, however, did not come out in English till 1631, under the altered title of *A Conference of the Catholike and Protestante Doctrine*. In its Preface the author recalls how many years have passed 'since I published the first parte of the Prudential Balance of Religion', and yet it 'hath never since bene answered by anie Protestant albeit divers ministers, and superintendents have carped at it both in Pulpits and printed books'. Meanwhile, a Latin version of both parts together – the translation of the first part and the original language of the second – came out in 1621 under the title, *Collatio Doctrinae Catholicorum ac Protestantium*.

589. *The Prudentiall Ballance of Religion, Wherin the Catholike and Protestant religion are weighed together with the weights of Prudence, and right Reason. The First Part, In which the foresaide Religions are weighed together with the weights of Prudence and Right Reason accordinge to their first founders in our Englishe Nation, S. Austin and Mar. Luther. And the Catholike Religion evidently deduced through all our Kings and Archbishops of Canterburie from S. Austin to our time, and the valour and vertue of our Kings, and the great learninge and Sanctitie of our Archbishopps, together with divers Saints and miracles which in their times proved the Catholike faith; so sett downe as it may seeme also an abridgment of our Ecclesiasticall Histories. With a Table of the Bookes and Chapters conteyned in this Volume.* 1609
(STC 22813, AR 777, ERL 269)

590. *A Conference of the Catholike and Protestante Doctrine with the expresse words of Holie Scripture. Which is the second parte of the Prudentiall Balance of Religion. Wherein is clearely shewed, that in more then 260. points of controversie, Catholiks agree with the holie scripture, both in words and in sense: and Protestants disagree in both, and deprave both the sayings, words, and sense of Scripture. Written first in Latin, but now augmented and translated into English.* 1631
(STC 22810, AR 774, ERL 334)

591. *Collatio Doctrinae Catholicorum ac Protestantium cum expressis S. Scripturae verbis, duobus libris comprehensa. In qua ad oculum ostenditur, in plusquam ducentis quinquaginta dogmatibus controversis,*

> *Catholicos cum expresso Verbo Dei & sensu & verbis etiam convenire,*
> *Protestantes autem & sensu & verbis ipsis eidem directe contradicere, &*
> *modi quibus Scripturae verba ac sensum sibi adversantia depravant,*
> *deteguntur. Quae summa controversiarum merito censeatur, ac*
> *Concionatoribus, & Controversiarum seu conversionis Haereticorum*
> *studiosis perutilis. Per Richardum Smitheum Lincolniensem, S.*
> *Theologiae Doctorem.* 1621

The year 1614 was particularly fruitful in such manuals of controversies. It was in this year that Edward Weston, one of the professors at Douai, brought out the first part of his *Triall of Christian Truth*, dealing with the virtue of faith. He went on to deal with the virtue of hope in the second part, which appeared in the following year. But there he ended, without going on to complete his plan for the virtues of charity and religion. Neither part, however, elicited any refutation from the Protestants.

592. *The Triall of Christian Truth by the Rules of the Vertues, namely these*
principall Faith, Hope, Charitie, and Religion: serving for the discoverie
of heresie, and Antichrist in his forerunners and misteries of iniquitie.
The first parte, Entreating of Faith. Wherin is evidentlie proved, that
the pretended Faith of the Protestant overthroueth all groundes, all
necessarie and essentiall partes of our Christian and Devine Beleefe. By
Edward Weston Doctor and Professor of Divinitie. 1614   (STC 25290,
AR 885, ERL 62)

593. *The Triall of Christian Truht, by the rules of the vertues, namelie these*
principall, Faith, Hope, Charitie, and Religion: serving for the
discoverie of heresie, and Antichrist, in his forerunners and misteries of
iniquitie. The Second Parte, Entreating of Hope. Wherein is made
manifest, that the pretended Hope of the Protestant, empeaching the
merits of Christ, his holy grace, and man his vertuouse life, destroyeth
all true confidence in Allmightie God, either exceding in presumption,
or wanting in Desperation. By Edward Weston Doctor and Professor of
Divinitie. 1615   (STC 25290, AR 886, ERL 366)

Also in that year a series of controversial treatises was published in pamphlet form by the Scottish Jesuit theologian, James Gordon Huntley, and translated from Latin into English by his fellow Jesuit, William Wright. They were variously entitled: *of the Written Word of God, of the Unwritten Word of God, concerning the Properties and Offices of the true Church, concerning The Ground of Faith*, and *concerning the Church* – and distributed into two 'controversies', with two parts in the first and three in the second. These five pamphlets were subsequently gathered together in 1618, and published as *A Summary of Controversies*. At the same time, the Latin original was coming out successively in three volumes, under the title of *Controversiarum Epitomes:* the first volume in 1612, the second in 1618, and all three together in 1620.

594. *A Treatise of the Written Word of God. Composed In Latin, by the Reverend Father Iames Gordon Huntley of Scotland, Doctour of Divinity, of the Society of Iesus. And translated into English, by I. L. of the same Society. The first Part of the first Controversy.* 1614 (STC 13996, AR 360)

595. *A Treatise of the Unwritten Word of God, commonly called Traditions. Written in Latin by the R. Father Iames Gordon Huntley of Scotland, Doctour of Divinity, of the Society of Iesus. And translated into English by I. L. of the same Society. The second Part of the first Controversy.* 1614 (STC 13996a, AR 361)

596. *A Treatise concerning the Properties and Offices of the true Church of Christ. Written In Latin, by the Reverend Father Iames Gordon Huntley of Scotland, Doctour of Divinity, of the Society of Iesus. And translated into English, by I. L. of the same Society. The first Part of the second Controversy.* 1614 (STC 13997, AR 362)

597. *A Treatise concerning The Ground of Faith. Written In Latin, by the Reverend Father Iames Gordon Huntley of Scotland, Doctour of Divinity, of the Society of Iesus. And translated into English, by I. L. of the same Society. The second Part of the second Controversy.* 1614 (STC 13997a, AR 363)

598. *A Treatise concerning the Church. Wherin It is shewed, by the Signes, Offices, and Properties therof, that the Church of Rome (and consequently such particuler Churches as live in her Communion) is the only true Church of Christ. Written In Latin, by the Reverend Father Iames Gordon Huntley, Doctour of Divinity, of the Society of Iesus. And translated into English, by I. L. of the same Society. The third Part of the second Controversy.* 1614 (STC 13997b, AR 364)

599. *A Summary of Controversies. Wherein Are briefly treated the cheefe Questions of Divinity, now a dayes in dispute betweene the Catholikes & Protestants: especially out of the holy Scripture. Written in Latin By the R. Father, Iames Gordon Huntley of Scotland, Doctour of Divinity, of the Society of Iesus. And translated into English by I. L. of the same Society. The I. Tome, devided into two Controversies. The Second Edition. 1618* (STC 13998, AR 365, ERL 195)

(The first edition comprises all the pamphlets which had been published separately under different titles. No other tomes were published in English after this first tome.)

600. *Iacobi Gordoni Huntlaei Scoti, e Societate Iesu doctoris Theologi Controversiarum Epitomes, in qua de quaestionibus theologicis hac nostra aetate controversis, breviter disputatur; idque ex sacris praesertim literis. Tomus primus.* 1612

601. *Epitomes Tomus Secundus. In quo de Augustissimo Eucharistiae Sacramento contra Calvinianos breviter disputatur: idque ex ipsis sacris literis praesertim.* 1618

602. *R. P. Iacobi Gordoni Huntlaei Scoti, e Societate Iesu Doctoris Theologi, Controversiarum Epitomes.*
Tomus Primus: In quo de Quaestionibus Theologicis hac nostra aetate controversis breviter disputatur: idque ex sacris praesertim literis.
Tomus secundus: In quo de Augustissimo Sacramento contra Calvinianos breviter disputatur: idque ex ipsis sacris literis praesertim. Disputationum De Controversiis Christianae Fidei adversus huius temporis haereticos, ex sacris praesertim literis, Epitomes Tomus III . . . Ad S. D. N. Paulum V. Pont. Max. 1620

(Each tome has a separate title-page, but the first two tomes have continuous pagination over 455 pages — the second beginning at page 367. The third tome is distinct from the other two, and has 352 pages. But all tomes are bound together in one volume.)

Yet another *Manual of Controversies* was published in 1614 by the seminary priest, Anthony Champney, who was then lecturing at the Sorbonne in Paris. Though it was no less general than the preceding manuals, the author expressed his expectation of a Protestant answer. This actually appeared in 1618, when Richard Pilkington published his *Parallela*, in which (as he explained) 'the grounds of the Romane and Reformed Religion are compard together'. In 1620 Champney responded with a book entitled, *Mr. Pilkinton his Parallela Disparalled.* Another possible answer to Champney's *Manual* may be seen in Francis Dillingham's earlier book, *A Probleme, Propounded*, published in 1616. While not mentioning Champney by name, he seems to be challenging the priest's claim to have proved the Catholic position from holy Scripture; and in fact he deals with most of the controversies covered by Champney.

603. *A Manual of Controversies wherin the Catholique Romane faith in all the cheefe pointes of controversies of these daies is proved by holy Scripture. By A. C. S.* 1614   (STC 4958, AR 231, ERL 80)

(In his 'Preface to the Reader' Champney requests: 'I expect and exact of him, or them that shal goe about to answer this treatise, the same rounde sincere, and direct dealinge, which I have here used.')

604. *Parallela: or The Grounds of the New Romane Catholike, and of the ancient Christian Religion compared together, By Rich. Pilkington Doctor of Divinitie, In answere to a late Popish Pamphlet, entituled A manuel of Controversies, wherein the Catholike Roman Faith in all the chiefe points of Controversies of these dayes is proved by holy Scriptures. By A. C. S.* 1618   (STC 19933)

605. *Mr. Pilkinton his Parallela Disparalled and The Catholike Roman faith maintained against Protestantisme. By Ant. Champney Sorbonist, and author of the Manuall of Controversies, impugned by the said Mr. Pilkinton.* 1620   (STC 4959, AR 232, ERL 50)

606. *A Probleme, Propounded by Francis Dillingham, in which is plainely shewed, that the holy scriptures have met with Popish Arguments and opinions.* 1616   (STC 6887)

(The subjects dealt with in this work are: reading of holy Scripture; prayer in an unknown tongue; works of congruity and merit; fulfilling of God's commandments; images; purgatory; satisfaction for sin; transubstantiation; the sacraments; prayer to the saints; the Pope's temporal power; sins of necessity; and justification.)

In 1615 the Jesuit Silvester Norris began his long series of controversies entitled *An Antidote*. In an Epistle to the Reader he indicated his purpose, 'not severally to encounter any one particuler adversary, but to trace the steppes, and ioyntly to descry the errours of many' — with special reference to William Whitaker, William Fulke, Thomas Bilson, John Reynolds, Thomas Sparkes, and Richard Field. After publishing the First Part in 1615, he went on to the Second Part in 1619. Then in 1622 he brought out a second edition of both parts together, while altering the sub-title from 'Soveraigne Remedie' to 'Treatise of Thirty Controversies'. In 1621 he came out with the Third Part, entitled *The Guide of Faith*, including the above-mentioned criticism of Francis Mason. In the same year he added *An Appendix to the Antidote*, giving a 'catalogue' similar to that already compiled by his fellow Jesuit John Percy (490). This soon entered into the important controversy of the closing years of the reign, and called for a *Defence* by another Jesuit, John Sweet, in 1624 (743). Then in 1623 Norris followed the example of Martin Becanus (626–7) and published an additional treatise on the judge of controversies, entitled *The Pseudo-Scripturist*.

607. *An Antidote or Soveraigne Remedie against the pestiferous writings of all English sectaries. and In Particular against D. Whitaker, D. Fulke, D. Bilson, D. Reynolds, D. Sparkes, and D. Field, the chiefe upholders, some of Protestancy, some of Puritanisme. Devided into three Partes. In which the true Catholike Doctrine, in the chiefest points of Faith,*

called in Question by the Protestants of our time, is explained,
defended, and their principall Obiections answered. By S. N. Doctour
of Divinity. The First Part. 1615   (STC 18657, AR 572a)

608. *An Antidote . . . The Second Part.* 1619   (STC 18658, AR 572b)

609. [= 586] *The Guide of Faith. Or, A Third Part of the Antidote against
the Pestiferous Writings of all English Sectaries. And in particuler,
agaynst D. Bilson, D. Fulke, D. Reynoldes, D. Whitaker, D. Field, D.
Sparkes, D. White, and M. Mason, the chiefe upholders, some of
Protestancy, and some of Puritanisme, Wherein the Truth, and
perpetuall Visible Succession of the Catholique Roman Church, is
cleerly demonstrated. By S. N. Doctour of Divinity.* 1621
(STC 18659, AR 574, ERL 210)

(Two Anglican divines have their names added to the title of the Third
Part: John White, for his *Way to the True Church* (1608), and Francis
Mason, for his *Of the Consecration of the Bishops* (1613); cf. 487, 577)

610. *An Appendix to the Antidote. Conteyning A Catalogue of the visible
and perpetuall Succession of the Catholique Professours of the Roman
Church, by whom the doctrine now taught under Pope Gregory the
XV. hath beene in all Ages, and Countreyes, since Christ, constantly &
uniformely maintayned. Togeather with A Counter-Catalogue
discovering the interruption of Hereticall Sectes, amongst whome the
chiefe Protestant Articles, and their Authours, have beene in divers
Ages, upon sundry occasions, contradicted, and condemned, by the
Watchmen of the true Church. By S. N. Doctour of Divinity.* 1621
(STC 18659, AR 575, ERL 172)

611. *An Antidote or Treatise of Thirty Controversies: With a large Discourse
of the Church. In which The soveraigne truth of Catholike doctrine, is
faythfully delivered: against the pestiferous writinges of all English
Sectaryes. AND In particuler, against D. Whitaker, D. Fulke, D.
Reynolds, D. Bilson, D. Robert Abbot, D. Sparkes, and D. Field, the
chiefe upholders, some of Protestancy, some of Puritanisme, some of
both. Devided into three Partes. By S. N. Doctour of Divinity.* 1622
(STC 18658, AR 573, ERL 185)

(The First Part is bound with The Second Part, with distinct title-pages
and pagination, and the date of 1622. The First Part covers Controversies 1–15 in 333 pages; and the Second Part covers Controversies
16–30 in 307 pages. The two together are sometimes bound with The
Third Part of 1621, with 229 pages, and the Appendix of 107 pages.)

612. *The Pseudo-Scripturist. or A Treatise wherein is proved, That the*

Wrytten Word of God (though most Sacred, Reverend, and Divine) is not the sole Iudge of Controversies, in Fayth and Religion. Agaynst the prime Sectaries of these Tymes, who contend to maintayne the Contrary. Written by N. S. Priest, and Doctour of Divinity. Devided into two parts. And dedicated to the Right Honorable, and Reverend Iudges of England, and other grave Sages of the Law. 1623
(STC 18660, AR 576, ERL 93)

Another volume of the same kind, entitled *A Summarie of Controversies*, appeared in 1616 under the initials C. W. — which is attributed by John Gee, in his *Foot out of the Snare* (689), to Richard Smith. Like *The Pseudo-Scripturist*, it was directed generally against 'the Sectaries of this Age'. The author professed to follow the great Catholic controversialists of the preceding age: Sanders, Allen, Heskins, Stapleton, Martin, Bristow, Harding and William Reynolds. Among contemporary Catholic writers he singled out 'the Author of that most worthy and laborious Treatise, intituled, The Protestants Apologie for the Roman Church'. Their arguments he aimed at reducing to a more compendious form.

613. *A Summarie of Controversies: Wherein the chiefest points of the holy Catholike Romane Faith, are compendiously and methodically proved, against the Sectaries of this Age. By C. W. /B.* 1616   (STC 26047, AR 866, ERL 190)

(A second edition was published in 1623, with a somewhat different spelling of the title, and the omission of B. after the author's name. (STC 26048, AR 867))

Two years later yet another manual was published under the title of *An Anker of Christian Doctrine* and the initials T. W. S. T. D. P. A. — standing for Dr. Thomas Worthington, the former President of Douai. It came out in four successive parts: the first, on the Articles of Faith, in 1618; the second, on the Sacraments, in 1620; and the third and fourth together, on the Ten Commandments and Prayer, in 1622. All four parts were finally published in two volumes in 1622, with the first part occupying the first volume and the other three parts together the second volume, making a total of more than fifteen hundred pages.

614. *An Anker of Christian Doctrine. Whearein the most principal pointes of Catholique Religion are proved by the only written word of God. Not abandoning Divine, nor Apostolical Traditions, Authentical Councels, Popes Decrees, Auncient Fathers, nor other ordinary proofes; but abstracting from them in this Encounter: For better satisfaction of those, who will admitte none other tryal of true Religion, but Scriptures only.* 1618   (STC 26000, AR 910)

(The Preface 'To the right welbeloved Christian Reader' is dated 1616, and signed 'Th. W.'
Only in the inner title is the book said to be 'Divided into foure partes', and that this is 'The First Part concerning Faith'.)

615. *The Second Part of an Anker of Christian Doctrine. Wherein, the most principal pointes of Catholique Religion, are proved: By the onlie written word of God. Not abandoning . . . Auctore T. W. S. T. D. P. A.* 1620   (STC 26000, AR 912)

616. *An Anker of Christian Doctrine. Wherein the most principal Points of Catholike Religion, are proved: by the only written Word of God. Not reiecting Divine, nor Apostolical Traditions; authentical Councels; Popes Decrees; ancient Fathers; nor other ordinarie Proofes; but abstracting from them in this Encounter. For better satisfaction of those, who wil admit no other trial of true Religion, but Scriptures onely. Auctore T. W. S. T. D. P. A.* 1622   (STC 26000, AR 915, ERL 376)

A possible reply to these manuals of controversy, whether of C. W. or of Worthington, may be seen in Thomas Clarke's *The Popes Deadly Wound*, which appeared in 1621 and professed to deal (like them, but from the opposite side) with 'the Chiefe and principall Points now in controversie betweene the Papists and Us'. Like them also, the author refrained from explicit mention of opposing books and authors (cf. also 705).

617. *The Popes Deadly Wound: Tending to resolve all men, in the Chiefe and principall Points now in controversie betweene the Papists and Us. Written by T. C. and now published by Master Doctor Burges, now Preacher to the English troopes in the Pallatinate.* 1621   (STC 5364)

(In his Preface, John Burges informs the Reader that 'The Author thereof, Master Thomas Clarke' is 'one of my parishioners in Sutton-Coldfield'.)

Finally, supplementing these Catholic manuals of controversy were a number of theological treatises by continental Jesuit writers, such as Leonard Lessius and Martin Becanus. Originally in Latin, they were soon translated into English — many of them by the Jesuit William Wright — for the benefit of English Catholics. A crucial topic of controversy dealt with by Lessius was the question, 'Whether every man may be saved in his own faith and religion?' This he discussed at length in his treatise, *Quae fides et religio sit capessenda, Consultatio*, which first appeared in 1609. At first, only the Appendix was translated into English by William Wright, under the title of *A Controversy . . . Whether Every Man may be saved in his owne Faith and*

Religion? Significantly, it was published in 1614, in the same year as William Bishop's *Disproofe* against Robert Abbot (482), which also deals with the question, 'whether every Christian can be saved in his owne religion'. The whole work was subsequently published in Wright's English translation in 1618, under the the title of *A Consultation*, and a second edition followed in 1621. About the same time, another translation by the Scottish Jesuit, Patrick Anderson, appeared in 1619.

618. *Quae fides et religio sit capessenda, Consultatio: Auctore Leonardo Lessio Soc. Iesu, S. Theologiae Professore.* 1609

(This consists of 'Decem considerationes' and (as part of the 'Nona consideratio, ex variis causis ob quas novae sint suspectae, & declinandae') 'Duodecim rationes'.)

619. *A Controversy, in which is examined, Whether Every Man may be saved in his owne Faith and Religion? Written by Leonard Lessius of the Society of Iesus.* 1614   (STC 15519, AR 459, ERL 106)

(The Printer introduces this work as 'This Appendix of F. Lessius to his Treatise intituled, of Consultation &c.')

620. *A Consultation what Faith and Religion is best to be imbraced. Written in Latin By the R. Father Leonard Lessius, Professour in Divinity, of the Society of Iesus. And Translated into English by W. I.* 1618 (STC 15517, AR 456)

(The second edition of 1621 also includes the second edition of Becanus' *Defence of the Roman Church* as an Appendix. (STC 15518, AR 457, ERL 236)

621. *A Consultatione which Faith is to be beleved which Religione is to be imbraced. Wryttin be M. Patrike Andersone I. 1618. With certane prayeris, to be said ewerie ewening, and Morning.* 1619   (Not in STC, AR 458, ERL 251)

(In the Preface the translator says he is following the book of the 'learned father Lessius'.)

A work of a somewhat similar nature, on the question 'An Romana Ecclesia defecerit a fide?', was by Martin Becanus. This had first appeared as an Appendix to his above-mentioned *Disputatio Theologica de Antichristo* in 1608. It was published in English translation in 1612, under the general title of *A Defence of the Roman Church;* and a second edition came out as an Appendix to the 1621 edition of Lessius' *Consultation.*

622. [= 447] *Disputatio Theologica De Antichristo Reformato. In qua tum*

*alii, tum Marpurgensis quidam Calvinista refutatur, qui nuper duplici
Elencho conatus est probare, Papam esse Antichristum. Cum
Appendice, An Romana Ecclesia defecerit a fide? Authore Martino
Becano Societatis Iesu Sacerdote & Theologo. 1608.*

623. [= 448] *A Defence of the Roman Church. Wherin Is treated, Whether
the said church of Rome hath fallen in faith, or no? Written in Latin by
the R. F. Martinus Becanus of the Society of Iesus, Professour in
Divinity: And Now translated into English.* 1612   (STC 1700, AR 79,
ERL 28)

(The second edition appeared as an Appendix to the second edition of
Lessius' *Consultation* in 1621, with the following announcement on the
title-page:

*Whereunto is also annexed a little Treatise Whether the Church of
Rome hath fallen in Fayth, or no?*

It also had a title-page of its own, with continuous pagination from the
preceding treatise. The translator's name was given in the initials W. W.
(for William Wright).)

Two other works by Becanus, which were translated into English by William
Wright and published for their controversial relevance, were his *Disputatio
theologica de triplici Coena* of 1608 and his treatise *De Judice Controversi-
arum* of 1616. The former appeared in 1614 in its English form as *A
Controversy;* and the latter in 1619 as *A Treatise.* It was evidently used by
Silvester Norris in his *Pseudo-Scripturist* of 1623, as mentioned above (612).

624. *Disputatio theologica de triplici Coena Calvinistica, Lutherana,
Catholica Moguntiae proposita a Rev. et Nob. Dn. M. Ioanne Ludovico
ab Hogen, SS. Theologiae Baccalaureo, ad Licentiam consequendam.
Praeside R. P. Martino Becano, Societatis Iesu Theologo. 1608.*

625. *A Controversy, in which the Communion of Calvin is wholy overthrowne, and The Reall Presence of Christs body in the Eucharist
confirmed. Written By Martin Becanus of the Society of Iesus.* 1614
(Not in STC, AR 78, ERL 46)

626. *De Judice Controversiarum, id est an Scriptura sit Judex Controversiarum ut volunt adversarii, an potius Ecclesia ut docent Catholici.
Authore Martino Becano Societatis Iesu Theologo. 1616*

627. *A Treatise of the Iudge of Controversies. Written In Latin, by the R.
Father Martinus Becanus of the Society of Iesus, Professour in Divinity.
And Englished by W. W. Gent.* 1619   (STC 1707, AR 81, ERL 159)

j) Recantations of an Archbishop

The most notorious of all the recantations of this reign was that of a Catholic archbishop, the Italian Marc'Antonio De Dominis, Archbishop of Spalato in Dalmatia; and like Theophilus Higgons, he made a double recantation in the opposite direction — from Catholic to Anglican, and back again to Catholic. His main quarrel was against the Pope of the time, Paul V; and he may well have been the anonymous author of the strange *Supplicatio Ad Imperatorem* of 1613, which William Crashaw translated into English as *The New Man* in 1622 (317—18). He finally broke with the Pope and made his way to England in 1616. Here he embraced the Anglican religion and was made Dean of Windsor by the King in the following year. Almost immediately he set about publishing a series of writings defending these actions. Already before leaving Italy he had written a Latin 'apology', entitled *Suae Profectionis Consilium Exponit;* and this he published in London on his arrival in 1616. It was translated into English and published in the same year as *A Manifestation of the Motives*, with an announcement of a forthcoming book 'concerning the Ecclesiastique Commonwealth'. (The translator could not help noting the parallel between this defection of the Archbishop from Rome and that of Carier from the Church of England.) Both books, Latin and English, were reissued the following year, 1617, in Edinburgh with more elaborate titles.

628. *Marcus Antonius De Dominis, Archiepiscopus Spalatensis, Suae Profectionis Consilium Exponit.* 1616   (STC 6996)

(The Scottish edition of 1617 is entitled:

Reverendissimi in Christo Patris Marci Antonii de Dominis, Archiepiscopi Spalatensis, Consilium. Caussas discessus sui ex Italia, & e Psychotyrannide Pontificis Romani exponit longe gravissimas. Excusum primo Venetiis 20. die Septemb. Anno 1616. Iam denuo ad primum exemplar fideliter recusum 12 Ianuarii Anno 1617. (STC 6997))

629. *A Manifestation of the Motives, Whereupon the most Reverend Father, Marcus Antonius De Dominis, Archbishop of Spalato, (in the Territorie of Venice) Undertooke his departure thence. Englished out of his Latine Copy.* 1616   (STC 6998)

(An Appendix gives the Decree of Pope Paul V prohibiting both this book and the promised *De Republica Christiana*, together with 'A parcell of Observations upon some considerable points in this Decree'. In it the author expresses warm support for Roger Widdrington, in his defence of the Oath of Allegiance and his opposition to 'the Popes temporall encrochments'.

The Scottish edition of 1617 is entitled:

> *A Declaration of the Reasons which moved Marcus Antonius de*
> *Dominis, Archbishop of Spalato or Salonas, Primate of Dalmatia and*
> *Croatia, to depart from the Romish Religion and his Countrey. Written*
> *by himselfe in Latine, and now for the Populare use translated.* 1617
> (STC 6999))

This apostasy of the archbishop, with his explanation, was immediately attacked by two English Jesuits, John Floyd and John Sweet. The former published his *Synopsis Apostasiae* in 1617, and shortly followed it with an English translation by Henry Hawkins, entitled *A Survey of the Apostasy*. Referring to himself as 'Fidelis Annosus, Verementanus Druinus', Floyd criticized the archbishop for the pompous style adopted in his title, 'as if you were the Pithian Apollo ready to give Oracles', or as if 'that olde Marke Antony' is 'revived againe, and fled from Rome to Aegipt'. The other Jesuit also brought out his reply in 1617, oddly entitling it *Monsigr. fate voi* (Monsignor, do it yourself!) and presenting it in the form of a letter to a friend in London. He discusses the matter mainly as concerning the issue of Papal supremacy. Another attack in Latin on the same book of the archbishop came from the pen of a Flemish divine, Laurence Beyerlinck of Antwerp; and it was published in the same year, 1617, with a title parodying that of De Dominis.

630. *Synopsis Apostasiae Marci Antonii De Dominis, olim Archiepiscopi*
     Spalatensis, nunc apostatae, ex ipsiusmet libro delineata, Auctore Fideli
     Annoso Verimentano Theologo. 1617

631. *A Survey of the Apostasy of Marcus Antonius De Dominis, Sometyme*
     Arch-bishop of Spalato. Drawne out of his owne Booke, and written in
     Latin, by Fidelis Annosus, Verementanus Druinus, Devine: And
     Translated into English by A. M. 1617   (STC 11116 = 70008, AR 331,
     ERL 58)

632. *Monsigr. fate voi. or A Discovery of the Dalmatian Apostata, M.*
     Antonius de Dominis, and his Bookes. By C. A. to his friend P. R.
     Student of the Lawes in the Middle Temple. 1617   (STC 23529,
     AR 803, ERL 48)

     (The inner title reads:

     The Dalmatian Bishop Discovered.)

633. *Laurentius Beyerlinck Archipresbyter Antuerpiensis Profectionis Marci*
     Antonii de Dominis quondam Archiepiscopi Spalatensis Consilium
     Examinat. 1617

That year, 1617, was a busy one for the archbishop, though he never directly replied to his opponents. He further explained his position in a *Sermon*, which he preached in Italian in London for the benefit of Italian residents and others. He subsequently published it not only in Italian, but also in Latin and English. His position was that the religion of both the Roman and the Reformed churches 'is in the maine essentials and fundamentals the very same' – a position to which the Arminian party in the Church of England was also moving.

634. *Predica Fatta Da Monsr. Marc' Antonio de Dominis, Arcivo. Di Spalato, La prima Domenica dell' Avvento quest' anno 1617. in Londra, nella Capella detta delli Merciari, (ch'e la Chiesa degl' Italiani,) ad essa Natione Italiana.* 1617   (STC 7003)

635. *A Sermon Preached in Italian, By the most Reverend father, Marc' Antony De Dominis, Archb. of Spalato, the first Sunday in Advent, Anno 1617. In the Mercers Chappel in London, to the Italians in that City, and many other Honorable auditors then assembled. Upon the 12. Verse of the 13. Chapter to the Romanes, being part of the Epistle for that day. First published in Italian by the Author, and thereout Translated into English.* 1617   (STC 7004)

636. *Concio Habita Italice a Reverendo Patre Marco Antonio De Dominis, Archiepiscopo Spalatensi primo die dominico Adventus Anno 1617. Londini in Mercatorum Capella, coram Italis ibi commorantibus, & aliis honorificis in illa Synaxi & Convent.* 1618   (Not in STC)

De Dominis went on to publish a book in Latin against the Papal claims, entitled *Papatus Romanus*. Then, continuing a metaphor he had used in his *Sermon*, he warned English readers against *The Rockes of Christian Shipwracke*, in a book published the following year, 1618. Needless to say, his 'first Rocke' is 'The Papacie', followed by 'Temporall power'. His principal preoccupation, however, was with his promised treatise, *De Republica Ecclesiastica*. Promising ten books, he presented the first four in Tome I, which appeared in 1617, and the next two in Tome II, which appeared with another issue of Tome I in 1620. But there he brought his work to an end.

637. *Papatus Romanus: Liber de Origine, Progressu, atque extinctione ipsius.* 1617   (STC 7002)

(In Chap. X, 'De Papatus Diminutione, & extinctione ipsius', there is a significant reference to the book by 'Novus homo', entitled 'Supplicatio ad Imperatorem Reges Principes &c.' together with another by 'Adamus Mulseus, qui in illum commentatus fuit anno 1615'.)

638. *The Rockes of Christian Shipwracke, Discovered by the holy Church of Christ to her beloved Children, that they may keepe aloofe from them. Written in Italian by the most Reverend Father, Marc' Ant. De Dominis, Archb. of Spalato, And thereout translated into English.* 1618 (STC 7005)

639. *De Republica Ecclesiastica Libri X. Auctore Marco Antonio de Dominis Archiepiscopo Spalatensi. Cum suis Indicibus.* 1617 (STC 6994)

(At the beginning by way of Preface there appears:

Marcus Antonius de Dominis Archiepiscopus Spalatensis suae profectionis consilium exponit.)

640. [= 328] *De Republica Ecclesiastica Pars Secunda: continens Libros quintum, et sextum. Cum Appendicibus in sexto capite quinti Libri. In quibus Appendicibus Refellitur opus imperfectum D. Cardinalis Perronii, in ea Parte in qua agitur De sanctissima Eucharistia. Additur in fine post sextum Librum Responsio ad magnam partem Defensionis Fidei P. Francisci Suarez. Autore Marco Antonio de Dominis Archiepiscopo Spalatensi.* 1620 (STC 6995)

(The work of Cardinal du Perron mentioned here seems to be his *Letter* of 1612 to Isaac Casaubon (431–34). The *Defensio Fidei* of Suarez in 1613 is dealt with above (323), followed by De Dominis' criticism.)

It was not long before this work was formally condemned by the universities of Paris and Cologne in 1618; and an English translation of the Paris condemnation was published in the same year. Two continental theologians added more detailed refutations: Leonard Marius of Cologne, with his *Catholica Hierarchiae Ecclesiasticae Assertio* in 1618; and the Jesuit Eudaemon-Joannes, with his *Admonitio ad Lectores* in 1619. In 1620 John Floyd returned to the attack on the archbishop, with his *Hypocrisis Marci Antonii De Dominis detecta*, which he offered as a preamble to a fuller refutation. This appeared in 1622, in the form of a *retorsio argumenti*, turning the reasons of his opponent against him, with the title *Monarchiae Ecclesiasticae . . . Demonstratio.*

641. *Censura Sacrae Facultatis Theologiae Parisiensis, in quatuor priores libros De Republica Ecclesiastica, Auctore Marco Antonio de Dominis quondam Archiepiscopo Spalatensi: Londini apud Ioannem Billium. typis excussos; Anno MDCXVII.* 1618

642. *The Censure of the Sacred Facultie of Divinitie of Paris, Against the Foure Bookes concerning the Ecclesiastical commonwealth, Composed*

*by Marcus Antonius de Dominis, Archbishop of Spalata: Printed at
London by Iohn Bill. 1617. Translated by a Student in Divinitie. To
which also is added a Preface to the Reader. 1618* (Not in STC or AR,
ERL 57)

(The Censure itself is dated December 1617.)

643. *Censura Sacrae Facultatis Theologicae Coloniensis; in quatuor priores
libros de Republ. Ecclesiastica M. Antonii de Dominis, quondam
Archiepiscopi Spalatensis.* 1618

644. *Catholica Hierarchiae Ecclesiasticae Assertio, in qua B. Petri et Romanae
Sedis Primatus, contra Heresim et Schisma M. Antonii Spalat: quondam
Archiep. ex Scriptura, SS.PP. & Conciliis defenditur, Ac simul illius
mendacia, imposturae & fraudes deteguntur. Authore Admodum
Reverendo & Doctissimo D. D. Leonardo Mario, SS. Theol. D.
eiusdemque in univers. Colon. Profess. Ordin.* 1618

645. *R. P. Andreae Eudaemon-Ioannis Cydonii e Societate Iesu Admonitio
ad Lectores Librorum M. Antonii de Dominis.* 1619

646. *Hypocrisis Marci Antonii De Dominis detecta, seu Censura in eius libros
De Republica Ecclesiastica, praeambula pleniori responsioni. Auctore
Fideli Annoso Veremontano Theologo.* 1620

647. *Monarchiae Ecclesiasticae, ex scriptis M. Antonii de Dominis Ex-Archi-
episcopi Spalatensis, Demonstratio, duobus libris comprehensa, seu
Respublica Ecclesiastica M. Antonii de Dominis, per Ipsum a fundamentis eversa. Auctore Fideli Annoso Verementano Theologo.* 1622

To all these attacks the archbishop answered not a word; but his secretary, a
Frenchman named Daniel Lohetus, published a Latin reply to Leonard
Marius, entitled *Sorex Primus* — treating him contemptuously as a shrew-
mouse. This was printed in London, and came out in 1618.

648. *Sorex Primus Oras Chartarum primi libri De Republica Ecclesiastica
Illustrissimi & Reverendissimi D. Archiepiscopi Spalatensis corrodens
Leonardus Marius Theologaster Coloniensis A Daniele Loheto
Burgundo Laudonensi, eiusdem D. Spalatensis Amanuensi, in muscipula
captus, & eiusdem scalpello confossus.* 1618

The next development in this controversy was that the archbishop
himself returned to Italy (now that Paul V had been succeeded in 1621 by
Gregory XV) and retracted everything he had written against Rome in
defence of the Anglican Church. The year after his return, in 1623, he

published his second recantation, first in Latin (with a title echoing his first recantation), *Sui reditus ex Anglia Consilium exponit*. This appeared in two separate English translations in that year: one at Rome by the Jesuit Edward Coffin, entitled *M. Antonius de Dominis . . . Declares the cause of his Returne;* and the other at Liege by G. K., entitled *The Second Manifesto*. He now denounced England as 'the Schoole of errours, lyes, and heresies', and again embraced 'the holy Romane Church' as 'the one, and onely piller and excellent ground of Catholike truth'. At the same time he promised to undertake 'the confutation of my bookes of the Ecclesiasticall Common-wealth and of the other bookes which I have written'. He was, however, unable to carry out his promise, as he died shortly afterwards. In 1624 there appeared *A Relation Sent from Rome* describing the circumstances of his imprisonment and death in that city. He was posthumously condemned by the Inquisition for having held the following heresies:

1. That the Councell of Trent had declared many things to be de fide which were not.
2. That all the Sects of Heretickes might be reduced unto one Church, if the Church of Rome would remit some of those things, which in processe of time she had determined to be de fide, instancing in particular in the Article of Transubstantiation.
3. That there might be made an union betweene the Church of Rome and the Protestant Heretickes, they both agreeing in articulis fundamentalibus.

649. *Marcus Antonius de Dominis Archiepisc. Spalaten. Sui reditus ex Anglia Consilium exponit.* 1623

650. *M. Antonius de Dominis Archbishop of Spalato, Declares the cause of his Returne, out of England. Translated out of the Latin Copy, printed at Rome this present yeare.* 1623   (STC 7000, AR 272, ERL 363)

(The running title is: *M. Antonius de Dominis His Recantation.*)

651. *The Second Manifesto of Marcus Antonius De Dominis, Archbishop of Spalato: wherein for his better satisfaction, and the satisfaction of others, he publikely repenteth, and recanteth his former errors, and setteth downe the cause of his leaving England, and all Protestant Countries, to returne unto the Catholicke Romane Church; Written by himselfe in Latine, and translated into English by M. G. K.* 1623 (STC 7001, AR 273, ERL 128)

652. *A Relation Sent from Rome, of the Processe, Sentence, and Execution, Done upon the Body, Picture, and Bookes, Of Marcus Antonius de Dominis, Archbishop of Spalato, after his death. Published by Command.* 1624   (STC 7007)

Consequent on this second recantation, there now arose a loud chorus of criticism from Anglican writers, not unlike that which his first had elicited from Catholic writers. The official refutation was compiled by Richard Neile, Bishop of Durham, in the form of 'a plaine and true Narration of the passages, which have beene betwixt his Maiestie & the Archbishop of Spalata ... after the first discovery of the said Archbishops purpose, to returne to the Church of Rome'. After being published in English in 1624, as *M. Ant. de Dnis ... his Shiftings in Religion*, it was translated into Latin and published in the same year, as *Alter Ecebolius*. Richard Montague, then Canon of Windsor, also felt obliged to publish a sermon of his on 'the Invocation of Saints', under the title *Immediate Addresse unto God Alone*, in order to defend himself against an imputation made by the archbishop in his recent recantation:

> 'I myselfe heard in England with great pleasure, one of my Chanons of Windsor preaching before the King, and expressely affirming, that there was no cause why every faithfull man should not turne himselfe unto his Angel-keeper, and say, O holy Angel-keeper pray for me.'

Finally, in the following year, 1625, there appeared a fuller refutation by Richard Crakanthorpe, entitled *Defensio Ecclesiae Anglicanae* – shortly after the author's own death.

653. *M. Ant. de Dnis Arch-bishop of Spalato, his Shiftings in Religion, A Man for many Masters.* 1624   (STC 18421)

654. *Alter Ecebolius M. Ant. de Dominis Arch. Spalatensis. Pluribus Dominis inservire Doctus.* 1624   (STC 7006)

(The Ecebolius of this title refers to a sophist of Constantinople in the time of Julian the Apostate.)

655. *Immediate Addresse unto God Alone. First delivered in a Sermon before his Maiestie at Windsore. Since revised and inlarged to a just Treatise of Invocation of Saints. Occasioned by a false imputation of M. Antonius De Dominis upon the Authour, Richard Mountagu.* 1624 (STC 18039)

(Echoing the title of 654, the author refers to the archbishop as 'that infamous Ecebolius of these times'.)

656. *Defensio Ecclesiae Anglicanae, Contra M. Antonii de Dominis, D. Archiepiscopi Spalatensis Iniurias: Viri omni virtute, doctrinaque Spectatissimi, D. Rich. Crakanthorp, S. T. D. & Regiae M. nuper Sacellani, Opus Posthumum. A. D. Iohanne Barkham, S. T. D. in Lucem editum.* 1625   (STC 5975)

(This was a substantial volume of 645 pages.)

By way of postscript, mention may be made here of three more converts from Rome to the Church of England in the aftermath of the archbishop's conversion – though he does not appear to have influenced their several decisions. In 1621 there appeared two recantations: one from a former Carthusian monk, Christopher Musgrave, entitled *Musgraves Motives*; the other from a Spanish physician, John de Nicholas, entitled *The Reformed Spaniard*.

657. *Musgraves Motives, and Reasons, for his Secession and Dissevering from the Church of Rome and her Doctrine, after that hee had for 20 yeares lived a Carthusian Monke, returning at Easter last into England. Wherein, after the Declaration of his Conversion, hee openeth divers absurdities practised in that Church, being not matters of report, but such things whereof he hath beene an eye and eare witnesse.* 1621 (STC 18316)

(His particular objections were to the Catholic doctrines of transubstantiation, auricular confession, and purgatory; also to repression within the Carthusian order.)

658. *The Reformed Spaniard: To all reformed Churches, embracing the true Faith, wheresoever dispersed on the Face of the Earth: And especially to the most reverend Archbyshops, and Worshipfull Reverend Byshops, Doctors, and Pastors, now gathered together in the venerable Synode at London, this yeare of our Lord, 1621. Iohn de Nicholas and Sacharles, Doctor of Physicke, wisheth health in our Lord. First published by the Author in Latine, and now thence faithfully Translated into English.* 1621 (STC 18530)

(The inner title reads:

The Reformed Spaniard, Declareth the reasons and motives, by which he was induced to forsake the Romish Church.)

The third convert was another Spaniard, Ferdinand Texeda, who came forward two years later to publish his recantation, both in English as *Texeda Retextus*, and in Latin as *Hispanus Conversus*. Like De Dominis, he was not content with a simple recantation, but went on to publish other anti-Roman writings. In 1624 he brought out *Scrutamini Scripturas: the Exhortation of a Spanish Converted Monke*; and in 1625 he followed it up with a criticism of 'Popish Miracles', entitled *Miracles unmasked*, drawing on his experiences in Spain. There he ended his writings; and there, too, the reign came to an end.

659. *Texeda Retextus: Or the Spanish Monke His Bill of Divorce against the Church of Rome: Together with other remarkable Occurrances.* 1623 (STC 23923)

(The inner title reads:

The Spanish Convert, or Ferdinandus Texeda his Conversion to the Reformed Church, with the cause moving him thereunto.

There is also a Preface 'To the Christian Reader', by Daniel Featley, who figures in the final controversy.)

660. *Hispanus Conversus.* 1623   (STC 23920)

(The author's name is given as 'Ferdinandus Texeda' at the end of the Dedicatory Epistle.

The inner title gives a fuller account:

Narrat causas quibus impulsus fuit ad deserendam Ecclesiam Romanam.)

661. *Scrutamini Scripturas: the Exhortation of a Spanish Converted Monke: collected out of the Spanish Authors themselves, to reade and peruse the holy Scriptures.* 1624   (STC 23922)

662. *Miracles unmasked. A Treatise Proving that Miracles are not infallible signes of the true and Orthodoxe Faith: That Popish Miracles are either counterfeit or divellish. Evidently confirmed by authorities of holy Scripture, of antient Doctors, of grave and learned Spanish Authors, by weighty reasons, manifest examples, and most true Histories which have happened in Spaine, and appeare in Bookes there Printed. By Ferdinando Texeda, Batchelar in Divinity.* 1625   (STC 23921)

k) *Sporadic Attack and Counter-Attack*

The controversies between Catholic and Anglican, which had tended to gather in clusters during the first half of James' reign, became increasingly sporadic during the latter half. Not that there was any notable diminution in the quantity of controversial literature; but challenges to controversy were no longer taken up and answered so readily as they had formerly been. In spite of the Gunpowder Plot and the subsequent Oath of Allegiance, the number of Catholic recusants, and of the seminary priests and Jesuits (as well as priests of other religious orders) ministering to them, had been steadily growing. The penal laws against them were less severely applied, especially since the deaths of their principal enemies, Archbishop Bancroft in 1610 and Robert Cecil, Earl of Salisbury, in 1614. This leniency came to a climax with the proposed 'Spanish match' for Prince Charles and his actual journey to Spain in 1623 with this in view. It brought increased self-confidence to Catholic authors, who now redoubled their assaults on the

Protestant position, with particular emphasis on the points of antiquity and apostolic succession. The Protestant authors inevitably responded with renewed attacks on Popery and claims of a Protestant succession opposed to that of Rome. But for the most part they refrained from replying to individual books or authors, till everything came to a head in the final controversy of the reign from 1623 onwards.

On the Catholic side, there were, to begin with, a number of books emphasizing the contrast between the Catholic and the Protestant religion. In 1620 John Copinger presented 'the manifest truth . . . of the Catholique Religion' as opposed to the 'falsitie and absurditie' of the Protestants in his *Theatre of Catholique and Protestant Religion*. In 1621 there appeared 'A Comparison of a true Roman Catholike with a Protestant', as an excerpt from Persons' *Treatise of Three Conversions*, and as the first part of *A Little Treatise concerning Trial of Spirits*. It may have been in response to this *Little Treatise* of Persons that there appeared in 1622 *A briefe Theologicall Discourse*, premitted to a criticism of Popish exorcisms entitled *The Boy of Bilson*. In 1623, on the occasion of 'the match with Spayn', one Patteson published *The Image of Bothe Churches*, the 'Babel, or Monarchomachia Protestantium', on the one hand, and 'Hierusalem, that Obedience, and Order, be the Eirenarchae of Catholiques', on the other.

663. *The Theatre of Catholique and Protestant Religion, divided into Twelve Bookes. Wherein The zealous Catholike may plainelie see, the manifest truth, perspicuitie, evident foundations and demonstrations of the Catholique Religion; Together with the motives and causes, why he should persever therin. The Protestant also may easilie see, the falsitie and absurditie, of his irreligious, and negative Religion; Together with many strong and convincing reasons, why he is bound to embrace the Catholique faith, and to returne againe to the true Church from whence he departed. Written by I.C. Student in divinitie.* 1620 (STC 4284 = 5558, AR 256, ERL 191)

664. *A Little Treatise concerning Trial of Spirits: taken for the most part out of the Works of the R. P. Robert Parsons, of the Societie of Iesus. Whereunto is added a Comparison of a true Roman Catholike with a Protestant, wherby may bee discovered the difference of their Spirits. With an Appendix taken out of a later Writer.* 1620 (STC 19410, AR 632, ERL 350)

(The first section bears the following title:

A Comparison of a true Roman Catholike with a Protestant, whereby may be discovered the difference of their Spirits, not only in things belonging to faith and beleefe, but also concerning their lives, conversation, and manners: taken out of a more simple discourse of this subject, made by that worthy and reverend Father, F. Parsons, in the 20. Chapter of his Examen of Fox his Calendar, the last six Moneths.

Another edition of the same year is without this section, and is more simply entitled:

A Little Treatise concerning Triall of Spirits. Written first by the R. F. Robert Parsons, of the Societie of Iesus, against Master Charke. Newly set forth, with an Appendix taken out of a later Writer. (Not in STC, AR 631)

The book mentioned here is Persons' *Defence of the Censure* (1582).)

665. *The Boy of Bilson: or, A True Discovery of the late notorious Impostures of certaine Romish Priests in their pretended Exorcisme, or expulsion of the Divell out of a young boy, named William Perry, sonne of Thomas Perry of Bilson, in the county of Stafford, Yeoman. Upon which occasion, hereunto is premitted*
A briefe Theologicall Discourse, by way of Caution, for the more easie discerning of such Romish spirits; and iudging of their false pretences, both in this and the like Practices. 1622 (STC 1185)

(The premitted *Discourse* is entitled:

A Discourse concerning Popish Exorcizing.

No explicit mention is made of Persons' book; but much use is made of Samuel Harsnet's 'Book intituled, A Declaration of egregious Impostures practized by Romish Priests', which came out in 1603.)

666. *The Image of Bothe Churches. Hierusalem and Babel, Unitie and Confusion. Obedienc and Sedition. By, P. D. M.* 1623 (STC 19480, AR 599, ERL 362)

(The name of the author is given by John Gee, *The Foot out of the Snare* (1624), as 'M. Pateson', and his book is described as 'a bitter and seditious book'.
It is divided into three parts, as follows:
a) *Babel, or, Monarchomachia Protestantium.*
b) *Hierusalem, that Obedience, and Order, be the Eirenarchae of Catholiques.*
c) *The Touchstone, Apotheosis Lutheri.*)

Other Catholic books merely insisted on the truth of the Catholic religion. In 1620 Thomas Doughty, a Carmelite priest, writing under the pseudonym of John Hunt, presented *An Humble Appeale to the Kings most excellent Maiestie* for this purpose. Later on, in 1623 two more books appeared out of their authors' imprisonment with a similar purpose. It was as a result of several disputes 'with sundry Bishops and Ministers of Scotland' during his imprisonment in Edinburgh in 1620–21 that the Scottish Jesuit, Patrick Anderson, published his *Ground of the Catholike and Roman Religion* together with 'A Table, or Catalogue of the Names of some Roman Catholiks, which shew that the Roman Church hath byn continually in all ages since Christ & his Apostles, untill our dayes, & shall continue to the end of the world'. Also from prison, in England, there appeared an anonymous *Epistle of A Catholicke Young Gentleman*, explaining the motives of his conversion to his father. Among them he stressed the need of a living rule of faith, to be found only in Rome which 'hath knowne continuance with succession of Pastors from the beginning of Christianity unto this day'.

667. *An Humble Appeale to the Kings most excellent Maiestie. Wherein is proved, that our Lord and Saviour Iesus Christ, was Authour of the Catholike Roman Faith, which Protestants call Papistrie. Written by Iohn Hunt, a Roman Catholike, in defence of his Religion against the Calumniations and persecutions of Protestant Ministers.* 1620 (STC 13986, AR 278, ERL 54)

668. *The Ground of the Catholike and Roman Religion in the Word of God. With the Antiquity and Continuance therof, throughout all Kingdomes and Ages. Collected Out of divers Conferences, Discourses, and Disputes, which M. Patrike Anderson of the Society of Iesus, had at severall tymes, with sundry Bishops and Ministers of Scotland, at his last imprisonment in Edenburgh, for the Catholike Faith. in the yeares of our Lord 1620 and 1621. Sent unto an Honourable Personage, by the Compyler, and Prisoner himselfe.* 1623   (STC 575, AR 20, ERL 165)

(The book is divided into three Parts, each with distinct pagination: respectively 60 pages, 552 pages, and 174 pages.)

669. *An Epistle of A Catholike Young Gentleman, (Being for his Religion imprisoned.) To his Father a Protestant. Who commaunded him to set downe in Writing, what were the motives that induced him to become a Catholicke.* 1623   (STC 10341 = 18330, AR 561, ERL 89)

(The letter is addressed 'To the worshipfull his very loving Father N. N. Esquire', and dated 15 August 1614.)

Yet other books were more directly critical of the Protestants, particularly their recent origins and heretical beliefs. In 1621 Richard Smith brought out an English translation of a work that had been published in Latin two years before, entitled *De Auctore et Essentia Protestanticae Ecclesiae et Religionis.* Also in that year Thomas Doughty followed up his *Humble Appeale* with *A Briefe Discoverie* of the corrupt translations in

Protestant Bibles, appealing (like Brereley and Broughton) to the admissions of the Protestants themselves.

670. *De Auctore et Essentia Protestanticae Ecclesiae et Religionis. Libri duo. Auctore Richardo Smithaeo, Lincolniense S. Theologiae Doctore.* 1619

(In his Dedication to Pope Paul V, the author speaks of two ways by which the Catholic religion is propagated in England: 'Sanguinis nimirum profusione, & Librorum conscriptione'.

Three lists are added as appendices:

Catalogus Librorum Lutheranorum.
Catalogus Sacramentariorum.
Catalogus Protestantium Anglorum.)

671. *Of the Author and Substance of the Protestant Church and Religion, Two Bookes. Written first in Latin by R. S. Doctour of Divinity, And Now reviewed by the Author, and translated into English by W. Bas.* 1621   (STC 22812, AR 776, ERL 258)

672. *A Briefe Discoverie of the Crafte & Pollicie which Protestant Ministers use in seducing theire Followers By Preaching and Publishing theire owne words for the word of God. Written By Iohn Hunt a Romaine Catholique, in defence of the true Gospell or Word of God.* 1621 (STC 13985, AR 277, ERL 62)

Three more works of this kind appeared a couple of years later, in 1623. The anonymous *Ruine of Calvinisme* was, like the *Humble Appeale*, confidently dedicated 'To the Kinges most Excellent Maiestie of great Brittanie'. It consisted of two parts: maintaining in the first 'that the church ought to be visible', and criticizing in the second the Calvinist doctrine of Predestination. In his *Uncasing of Heresie*, a work that went into two editions in two years and was often mentioned but never fully refuted by his opponents, Oliver Almond even declared 'that the God of the Protestants . . . is no other but a divell of hell'. Then there was the above-mentioned *Gagge of the New Gospel*, or (as it was retitled in the second edition of that year) *Gagge of the Reformed Gospell*, which became the occasion of the Arminian controversy among the Anglicans.

673. *The Ruine of Calvinisme.* 1623   (Not in STC, AR 743, ERL 192)

(The second part has a new title-page and new pagination.)

674. *The Uncasing of Heresie, or The Anatomie of Protestancie. Written and Composed by O. A.* 1623   (STC 12 = 535, AR 15)

(The author criticizes various Protestant catalogues proposed by Illyricus, Foxe, Fulke, and White. He also mentions the report 'that (D. King Bishop of London) desired a Priest before his death, and to die a member of the Catholike Roman Church' — to be considered later.

The second edition of 1624 is presented in the title as 'Reviewed and augmented, by the Author of the first'. STC 13, AR 17, ERL 113)

675. [= 137] *The Gagge of the New Gospel: contayning a briefe abridgement of the errors of the Protestants of our time. With their refutation, by expresse texts of their owne English bible.* 1623 (Not in STC, AR 422, see ERL 336)

John Brereley now reappeared in 1620 with two more learned books, in which he followed his old method of defending the Catholic and attacking the Protestant position by means of a skilful selection of quotations from the writings of his adversaries. In *The Lyturgie of the Masse* he aimed at showing how the ceremonies of the Catholic Mass were derived from the primitive age of the Church, and how in general the ancient is Catholic and the modern Protestant. Similarly, in *Sainct Austines Religion* he drew both on the saint's own writings and on 'the confessions of the learned Protestants' to demonstrate his substantial agreement with the present teaching of the Roman Church. This work alone elicited a reply from a Protestant, William Crompton, who published his reply with the identical title of *Saint Austins Religion* in 1624 — not only as a particular refutation of Brereley, but also as a general reply to the insistent question then being raised by the Catholics: 'Where was your religion before Luther?'

676. *The Lyturgie of the Masse: Wherein are treated three principal pointes of faith. 1. That in the Sacrament of the Eucharist are truly and really contained the body and bloud of Christ. 2. That the Masse is a true and proper sacrifice of the body and bloud of Christ, offered to God by Preistes. 3. That Communion of the Eucharist to the Laity under one kind is lawful. The ceremonies also of the Masse now used in the Catholicke Church, are al of them derived from the Primitive Church. By Iohn Brereley Preist.* 1620 (STC 3607, AR 137, ERL 184)

677. *Sainct Austines Religion. Collected from his owne writinges, & from the confessions of the learned Protestants: Whereby is sufficiently proved and made knowen, the like answearable doctrine of the other more auncient Fathers of the Primitive Church. Written by Iohn Brereley.* 1620 (STC 3608, AR 138, ERL 30)

678. *Saint Austins Religion. Wherein is manifestly proved out of the Works of that Learned Father, that he dissented from Popery, and agreed with*

*the Religion of the Protestants in all the maine Points of Faith and
Doctrine. Contrary to that Impudent, Erronious, and Slanderous
Position of the bragging Papists of our Times, who falsely affirme, we
had no Religion before the Times of Luther and Calvine.* 1624
(STC 6059)

(The inner title begins:

St. Augustines Religion: Wherein is prooved that hee dissented . . .)

Brereley went on to publish two more direct attacks on his opponents: first,
in 1621, on *The Reformed Protestant* in general, as abetting 'the ruine of all
religion'; and then, in 1624, on the author of Protestantism, in a book
entitled *Luthers Life*, once more drawing on 'the onely reporte of learned
Protestants themselves' as his authorities.

679. *The Reformed Protestant, tending directly to atheisme, and all
impietie. This treatise proveth, that the reformation of the Romane
Church, pretended by Protestants, is indeede the destruction of
themselves, the ruine of all religion, and the decay of good life. With
further particuler instances hereof, by their deniall of freewill, by their
pretended certaintie of salvation, and by their most dangerous doctrine
of reprobation. Written by I. B. P.* 1621   (Not in STC or AR, ERL 383)

(cf. *Recusant History* 7 (1963–4), p. 144: Note by A. F. Allison.)

680. *Luthers Life Collected from the Writinges of him selfe, and other learned
Protestants, Together With a further shorte discourse, touchinge
Andreas Melanchton, Bucer, Ochine, Carolostadius, Suinglius, Calvine
and Beza, the late pretended Reformers of Religion. Taken from the
onely reporte of learned Protestants themselves. By Iohn Brereley Priest
and Author of the Protestants Apologie.* 1624   (STC 3606, AR 136,
ERL 172)

The reappearance of John Brereley was soon followed, once more, by that
of Richard Broughton. On the reassembling of Parliament in 1621 James
Ussher had preached a *Sermon*, which he published soon afterwards, strongly
attacking the Papists as idolaters and king-killers and therefore not to be
tolerated. Broughton, therefore, published his *English Protestants Plea* for
the toleration of Catholics, emphasizing the truth, admitted by his
Protestant adversaries, that theirs was the religion of all Englishmen up till
comparatively recent times. This was only the first part of the work; but the
second did not come out until 1625, dealing more particularly with the
Catholic priesthood. By that time he had also brought out *An Ecclesiastical
Protestant Historie* in 1624, using a similar method to show the continuity
of the Catholic religion in England through the testimony of such Anglican

antiquarians as Matthew Parker, Francis Godwin and William Camden, and even Francis Mason.

681. *The Substance of that which was delivered in a Sermon before the Commons House of Parliament, in St. Margarets Church at Westminster, the 18. of February, 1620. By Iames Ussher, Professor of Divinity in the University of Dublin, in Ireland.* 1621   (STC 24556)

682. *English Protestants Plea, and Petition, for English Preists and Papists, to the present Court of Parlament, and all persecutors of them: divided into two parts. In the first is proved by the learned protestants of England, that these Preists and Catholiks, have hitherto been uniustly persecuted, though they have often and publickly offered soe much, as any Christians in conscience might doe. In the second part, is proved by the same protestants, that the same preistly sacrificinge function, acknowledgeing and practize of the same supreame and spirituall Iurisdiction of the Apostolick See of Rome, and other Catholick doctrines, in the same sence wee now defend them, and for which wee ar at this present persecuted, continued and were practized in this Iland without interruption in al ages, from S. Peter the Apostle, to these our tymes.* 1621   (STC 10415, AR 159, ERL 218)

(The book ends abruptly with the words: 'And soe much for this first part of this protestant Plea and petition' — without any warning in the title.
It presents an interesting version of the Gunpowder Plot, as largely a propaganda device of Sir Robert Cecil against the Catholics: pp. 55f.)

683. *The Second Part of the Protestants Plea, and Petition for Preists and Papists. Beeing an historie of the holy preisthood, and sacrifice of the true Church of Christ. Invincibly proving them to be, the present sacrificing preisthood: proving also the sacrifice of the Masse, used in the Catholike Roman Church: and that these were promised, and foretold by the Prophets, instituted by Christ, and exercised by all his Apostles. Moreover that they have ever from the first plantinge of Christianitie in this our Britanye, in the dayes of the Apostles, in every age, and hundred of yeares, beene continued and preserved here. All for the most part, warranted by the writinges, and testimonies of the best learned Protestant Doctors, and antiquaries of England, and others.* 1625   (STC 20445, AR 169, ERL 257)

684. *An Ecclesiastical Protestant Historie, of the high pastoral and fatherly chardge and care of the Popes of Rome, over the Church of Britanie, from the first planting of the christian faith there, by S. Peter the Apostle, and his Disciples: continued in every age, and hundred of*

yeares, by holy Bishops, and cleargie men, sent hither and consecrated by them, his Successors in the See Apostolicke. Evidently deduced and proved by historicall narration, from the published and priviledged writings (to appease al protestants) of the most learned & allowed English protestant pretended Bishops, Doctors, Antiquaries, & others of that Religion. 1624 (STC 3895 = 20446, AR 157, ERL 179)

(The theory of St. Peter's coming to Britain is here based on Camden's *Britannia*, 6th ed. 1607; cf. also Person's arguments in the *Treatise of Three Conversions*, Vol. I (1603), page 17.)

The first of these books, the first part of *English Protestants Plea*, gave rise to a minor controversy, not in view of its main thesis, but of a rumour to which it gave currency: that the Bishop of London, John King, had made a death-bed conversion to the Church of Rome in 1621. This was immediately taken up and refuted by the bishop's son, Henry King, in *A Sermon preached at Pauls Crosse*, which was published soon afterwards. The Benedictine priest and author, Thomas Preston, was also involved, since he had been named as the priest who had reconciled the bishop to Rome, according to the 'Book not long since published, which is intituled, *Protestants Plea*'. This was not enough, however, to kill the rumour; and it reappeared with renewed vigour in 1623, when a seminary priest, George Musket, brought out *The Bishop of London His Legacy*. Taking it as a certain truth that the bishop had 'altered his Religion before his death, and dyed Catholike', he went on to develop his motives and apply them 'by a Poeticall freedome' to the bishop himself. His book, which had two editions in two years, won considerable notoriety and was echoed (as has been noticed) by Oliver Almond in his *Uncasing of Heresie* in the same year.

Another Anglican rejection of the rumour came from the pen of the Bishop of Hereford, Francis Godwin, in a separately published appendix to his recent commentary *De Praesulibus Angliæ* (1616), including denunciations both of the *Protestants Plea* and of *The Bishop of London his Legacy*. A fuller refutation of the latter book was undertaken in 1624 by Henry Mason in his *New Art of Lying*. In it he made the mistake (through association of ideas) of regarding Musket as a Jesuit — a mistake which was again made by John Gee in the Catalogue of Popish books which he added to his *Foot out of the Snare* in 1624. Here he speaks of 'The lewd lying Pamphlet, tearmed, The Bishop of Londons Legacie, written by Musket a Iesuite'; but in a third edition of his book, printed in the same year, he added 'a gentle Excuse unto Master Musket, for stiling him Iesuite'.

685. *A Sermon preached at Pauls Crosse, the 25. of November. 1621. Upon occasion of that false and scandalous Report (lately Printed) touching the supposed Apostasie of the right Reverend Father in God, Iohn King, late Lord Bishop of London. By Henry King, his eldest Sonne.*

> *Whereunto is annexed the Examination, and Answere of Thomas*
> *Preston, P. taken before my Lords Grace of Canterbury, touching this*
> *Scandall.* 1621 (STC 14969)

(It is in connection with 'The Examination of Thomas Preston' that
mention is made of a 'Book not long since published, which is intituled,
Protestants Plea, and Petition for Priests and Papists'.)

686. *The Bishop of London his Legacy. or Certaine Motives of D. King, late*
Bishop of London, for his change of Religion, and dying in the
Catholike, and Roman Church. With a Conclusion to his Brethren, the
LL. Bishops of England. 1623 (STC 18305, AR 555, ERL 160)

(The book begins with 'An Advertisement of the Publisher of this
Treatise to the Reader', explaining the 'Poeticall freedome' assumed by
the author in putting words and motives into the mouth of the dead
bishop. There follows an 'Epistle to the Reader', as if spoken by the
bishop himself, before going on to recount his motives — among them
being 'the many astonishing Miracles wrought these late yeares in the
low Countryes at Sichem', as recorded by Justus Lipsius (542).)

687. *Ad Commentarium de Praesulibus Angliae, per Franciscum Godwinum,*
Episcopum tunc Landavensem, modo Herefordensem, editum Anno
1616. 1623? (STC 11942)

(The context in which the rumour is rejected is where the succession of
bishops of London is brought up to date. The main work is entitled:

De Praesulibus Angliae Commentarius: Omnium Episcoporum, necnon
et Cardinalium eiusdem gentis, Nomina, Tempora, Seriem, Atque
actiones maxime memorabiles ab ultima antiquitate repetita complexus.
Per Franciscum Godwinum, Episcopum Landavensem. 1616
(STC 11941))

688. *The New Art of Lying, covered by Iesuites under the Vaile of*
Equivocation. Discovered and disproved By Henry Mason. 1624
(STC 17610)

(The author recalls those Jesuits who have formerly defended the use of
equivocation: Garnet, who gave his licence to a 'Treatise of Equivocation'; and Persons, who further justified it in his *Treatise tending to*
Mitigation (1607) (264). But of them all, he adds, 'hee that wrote the
Bishop of Londons Legacie, is the most shamelesse and impudent lier'.
He goes on to give his account of its publication, referring to an earlier
edition of 1622, which does not seem to have survived: 'He hath made
two publications of one individuall Booke. . . . For, in the yeare 1622.
when hee first divulged this Libell, he made the worthy Bishop to
speake those silly Motives, which his worthlesse selfe had devised . . .

And then in the yeere following 1623. hee made a new publication of the same worthy Worke, changing only the Title-leafe, and the Preface to the Reader. And in this second publication, hee is contented to owne his owne abortive Brat.')

689. *The Foot out of the Snare: with A Detection of sundry late practices and Impostures of the Priests and Iesuits in England. Whereunto is added a Catalogue of such bookes as in this Authors knowledge have been vented within two yeeres last past in London, by the Priests and their Agents. As also a Catalogue of the Romish Preists and Iesuites now resident about London. By Iohn Gee, Master of Arts, of Exon-Colledge in Oxford. 1624* (STC 11701)

(The appendix, which is of great value to the bibliographer, is entitled:

A Catalogue or Note of such English bookes (to the knowledge of which I could come) as have been printed, reprinted, or dispersed by the Priests and their Agents in this Kingdome, within these two yeeres last past, or thereabouts.

Several of the books mentioned in this Catalogue are recorded neither in STC nor in AR: viz.
'The new Religion, no Religion, written by one Floud . . . The Protestants Consultation, a dangerous book, lately written by an unknowne Author . . . The unity of Gods Church, by one Master Stevens, a Iesuite . . . The Reconcilement of the Dalmatian Bishop . . . Saint Peters Keyes, by Edmund Gill, Iesuite . . . The Reformed Protestant, by Brerely . . . A Watch-word, by F. Baker . . . The Apologist, by Richard Conway . . . The Principles of Catholick Religion, by Richard Stannihurst . . . Flagellum Dei, or A Sword for Contradictors: a ridiculous pamphlet written by P. D. M. . . . I. Markes Iesuite, in a book of his written of late, and intituled, The Examination of the new Religion . . .'
What made this book particularly sensational, however, was the other 'Catalogue of the Romish Preists and Iesuites now resident about London', for which reason (as he complained in his enlarged second edition) 'the first impression, consisting of 1500, is vanished in a week', having been bought up by the Papists and burned. For the same reason he had to bring out a third edition in the same year, adding his 'Gentle Excuse made to Master Musket, for stiling him Iesuite', together with yet another 'Catalogue of such Popish Physicians in and about the City of London, as the Author either knoweth, or by good information heareth of'.
He also went on to publish the sequel which follows.)

690. *New Shreds of the Old Snare. Containing The Apparitions of two new female Ghosts. The Copies of divers Letters of late intercourse*

concerning Romish affaires. Speciall Indulgences purchased at Rome,
granted to divers English gentle-beleeving Catholiques for their ready
money. A Catalogue of English Nunnes of the late transportations
within these two or three yeares. By Iohn Gee, Master of Arts, late of
Exon-Colledge in Oxford. 1624   (STC 11706)

Two other Catholic authors, both writing in 1623, followed the example
of Brereley and Broughton in using the Protestants to refute them-
selves — this time using the legal image of a 'Grand Jury'. In his
Application of the Lawes of England for Catholike Priesthood William
Pendryck appealed to 'The Confession of twelve of the learnedest of the
Adversarie parties' to prove the Catholic claims to 'Prioritie of possession', to
'Praescription', and to 'Continuall claime' — the twelve being: Calvin, Beza,
Melanchthon, Whitaker, Fulke, Napier, Gifford, Field, Godwin, Jewel,
Ridley, and Hooker, with the addition of Dove, Middleton, Sutcliffe, Willet,
Covell, Morton, Parkes and Downame, for good measure. William Wright, the
Jesuit, also appealed in his *Briefe Treatise* to 'A Grande Iury Of most famous
and learned Protestants, assuring all Catholiques of their Salvation, if they
live and dye well, in the Catholique Roman Fayth and Church' — naming in
particular: Whitaker, Covell, Morton, Hooker, Bunny, Saravia, White, Willet,
Stubbes, Foxe, Godwin, Camden, Holinshed, Sir Edwin Sandys, and the
anonymous author of the *Theater of Great Britaine.*

691. *The Application of the Lawes of England for Catholike Priesthood,*
     And the Sacrifice of the Masse. Directed to the Lords of his Maiesties
     most Honourable privie Counsell, Judges, Justices, and other Studients
     of the Law. 1623   (STC 7435, AR 601, ERL 118)

     (The author signs himself, 'Your poore Countryman, M. E.')

692. *A Briefe Treatise in which, Is made playne, that Catholikes living and*
     dying in their Profession, may be saved, by the Iudgment of the most
     Famous and Learned Protestants that ever were. Agaynst a Minister
     (N. E.) who in his Epistle exhorteth an Honourable Person, to forsake
     her ancient Catholike Roman Religion, & to become one of his
     new-found-out Protestant Congregation. 1623   (STC 26044, AR 926,
     ERL 143)

     (The identification of this Epistle is uncertain; but the 'Honourable
     Person' appears to be the Countess of Buckingham.)

This thesis of Wright's, that salvation is to be found only in the Catholic
Church, is taken up in two books of 1625 — not so much against the
Anglicans, as against so-called 'Adiaphorists' or 'Ambidexter Christians' who
hold that 'Salvation may be obtayned in any Religion, if so the Professours
thereof do believe only in the Trinity, the Incarnation, and such funda-

mentall points of Christianity'. Against such 'Omnifidians in Religion' the Jesuit, Lawrence Anderton, who is often identified with John Brereley, published his *One God, One Fayth*. Likewise the seminary priest, William Smith, brought out an English treatise under the Latin title, *Qui non Credit Condemnabitur*, against 'these Adiaphorists (whose secret pulse doth indeed beate upon Atheisme)'. Both these books were probably occasioned by the publication in 1623 of the English translation of Henry Constable's *Examen Pacifique de la Doctrine des Huguenots* (1590) under the title of *The Catholike Moderator*. Constable's plea that the Huguenots should not be condemned as heretical was taken up by Thomas James in his *Manuduction*, in 1625, with the remark: 'I am not ignorant, that there be some in the world moderate Papists, that have taken as iust, and as great exception, as we doe, or can, unto the Councell of Trent' (page 123). In this way James was aiming at a 'Confutation of Papists by Papists'; and he may thus have provided added stimulus to Anderton and Smith in their attack, not just on Constable's book in particular, but the whole tendency which he illustrated.

693. *One God, One Fayth. Or A Discourse against Those Lukewarm-Christians, who extend Salvation to all kinds of Fayth and Religion; so, that the Professours do believe in the Trinity, the Incarnation, the Passion &c. howsoever they differ in other inferiour Articles. Written by W. B. Priest.* 1625   (STC 578, AR 23, ERL 183)

694. *Qui non Credit Condemnabitur. Marc. 16. Or A Discourse proving, that a man who beleeveth in the Trinity, the Incarnation, the Passion &c. & yet beleeveth not all other inferiour articles of Christian fayth, cannot be saved. And Consequently, that both the Catholike, and the Protestant (seeing the one necessarily wanteth true fayth) cannot be saved. Written by William Smith, Priest.* 1625   (Not in STC, AR 779, ERL 128)

(These two books have much in common, besides the wording of their titles.)

695. *The Catholike Moderator: or A Moderate Examination of the Doctrine of the Protestants. Proving against the too rigid Catholikes of these times, and against the Arguments especially, of that Booke called, The Answer to the Catholike Apologie, That we, who are members of the Catholike, Apostolike, and Roman Church, ought not to condemne the Protestants for Heretikes, untill further proofe be made. First written in French by a Catholike Gentleman, and now faithfully translated. See the occasion of the name of Huguenots after the Translaters Epistle.* 1623   (STC 6377)

(The book mentioned in the title as 'The Answer to the Catholic Apologie' seems to be John Brereley's response to Thomas Morton's

Apologia Catholica, entitled *The Protestants Apologie for the Roman Church* and published in 1608 (513–14). The title and the Preface to this translation are, of course, the work of the Protestant translator, W. W.

The occasion of the name of Huguenots, announced in the title, is given as King Hugon's Gate in Tours (derived from the 'night spirit called King Hugon') through which the Protestants used to pass on their way to assemblies outside the city.)

696. *A Manuduction, or Introduction unto Divinitie: Containing A Confutation of Papists by Papists, throughout the importantArticles of our Religion; their testimonies taken either out of the Indices Expurgatorii, or out of the Fathers, and ancient Records; But especially the Manuscripts. By Tho. Iames, Doctor of Divinitie, late Fellow of New-Colledge in Oxford, and Sub-Deane of the Cathedrall Church of Welles.* 1625 (STC 14460)

On the Anglican side, the more serious replies to Catholic demands for a 'Catalogue of Protestant Professors' comparable to their own – that is, to the insistent Catholic question, 'Where was your Church before Luther?' – were mainly drawn into the final controversy of the reign; and so their treatment may be postponed till then. Meanwhile, there was a notable increase of books attacking Popery in general, and so entering into the atmosphere of the final controversy of the reign. An almost regular series of such books, though of little controversial value, came from the pen of Alexander Cooke, vicar of Leeds. As early as 1610 he had appeared in print with a revival of the old story or scandal of *Pope Joane*, and in his later books he returned to this theme from time to time. But the characteristic of his later writings, as of 'maister Bel' before him, was a series of challenges to an unspecified 'Masse-priest'. In 1617 he published *Worke for A Masse-priest*, addressing him boldly as 'Sir Priest'. In 1621 he produced an enlarged edition (from fourteen to seventy-four pages, and from thirty-four to ninety-one queries) under the altered title, *More Worke for A Masse-priest;* and this went into another edition in 1622. Also in 1622 he brought out *Yet More Worke for A Masse-Priest,* repeating his former queries with forty-two pages of additional material. Here he admitted his authorship for the first time, at the end of a Dedicatory Epistle, in which he speaks of a report that 'there is an answer made, or in making' to his book. But this answer, if it ever appeared, has not survived. For the most part the Catholics treated him, as they had treated Thomas Bell, with silence. At the most, he received 'an Epistle of an unknowne Priest remaining in London', which he not only answered but also printed with his answer in yet another enlarged edition of his book in 1628, under the title, *Worke, More Worke, and A Little More Worke for a Masse-Priest;* and this went into two more editions in 1630.

697. *Pope Joane. A Dialogue betweene a Protestant and a Papist. Manifestly proving, that a woman called Ioane was Pope of Rome; against the surmises and obiections made to the contrarie, by Robert Bellarmine and Caesar Baronius Cardinals: Florimondus Raemondus, N. D. and other Popish writers, impudently denying the same. By Alexander Cooke.* 1610   (STC 5659)

(The author praises 'maister Bel', particularly 'his book of Motives' and 'his Survey of Poperie: whereunto never a Papist of you all dare answer'.
A second edition came out in 1625.)

698. *Worke for A Masse-priest.* 1617   (STC 5662)

(Thirty-two points are listed, 'in which the author desires to be satisfied'.)

699. *More Worke for A Masse-priest.* 1621   (STC 5663)

(The former *Worke* is extended to ninety-one queries, but no mention is made of it — apart from the 'More' of the title. A second edition came out in 1622.)

700. *Yet More Worke for A Masse-Priest. Published by the Author of the other Bookes.* 1622   (STC 5664)

(In his signed Dedication to Sir Thomas Savile, Cooke says: 'The former partes of this Booke hath been printed and reprinted, yet without my name, though not without the knowledge of many that it was mine, who now do father it.')

701. *Worke, More Worke, and A Little More Worke for a Masse-Priest, Reviewed and augmented by the Authour. With an Epistle of an unknowne Priest remaining in London, sent to the Authour, excepting against five points therein. With the Authours Answere thereunto: returned unto the Priest within twelve dayes after the receipt of the Priests Exceptions.* 1628   (STC 5665)

(The author's name is again relegated to the Dedication. This *Worke* is, in fact, a combination of *Worke and More Worke* (pp. 1–86) and *Yet More Worke* (pp. 86–135). Then on page 136 there follows 'the Letter of an unknowne Priest', whose initials are given as 'Th.Bl. a Masse-priest'; and Cooke's answer is from page 141.)

Two more books were published by Cooke in the last year of the reign. At least, one appeared with his name on the title-page, *The Abatement of Popish Braggs;* and in the main text, 'A Dialogue betwixt a Protestant and a

Papist', he looks back to the time when 'wee talked about Pope Ioane'. The other book, entitled *The Weather-Cocke of Romes Religion*, was anonymous, but attributed to his authorship.

702. *The Abatement of Popish Braggs, Pretending Scripture to be theirs. Retorted by the hand of Alexander Cooke.* 1625   (STC 5658)

703. *The Weather-Cocke of Romes Religion: with her severall changes, or: The World turn'd Topsie-turvie by Papists.* 1625   (STC 5661)

Also from the North, from the nearby parish of Halifax, came a more substantial work by John Favour, entitled *Antiquitie triumphing over Noveltie.* Published in 1619, this book of six-hundred-and-two pages countered 'the false imputation of Noveltie' made by the Catholics (in general) and renewed the Anglican claim to 'antiquitie'. But as it was written against no author in particular, it remained unanswered.

704. *Antiquitie triumphing over Noveltie: Whereby it is proved that antiquitie is a true and certaine Note of the Christian Catholicke Church and verity, against all new and late upstart heresies, advancing themselves against the religious honour of old Rome, whose ancient faith was so much commended by S. Pauls pen, and after sealed with the bloud of so many Martyrs and worthy Bishops of that Sea. With other necessarie and important questions incident and proper to the same subiect. By Iohn Favour Doctor of the Lawes, sometimes Fellow of New College in Oxford, now Vicar of Halifax.* 1619   (STC 10716)

(Like Alexander Cooke, the author dedicates his book to Tobie Mathew, Archbishop of York. He notes how 'many of our adversaries bookes . . . are divulged either without names at all, like speechlesse idols, or onely with a paire of letters . . . for the most part transposed, that Oedipus himselfe could not find out the riddle: or a plaine counterfet name, as Matthaeus Tortus for Robert Bellarmine.')

In 1621 there appeared three or four books attacking the Papists on a somewhat lower level. One R. W., describing himself as 'a poore Minister in Norffolke', published *A Looking-Glasse for Papists*, together with 'a briefe History of the Popes lives'. The printer of this book, T. S. (Thomas Snodham), had only recently — as he confided to the reader — brought out the above-mentioned *Pope's Deadly Wound* by Thomas Clarke (617); and he draws attention to the fact that both books are of much the same nature, and had both been committed to his care by 'that Reverend & worthy man, master Doctor Burges' (of Sutton Coldfield in Warwickshire). Also from an Eastern county came *The Roman-Catharist* by Timothy Rogers, a minister in Essex. In his work he refers with approval to the 'Supplicatio ad

Imperatorem. contra Paul. Quintum by one that calls himself Novus Homo'. The English translator of that *Supplicatio,* William Crashaw, also produced one of his many anti-Popish writings, or rather a second edition of one, entitled *Fiscus Papalis,* which had first appeared in 1617. Calling himself 'a Catholike Divine', he professed to have discovered an ancient document of this title, which he was now translating into English for the benefit of good Catholics, to show them the errors of Romish ways.

705. *A Looking-Glasse for Papists: To see their owne Deformities in matters of Faith, and Religion. And for formall Protestants, to make them more carefull of the true profession of Iesus Christ: lest at any time they fall away from the sinceritie of the Gospell of Christ. With a briefe History of the Popes lives, from the first three hundred yeeres after Christ, until Paul the fift.* 1621   (STC 24912)

706. *The Roman-Catharist: or, The Papist is a Puritane. A Declaration, shewing that they of the Religion and Church of Rome, are notorious Puritans. By Timothy Rogers, Preacher of the word of God at Steple in Essex.* 1621   (STC 21250)

707. *Fiscus Papalis. Sive, Catalogus Indulgentiarum & Reliquarum septem principalium Ecclesiarum urbis Romae. Ex vetusto Manuscripto codice vere & fideliter descriptus. A part of the Popes Exchequer. That is, A Catalogue of the Indulgences and Reliques belonging to the seven principall Churches in Rome. Laying downe the spirituall riches and infinite treasure which (as sure as the Pope is holy and true) are to be found in the Catholike Roman Church, whereof the poore Heretikes in England have not one Mite. Taken out of an ancient Manuscript, and translated: Together with Certaine notes and Comments, explaining the more difficult places, for the ease and helpe of good Catholikes, who had best goe to Rome, to try the vertue of the glorious Indulgences. By a Catholike Divine.* 1617, 1621   (STC 19174–74a)

After a temporary lull on both sides during the year 1622, the opponents to the Papists – no less than the Papists themselves – returned to the attack, especially as the news came of the failure of the 'Spanish match' in 1623. An attack on Catholic priests was published that year by the Scottish poet, George Lauder, under the title of *The Anatomie of the Romane Clergie,* as an English translation of various Latin satires 'by sundrie Authors of their owne profession'. An attack on the Jesuits, *The State-Mysteries of the Iesuites,* was also a translation 'extracted out of their owne Writings' – first into French by Pierre Gosselin and then into English. A more general attack on Popery in dialogue form, entitled *A Pill to Purge out Poperie,* and attributed to John Mico, was particularly popular and went into three editions before the end of the reign. A similar book came out the following year, entitled *A Gagge for the Pope, and the Iesuits*, with the old cry of Antichrist.

708. *The Anatomie of the Romane Clergie: or A Discoverie of the Abuses Thereof. Written in Latine by sundrie Authors of their owne profession. And Translated into English verse by G. L.* 1623   (STC 15311)

(The initials G. L. are identified as those of George Lauder.)

709. *The State-Mysteries of the Iesuites, By way of Questions and Answers. Faithfully extracted out of their owne Writings by themselves published. And A Catalogue prefixed of the Authors names which are cited in this Booke. Written for a Premonition in these times both to the Publike and Par.:icular. Translated out of French.* 1623   (STC 12092)

(The name of Peter Gosselin is added to the Dedication.)

710. *A Pill to Purge out Poperie: Or, A Catechisme for Romish Catholikes; Shewing that Popery is contrarie to the grounds of the Catholike Religion, and that therefore Papists cannot be good Catholikes.* 1623 (STC 17858)

(The dialogue is between 'A Weake Christian' and 'A Minister'.)

711. *A Gagge for the Pope, and the Iesuits: or The Arraignement, and Execution of Antichrist. Shewing plainely, that Antichrist shall be discovered, and punished in this World: to the amasement of all obstinate Papists.* 1624 (STC 20111)

(The inner title gives only:

The Arraignement and Execution of/Antichrist.)

Also in 1623, towards the end of the year, there took place a tragedy known as 'the fatal Vesper' or 'doleful Evensong', when many Catholics had assembled in the Blackfriars to hear a sermon by the Jesuit Robert Drury. The floor gave way under the weight of the crowd, and over eighty persons were killed. A surprisingly impartial account of the disaster was given by a Protestant author, signing himself W. C. under the title of *The Fatall Vesper;* but he could not help seeing in it a sign of divine providence and advising his readers to draw their own conclusions. Another book of the same kind, which does not seem to have survived (unless it is identical with the former), is mentioned by a contemporary with the title of *The Doleful Even-Song* and attributed to Samuel Clarke (Foley I 77–78). A Catholic view came out in the same year in the form of *A word of Comfort* by the Jesuit John Floyd.

712. *The Fatall Vesper, or A True and punctuall relation of that lamentable and fearefull accident, hapning on Sunday in the afternoone being the*

26. of October last, by the fall of a roome in the Black-Friers in which
were assembled many people at a Sermon, which was to be preached by
Father Drurie a Iesuite. Together with the names and number of such
persons as therein unhappily perished, or were miraculously preserved.
1623   (STC 6015)

(The Dedication and Preface are both signed W. C. — which the STC
interprets as the initials of William Crashaw. The account of this
incident given in Foley I 77 is from the pen of the Jesuit Edward
Coffin, who refers to a similar book entitled *The Doleful Even-Song* by
Rev. Samuel Clarke.)

713. *A word of Comfort. or A Discourse concerning The late lamentable*
   Accident of the fall of a roome, at a Catholike Sermon, in the
   Black-friars at London, wherwith about fourscore persons were
   oppressed. Written for the Comfort of Catholiks, and Information of
   Protestants, By I. R. P. 1623   (STC 11118, AR 333, ERL 193)

Mention may be made here of a couple of sermons against Popery
published respectively in 1623 and 1625 by another Robert Abbot,
'preacher of the Word of God at Cranbrook in Kent'. The first was entitled
The Trial of True Religion, and appeared in a collection of sermons under
the general title of *A Hand of Fellowship*. The second was entitled *The
Danger of Popery*.

714. *The Trial of True Religion. upon Iames 1.27. By Robert Abbot.* 1623
   (Published with its own title-page as part of:

   A Hand of Fellowship, to helpe keepe out sinne and Antichrist. In
   certaine Sermons preached upon severall occasions. By Robert Abbot,
   Preacher of Gods Word at Cranebrooke in Kent. 1623   (STC 59)

715. *The Danger of Popery: or, A Sermon Preached at a Visitation at*
   Ashford in Kent, upon 2. Thess. 2.12. Wherein the marks of Anti-
   christianisme and signes of truth are opened and applied, and the
   Question of the saving and damning of those that follow Antichrist is
   explained by the Scriptures. By Robert Abbott, Preacher of the Word of
   God at Cranebrooke in Kent. 1625   (STC 57)

In 1624, in the aftermath of the breakdown of negotiations with Spain,
the King changed his attitude towards the Catholics for a time and issued a
proclamation dated 6 May 1624, 'charging all Iesuites, Seminaries, &c. to
depart the Land' — at the express petition of Parliament. It was followed by
another, dated 15 August 1624, against 'the printing, importing, and
dispersing of Popish and seditious Bookes and Pamphlets'. These were

acclaimed by Thomas Scott, who had recently been publishing numerous pamphlets (of a political nature) against Spain and Rome, in yet another one entitled *Englands Ioy*. It was just in time to be included in his *Workes*, which were published together in one volume that same year at Utrecht in Holland.

716. *By the King. A Proclamation charging all Iesuites, Seminaries, &c. to depart the Land.* 6 May 1624   (STC 8276)

(This was followed soon after by a second proclamation, as follows:)

717. *By the King. A Proclamation against Seditious, Popish and Puritanicall Bookes and Pamphlets.* 15 August 1624   (STC 8736)

718. *Englands Ioy, for suppressing the Papists, and banishing the Priests and Iesuites.* 1624

(The author, Thomas Scott, had become notorious for his outspoken criticism of the Spanish ambassador in London, Count Gondomar, in *Vox Populi* (1620); and this led to his exile in Holland.)

719. *The Workes of the most famous and reverend divine Mr. Thomas Scot. Batcheler in Divinitie: Sometimes Preacher in Norwich.* 1624

(Only this general title-page was printed, and bound with a collection of Scott's pamphlets.)

A supposed translation from the French, attacking the corruptions of the Romish Mass, and entitled *The Originall of Idolatries*, appeared in 1624. Translated by Abraham Darcie, it was attributed to 'that famous and learned Isaac Casaubon' and dedicated to Prince Charles. At once its authenticity was challenged by Meric Casaubon in his father's name, not only by word, but also in a printed book entitled *The Vindication or Defence of Isaac Casaubon*. This was published in London 'by his Maiesties Command' simultaneously in English, French and Latin; and all copies of the offending book were called in. Apparently, such an attack on the Mass was not at all to the King's liking. Nevertheless, some years later a second edition was published abroad in 1630, entitled *The Originall of Popish Idolatrie*, and still 'under the name of Casaubon'.

720. *The Originall of Idolatries: or, The Birth of Heresies: A true, Sincere, and exact description of all such Sacred Signes, Sacrifices, and Sacraments as have been instituted and ordained of God since Adam; With the true source and lively Anatomy of the Sacrifice of the Masse. First faithfully gathered out of sundry Greeke and Latine Authors, as also out of divers learned Fathers; By that famous and learned Isaac Casaubon, and by him Published in French, for the good of Gods*

Church: And now translated into English for the benefit of this Monarchy: By Abraham Darcie. 1624   (STC 4747)

721. *The Vindication or Defence of Isaac Casaubon, Against Those Impostors that lately published an impious and unlearned Pamphlet, Intituled The Originall of Idolatries, &c. under his Name. By Meric Casaubon his Sonne. Published by his Maiesties Command.* 1624 (STC 4751)

722. *Meric Casaubon vangeur, Contre Les Imposteurs qui nagueres, souz le nom d'Isaac son Pere, ont publié un Livre inepte & impie, De l'Origine de l'Idolatrie, &c. Publié par commandement de S. M.* 1624 (STC 4752)

723. *Merici Casauboni Is.F. Vindicatio Patris, Adversus Impostores, qui librum ineptum, et impium, De Origine Idololatriae, &c. Nuper sub Isaaci Casauboni nomine publicarunt.* 1624   (STC 4750)

(This was the second time Meric came to his father's defence – the first having been in 1621 against the Papists:

Merici Casauboni Is.F. Pietas contra maledicos Patrii nominis, & religionis hostes.   (STC 4749))

724. *The Originall of Popish Idolatrie, or The Birth of Heresies. Published under the name of Casaubon, And called-in the same yeare, upon misinformation. But now upon better Consideration Reprinted with Alowance. Being a True and Exacte Description of such Sacred Signes, Sacrifices and Sacraments as have bene instituted and ordained of God since Adam. With a newe Source and Anatomie of the Masse, first gathered out of sundrie Greeke and Latine Authors, as also out of diverse learned Fathers. Published by S. O.* 1630   (STC 4748)

Three more scattered books, published at the end of the reign, may serve to bring these scattered controversies to a conclusion. In 1624 George Carleton, now Bishop of Chichester, looked back – as Matthew Sutcliffe had done in 1604, in his *Ful and Round Answer to N. D.* (252) – on the blessings of Queen Elizabeth's reign, in his *Thankfull Remembrance of Gods Mercy*. A second edition, 'revised, and enlarged', came out the following year, with two more editions in 1627 and 1630. Sutcliffe's book was also republished under the new title of *The blessings on Mount Gerizzim*, and shortly afterwards (at an unspecified date) as *A True Relation of Englands Happinesse*. In both these works there was an undercurrent of 'No Popery'. A third author who reappeared, after a long silence, in this last year of the reign was John Terry, who now brought out his third part of *The Tryall of Truth*, under the new title of *Theologicall Logicke*, 'Against the Heathenish

215

Atheist, and the Romish Catholick'. The first two parts had appeared in the closing years of the old reign of Elizabeth, in 1600 and 1602 respectively.

725. *A Thankfull Remembrance of Gods Mercy. In an Historicall Collection of the great and mercifull Deliverances of the Church and State of England, since the Gospell began here to flourish, from the beginning of Queene Elizabeth. Collected by Geo: Carleton, Doctor of Divinitie, and Bishop of Chichester.* 1624   (STC 4640)

(Subsequent editions came out in 1625, 1627 and 1630 (STC 4641–3))

726. *The blessings on Mount Gerizzim, and the curses on Mount Ebal. Or, the happie estate of Protestants, compared with the miserable estate of Papists under the Popes tyrannie. By M. S. Doctor of Divinitie.* 1625? (STC 23466)

727. *Theologicall Logicke: or The Third Part of the Tryall of Truth: Wherein is declared the excellency and aequity of the Christian Faith, and that it is not withstood and resisted; but assisted and fortified by all the forces of right reason and by all the aide that artificiall Logicke can yeeld. Against the Heathenish Atheist, and the Romish Catholick, whereof the one taketh exception against the Faith of Christ in generall; and the other against the doctrine thereof, as it is professed in the Reformed Churches, as being in their opinions absurd, and contrary to the evident and undeniable grounds of reason. By Iohn Terry Minister of the Word of God at Streton.* 1625   (STC 23914)

(The previous parts are simply entitled: *The Triall of Truth* (1600) and *The Second Part of the Trial of Truth* (1602). They are presented as 'A preservative for the simple against the poisoned doctrine of the Romish Antichrist' (STC 23913).)

l) *The Fisher Controversy*

The final controversy of James' reign largely arose out of the Catholic claim to antiquity and apostolic succession and the challenge they made to their Anglican opponents to produce any stronger credentials. This had been less of a problem for the Elizabethan Church, whose theology had been mainly Calvinist; but during the reign of James there had set in a strong movement of reaction away from Calvinism, and an increasing respect for patristic tradition – with its emphasis on the institution and succession of bishops. Elizabethan divines, like John Foxe, had sought to demonstrate the continuity of Protestantism through the various sects, such as the Waldensians, the Hussites and the Lollards, that had appeared in various places during the Middle Ages. But many of the Jacobean divines, like Francis

Mason, had preferred to trace the line of episcopal succession through the Popish prelates of the Middle Ages — thus recognizing the Roman Church as a true, if corrupt, Church of Christ. It was John Percy, alias John Fisher, who first recognized this weakness among his opponents and consequently insisted on this one point, with his Catalogues of Catholic 'professors' and his Challenges to the Protestants to produce corresponding Catalogues of their own. He was followed by his fellow-Jesuit, Silvester Norris, both in the Third Part of his *Antidote*, entitled *The Guide of Faith*, 'Wherein the Truth, and perpetuall Visible Succession of the Catholique Roman Church, is cleerly demonstrated' (609), and in the *Appendix to the Antidote*, which contained 'A Catalogue of the visible and perpetuall Succession of the Catholique Professours of the Roman Church' (610). These two contributions of Norris both appeared in 1621 — in the same year as yet another Jesuit, Anthony Clarke, brought out his *Defence of the Honor of God*. In his book Clarke contrasted 'the beginning of Protestants, and how they have begotten themselves', with 'the unity, visibility, succession, and universality of Catholique Church, faith, or seede in all ages, since it was planted by our Saviour'. In a chapter entitled 'Of the Throne and seede of David' (Chapter XI), he added his further Catalogue of Roman Catholic Professors, together with the unbroken line of the Popes from St. Peter's time, 'who in all ages taught the Catholique faith which wee now professe'.

728. *The Defence of the Honor of God, and of his only Sonne Iesus Christ our Lord, Of the Apostles, Prophets, Ancient Fathers, and all Catholike Christians. Against the iniurious Words, and Writings of Protestant Ministers; who affirme, That the Church of God hath erred, decayed, and beene invisible upon Earth. Written by Anthonie Clarke, a Catholike Christian.* 1621   (STC 5352, AR 240, ERL 69)

The Anglican reply, not to Clarke alone (who is only occasionally mentioned by name), but also to Percy and Norris, opened up in the years 1623 and 1624. In the former year Richard Bernard published his *Looke beyond Luther*, protesting against the 'Catalogue of chiefe Pastors, General Councels, and Catholike Professors, of which they much glory, seducing therewith the simple and unadvised', while reassuring his readers that 'it is not so difficult a matter, as they would make the world beleeve, to bring forth in every Age the Professours of this our Christian Faith'. A similar response to the same question appeared in 1624 in the anonymous book entitled *Luthers Predecessours*, which has been ascribed to Thomas Bedford. Here reference is made to 'the proceedings of the late conference betwixt D. White, and D. Featly, against Fisher, and Sweet', which is to be considered later. Another anonymous book which came out in 1624, on the question 'Of the Visibilitie of the true Church', was entitled *A Treatise Of The Perpetuall Visibilitie*, whose distinguished authorship did not long remain a secret: that of the Archbishop of Canterbury, George Abbot. This went into two editions in the same year. Yet another distinguished contribution, *A Briefe Declaration of the Universalitie of the Church*, came first from the mouth (in the form of 'a Sermon before His Maiestie the 20th of Iune, 1624') of the learned Bishop of Meath, James Ussher, the author of the Latin treatise *De Christianarum Ecclesiarum ... continua successione & statu* (1613) (579); and it was published the same year. Here he dealt with two great questions 'which trouble manie': first, 'What wee may judge of our Forefathers, who lived in the communion of the Church of Rome?'; and secondly, 'Where was your Church before Luther?' His answer, presented as it was in a learned manner, was further developed in 1625 by John Mayer in *An Antidote against Popery*, considering that, whereas the 'Reverend and learned Bishop of Meath' has fully dealt with the question, still 'Babes must have their provision as well as those that are stronger'.

729. *Looke beyond Luther: Or An Answere to that Question, so often and so insultingly proposed by our Adversaries, asking us: Where this our Religion was before Luthers time? Whereto are added sound props to beare up honest-hearted Protestants, that they fall not from their saving-faith. By Richard Bernard, of Batcombe in Sommersetshire.* 1623 (STC 1956)

(A second edition came out in 1624 (STC 1957).)

730. *Luthers Predecessours: Or An Answere To the Question Of the Papists: Where was your Church before Luther?* 1624 (STC 1787)

731. *A Treatise Of The Perpetuall Visibilitie, And Succession of the True Church in all Ages.* 1624 (STC 39)

(The page heading is simply: *Of the Visibilitie of the true Church.* A second edition came out in the same year (STC 40).)

732. *A Briefe Declaration of the Universalitie of the Church of Christ, and the Unitie of the Catholike Faith professed therein: Delivered in a Sermon before His Maiestie the 20th of Iune, 1624. at Wansted.* 1624 (STC 24545)

(There was a second Impression in 1625 (STC 24546).)

733. *An Antidote against Popery: Confected out of Scriptures, Fathers, Councels, and Histories. Wherein dialogue-wise are shewed, the points, grounds, and antiquitie of the Protestant Religion; and the first springing up of the points of Popery: together with the Anti-christianisme thereof. Being alone sufficient to inable any Protestant of meane capacitie, to understand and yeeld a reason of his Religion, and to incounter with and foyle the Adversary. By Iohn Mayer, B. D. and Pastor of the Church of little Wratting in Suffolke.* 1625 (STC 17729)

(The work is dedicated to King James.

The speakers in the dialogue are: Saul or Paul, Sergius Paulus, and Elymas.)

Of these writers, Bernard, Bedford, Abbot and Ussher were rather summarily answered by John Percy in his *Reply to D. White and D. Featly* in 1625, where he also dealt with two more books: *A Dialogue* by W.C. (published as an appendix to Henry Rogers' *Answer to Mr. Fisher* in 1623 (741), and an unidentified *Protestant Kalendar*. This *Reply* will be considered later (748). Ussher's *Sermon* alone provoked a full response a few years later, when the Irish priest, Paul Harris, published *A Briefe Confutation* in 1627.

734. *A Briefe Confutation of Certaine Absurd, Hereticall, and Damnable Doctrines, delivered by Mr. Iames Usher, in a Sermon, Preached before King Iames our late Soveraigne, at Wansted, Iune 20. Anno Domini. 1624. By Paulus Veridicus.* 1627 (STC 12813, AR 381, ERL 161)

At the same time, Ussher was drawn into a parallel dispute with the Irish Jesuit, William Malone, who had presented him with a brief 'Challenge' on the identity of the true Church some six years before; but it was only now that Ussher was prevailed upon by 'some of high place in both Kingdomes' to publish a detailed answer. This appeared in 1624 under the title, *An Answer to a Challenge*, in which the text of 'The Iesuites Challenge' is prefixed (in four pages) to his reply (of 527 pages). But already in 1623 he had covered much the same ground, though in a different context, in his *Discourse of the Religion Anciently professed by the Irish and British*. Malone's *Reply to Mr. Iames Ussher* came out in the same year as Harris' *Confutation* of the latter's *Sermon*.

735. *An Answer to a Challenge made by a Iesuite in Ireland. Wherein The Iudgement of Antiquity in the points questioned is truely delivered, and the Noveltie of the now Romish doctrine plainly discovered By Iames Ussher Bishop of Meath.* 1624 (STC 24542)

(The points questioned by Malone were: traditions, the real presence, confession, priests' power of forgiveness, purgatory, prayer for the dead, limbo, prayer to saints, free will, and merits.

A second edition came out in 1625, and a third (with other treatises) in 1631 (STC 24543–44).)

'36. *A Discourse of the Religion Anciently professed by the Irish and British. By Iames Ussher Bishop of Meath.* 1623

(This was first published in Dublin in 1623; but only the second edition of 1631 (in London) is recorded by the STC: STC 24549)

Among 'The chiefe Heads treated of in this discourse' are: the holy
Scriptures, free will, works, purgatory, prayer for the dead, the
sacrament of the Lord's Supper, sacramental confession, absolution, and
the Church.)

737. *A Reply to Mr. Iames Ussher his Answere Wherein it is discovered how
Answerlesse the said Mr. Ussher returneth. The uniforme consent also
of Antiquity is declared to stand for the Roman Religion: And the
Answerer is convinced of vanity in challenging the Patronage of the
Doctors of the Primative Church for his Protestancy. By William
Malone of the Societie of Iesus.* 1627   (STC 17213, AR 494,
ERL 244)

These controversies now came to their climax in 1623, at the house of a
Protestant gentleman, Sir Humphrey Linde, in London. It was in this year
that Linde undertook to republish an old translation of a treatise on the
Mass by the Carolingian monk Ratramnus (or Bertram), which he entitled *A
Booke of Bertram* and further glossed with a long Preface to bring out its
relevance to the Anglican teaching on the Eucharist against that of the
Catholics. He was refuted in the following year by the Jesuit, John Floyd,
who published *A Plea for the Reall-Presence.*

738. *A Booke of Bertram the Priest, Concerning the Body and Blood of
Christ, Written in Latin to Charles the Great, being Emperour, above
eight hundred yeeres agoe. Translated and imprinted in the English
Tongue. Anno Dni 1549. And now the third time published for the
profit of the Reader.* 1623 (STC 20752 – where the original translation
of 1549 is attributed to Sir H. Linde!)

739. *A Plea for the Reall-Presence. Wherein The preface of Syr Humfrey
Linde, concerning the booke of Bertram, is examined and censured.
Written by I. O. unto a Gentleman his friend.* 1624 (STC 11113,
AR 328, ERL 9)

This was, however, subsidiary to the main controversy, for which Sir
Humphrey Linde merely provided the occasion of a conference at his house,
on 27 June 1623. Then it was that two Jesuit priests, John Percy (or Fisher)
and John Sweet, faced two Protestant divines, Francis White and Daniel
Featley, on the question not so much of the Eucharist as of the true Church.
The origin of the conference was described by Featley in his narration,
entitled *The Fisher Catched in his owne Net* and published in that very year,
1623:

'Edward Buggs Esquire . . . was solicited by some Papists then about
him to forsake the Protestant faith, telling him there was no hope of

salvation without the Church, there was no Catholik Church but theirs,
and to beleeve the Catholike Church was the Article of his Creed, and
by it no other Church could be meant but the Church of Rome,
because it could not be proved by all the Protestants in the kingdome,
that they had any Church before Luther.'

Featley went on to present the Protestant side as victorious in the outcome;
and Mr. Buggs returned to the Anglican fold. His arguments against Percy
(Fisher) were further urged by Henry Rogers in *An Answer to Mr. Fisher*,
which also came out in 1623. In his Preface Rogers notes how 'Fisher,
Sweet, Brierly, Clerk, with others of that company, doe studie and strive
with all might and maine by divulging their written papers, as also their
Printed Bookes full of lyes and untruths'. He added an appendix, giving 'A
Dialogue concerning this Question, Where was your Church before Luther
and Calvin', by W. C.

740. *The Fisher Catched in his owne Net*. 1623   (STC 10732)

(The narration is entitled as follows:

*A Relation of what passed in a Conference touching the visibilitie of
the Church. Iun. 27. 1623.*)

741. *An Answer to Mr. Fisher the Iesuite, his Five Propositions concerning
Luther. By Mr. Rogers, that worthy Oxford Divine. With some passages
also of the said Mr. Rogers with the said Mr. Fisher. Hereunto is
annexed Mr. W. C. his Dialogue of the said Argument, wherein is
discovered Fishers Folly*. 1623   (STC 21177)

(There is a separate title-page for the *Dialogue*, though the pagination
continues:

*A Dialogue concerning this Question, Where was your Church before
Luther and Calvin. Giving good directions how to discover Fishers
Folly. By W. C.*

In reply, Percy (or his fellow-Jesuit, John Floyd) came out in the same
year, 1623, with *An Answer to a Pamphlet*, giving his account of 'the
occasion, progresse, and issue of that Conference'. He also added 'An
Appendix Containing An Answere to some Untruthes, obiected by D. White,
and D. Featly, against M. Fishers Relations, or Writings'. Sweet published his
answer in the following year, in the form of *A Defence of the Appendix* —
that is, Norris' *Appendix to the Antidote* (1621). He prefaced it with an
open letter to Sir Humphrey Linde, charging him with having written
'against a printed Catalogue of Catholike Professors, whereof a deare friend
of mine is the Author, given you upon a former Conference — concerning a
Protestant Catalogue; which Conference though privatly intended, was

afterwards victoriously printed'. His particular reply to Featley, in Section 1, is entitled: 'The Fisher freed, and the Catcher catcht'.

742. *An Answer to a Pamphlet, Intituled: The Fisher Catched in his owne Net. In which, by the way, is shewed, That the Protestant Church was not so visible, in al Ages, as the true Church ought to be: and consequently, is not the true Church. Of which, men may learne infallible Faith, necessarie to Salvation. By A. C. 1623* (STC 4957, AR 603; see ERL 312)

(A copy of this book in the university of Liege is inscribed in a contemporary hand, 'Author P. J. Floyd Soc. Jesu'; (cf. Sommervogel, under Floyd).)

743. *A Defence of the Appendix. or A Reply to certaine Authorities alleaged in Answere to a Catalogue of Catholike Professors, called An Appendix to the Antidote. Wherein Also the Booke fondly intituled, The Fisher catched in his owne Net, is censured. And the sleights of D. Featly, and D. White in shifting off the Catalogue of their owne Professors, which they undertooke to shew, are plainly discovered. By L. D. To the Rt. Worshipfull Syr Humphry Lynde. 1624* (STC 23528, AR 802, ERL 317)

In support of the two Jesuits, the former Douai professor, Edward Weston, came out against Featley in particular with his *Repaire of Honour* in 1624. Addressing his words to them, he recalled the 'disputation betwixt you, and a couple of Ministers White & Featlye', and alluded to a rumour that 'two English Earles present at your dispute' had thereby 'beene converted to the Catholike fayth'. He went on to show how their position was confirmed by the Letters of St. Ignatius of Antioch in the primitive Church.

744. *The Repaire of Honour, Falsely impeached by Featlye a Minister. Wherein (by occasion) the Apostles Disciple S. Ignatius Bishop & Martyr, his Religion, against Protestantisme, is layd open. By Ed. Weston Doctour of Theology: In a Letter, by him written unto two Fathers of the Society of Iesus, in England. 1624* (STC 25289, AR 884, ERL 59)

In reply to the two Jesuits, Featley published a book entitled like his previous one, *The Romish Fisher caught and held in his owne Net*. His main text was, in fact, limited to a censure of 'Master Fishers Answer'; and it was only after he had finished this task that he came across 'Master Sweets Censure' and answered it in what he calls 'an Appendix', though it is really a separate work bound with the former. In it he not only identifies L. D. as John Sweet, but also as Francis Walsingham — though they were two distinct individuals. To this he added, as a further Appendix, *A True Relation* of another conference on the subject of Transubstantiation, no doubt arising from *The Booke of Bertram*.

745. *The Romish Fisher caught and held in his owne Net. Or, A True*
  Relation of the Protestant Conference and Popish Difference. A
  Iustification of the one, and Refutation of the other. In matter
  of $\begin{cases} Fact \\ Faith \end{cases}$
  By Daniel Featly, Doctor in Divinity. 1624   (STC 10738)

746. *An Appendix to The Fishers Net: Together with a Description of the*
  Romish Wheele, or Circle. By Daniel Featly, Doctor of Divinitye.
  1624   (STC 10738)

747. *A True Relation of that which passed in a Conference, at the end of*
  Pater-noster-Rowe, called Amen: Touching Transubstantiation. 1624
  (STC 10738)

This prompted Percy to bring out yet another *Reply* in 1625, not only to Featley (whom he calls 'the first and principall Disputant who did in the Conference undertake to answer M. Fishers Question'), but also to White, who had published a book on another, more important conference which comes up next for consideration. He insisted on the main issue, 'Whether the Protestant Church had bene alwayes visible?' If so, then let the Protestant disputants 'confront those Catalogues of Catholique Romane professors, which are set downe by Gualterus in his Tabula Chronographica, by M. Fisher in his Reply to M. Wotton and M. White, by S. N. in his Appendixe to the Antidote (lately defended by L. D.) and others', with a better Catalogue of their own. After pointing out that neither Featley nor White had proposed any such Catalogue, he devoted several chapters to a confutation of the above-mentioned Protestant books on the subject: those of Bernard, Rogers, W. C., Abbot, Bedford, Ussher and the anonymous author of *The Protestant Kalendar*. Among these he notes that 'some make much account of D. Usher, and thinke this his Sermon to containe a better Answer, then is found in other mens writings'. His *Reply* is divided into two Parts, each with its own title-page, the one negative against the Protestant position, the other positive for the Catholic position.

748. *A Reply to D. White and D. Featly, who have undertaken to shew a*
  Visible Protestant Church in all Ages, by naming, proving, and
  defending Visible Protestants in all Ages, out of good Authors. The
  First Part. In which is shewed, that neither they, nor any other, have
  performed this undertaken Taske, in such methode and manner as
  M. Fishers Question (proposed to the sayd Doctours in a Conference)

> *required: And much lesse have they, or can they, or any other, shew*
> *such a Visible Protestant Church in all Ages, and Nations, as Christs*
> *true Church is (in the Prophesies and promises of holy Scripture)*
> *described. Whence it followeth, that the Protestant Church, is not the*
> *true Church of Christ.* 1625   (STC 10925 = 23530, AR 610)

749. *A Reply to D. White and Doctour Featly. The Second Part. In which is*
shewed, that the Cath. Roman Church can Name Prove and Defend
Visible Professours of her Fayth, in all Ages. And that, She only, and
such as agree in Fayth with her, is the True, Visible, Catholique Church,
out of which there is no Salvation. 1625   (references as 748)

The real climax to all these controversies, however, was occasioned by yet another conference, or series of conferences, which had been held earlier in 1622, but only came to light later on account of the secrecy in which it had been held. It all began (according to Percy's explanation in his *True Relations*) with 'a certaine written Paper, given by M. Fisher to an Honble Lady [the Countess of Buckingham], who desired somthing to be briefly written, to prove the Catholique Roman Church, & Faith, to be the only right'. The Dean of Carlisle, Francis White, was called in by the Duke of Buckingham to confer with the Countess, his mother; and this led to a preliminary disputation with the Jesuit. A second, more formal conference was arranged between the two disputants, this time in the presence of the King himself, who took a leading part in the discussion. There followed a third conference, again in the royal presence, when White's place as disputant was taken by the influential Bishop of St. David's, William Laud. Afterwards, the King delivered a Note to the Jesuit, containing nine questions in controversy under the title: 'Some of the principall points which with-hold my ioyning unto the Church of Rome, except she reforme her selfe, or be able to give me satisfaction'. At first, the proceedings of the conference and the questions of the King were kept strictly secret. But the Jesuit spread around certain written papers concerning the conference, with his answers to the nine questions raised by the King. This led White to publish his *Replie to Iesuit Fishers answere* in 1624, to which Percy responded in his above-mentioned *Reply to D. White and D. Featly*. The bishop's chaplain, Robert Baillie, also published his *Answere* on behalf of Laud, from whom he had received 'the Papers that were spread, and a Note what was mis-spread in them'.

750. *A Replie to Iesuit Fishers answere to certain questions propounded by*
his most gratious Matie. King Iames. By Francis White D. of Div. Deane
of Carlile, Chaplaine to his Matie. Hereunto is annexed a Conference of
the right R. B. of St. Davids with the same Iesuit. 1624   (STC 25382)

(In his preface 'To the Reader', the author gives the details of the three conferences from his viewpoint: 'It is now two yeeres, since I was first called, by my Lord Duke of Buckingham, to conferre with an Honourable Person, who as then began to make Revolt from the true Faith and Religion professed in our Church . . .')

751. *An Answere to Mr. Fishers Relation of a Third Conference betweene a certaine B. (as he stiles him) and himselfe. The Conference was very private, till Mr. Fisher spread certaine Papers of it, which in many respects deserved an Answere. Which is here given by R. B. Chapleine to the B. that was imployed in the Conference.* 1624 (STC 1204)

(The inner title reads:

A Briefe Relation of what passed in a third private Conference betweene a certaine B. and me, Before &c. Answered by R. B. Chaplaine to the B.)

A second edition was published in 1639 under the title, *A Relation of the Conference*, in which Laud acknowledged his real authorship of the book, though formerly published under the name of his chaplain, in the Dedication to Charles I.

A Relation of The Conference betweene William Lawd, Then, Lrd Bishop of St. Davids; Now Lord Arch-Bishop of Canterbury: And Mr. Fisher the Jesuite, by the Command of King James of ever Blessed Memorie. With an Answer to such Exceptions as A. C. takes against it. By the sayd Most Reverend Father in God, William, Lord Arch-Bishop of Canterbury. 1639 (STC 15298)

Concerning the identity of A. C. Laud writes: 'Whether These be two, or but One Iesuite, I know not; since scarce One amongst them, goes under One Name. But for my owne part . . . I thinke they are One, and that One, M. Fisher.')

With the assistance of his fellow-Jesuit John Floyd, Percy now published his *Answere unto The Nine Points of Controversy*, with an additional 'Reioynder Unto the Reply of D. Francis White Minister', in 1625. It went into a second edition the following year. Also in 1626 he published his account of the whole proceedings, entitled *True Relations of Sundry Conferences*, together with his answer to Baillie. And there the controversies of the reign came to an end, presided over by the King as he had done from the time of his accession in 1603.

752. *The Answere unto The Nine Points of Controversy, Proposed by our late Soveraygne (of Famous memory) unto M. Fisher of the Society of Iesus. And The Reioynder Unto the Reply of D. Francis White Minister.* 1625 (Not in STC, AR 604; see ERL 379)

(Prefixed to the main text is the following Note:

His Maiestyes Note delivered unto M. Fisher.
'Some of the principall points which with-hold my ioyning unto the Church of Rome, except she reforme her selfe, or be able to give me satisfaction, Are these.
1. The worship of Images.
2. The Praying & Offering oblations to the Blessed Virgin Mary.
3. Worshipping & Invocation of Saints, & Angels.
4. The Liturgy, & private Prayers for the Ignorant in an unknowne Tongue.
5. Repetitions of Pater Nosters, Aves, & Creeds, especially affixing a kind of merit to the number of them.
6. The Doctrine of Transubstantiation.
7. Communion under one kind, & the abetting of it by Concomitancy.
8. Workes of Supererogation, especially with reference unto the Treasure of the Church.
9. The Opinion of deposing Kings, and giving away their Kingdomes by Papall power.')

Percy himself is said to have answered these questions in a month; but what was published was 'a revised copy of them with a learned commentary by Fr. John Floyd' (Foley I 532). The second edition of 1626, dedicated to King Charles, had an altered title:

The Answere unto The Nine Points of Controversy, Proposed by our late Soveraygne (of Famous Memory) unto M. Fisher, of the Society of Iesus. And the Reioynder Unto the Reply of D. Francis White Minister. With the Picture of the sayd Minister, or Censure of his Writings prefixed. (STC 10911, AR 605, ERL 379)

753. *True Relations of Sundry Conferences had between certaine Protestant Doctours, and a Iesuite called M. Fisher (then Prisoner in London for the Catholique Fayth:) togeather with Defences of the same. In which Is shewed, that there hath alwayes beene, since Christ, a Visible Church, and in it a Visible Succession of Doctours & Pastours, teaching the unchanged Doctrine of Fayth, left by Christ and his Apostles, in all points necessary to Salvation. And that Not Protestants, but only Roman Catholiques have had, and can shew such a Visible Church; and in it such a Succession of Pastours and Doctours, of whome men may securely learne what points of Fayth are necessary to Salvation. By A. C. 1626* (STC 10915 = 23530, AR 610, ERL 312)

(The contents are divided into three sections:

The Occasion of a Certaine Conference had betweene D. Francis White, and M. Iohn Fisher.

A briefe Relation of what passed betweene D. White, and M. Fisher,
about the foresaid written Paper.
A Relation of the Conference betweene a certain B. & M. Fisher,
defended against the said B. his Chaplayne.

This is in turn bound with the two Parts of Percy's *Reply to D. White*
and D. Featly, complete with their old title-pages.)

CHAPTER 5

Fragments of Controversies

There still remain some controversial books and pamphlets which do not conveniently fit into the preceding categories; and they must now be added for the sake of completeness. The only way of putting them together is simply their chronological order of publication – though in some cases their composition was many years before.

754. *A Relation of the State of Religion: and with what Hopes and Policies it hath beene framed, and is maintained in the severall states of these westerne parts of the world.* 1605   (STC 21715)

(The author, Sir Edwin Sandys, formerly a pupil of Richard Hooker, had to recall the copies of the three editions of 1605, which had been printed without his leave; and only a few now remain. It was republished in 1629 under a new title, *Europae speculum, or a view or survey of the state of religion in the western parts of the world*; and again in 1632, according to the original copy, with a preface and appendix by L. O. (Lewis Owen). (STC 21718–19)
Rare though it was, it came into the hands of Catholic authors, who not infrequently cited it on their behalf in controversial writings, on account of the relatively favourable view Sandys presents of the Roman Church, and especially the Society of Jesus, on the continent. Possibly it was for this reason that he was obliged to recall the first editions.)

755. *Disputatio de Natura Poenitentiae adversus Bellarminum, per Franciscum Dillinghamum baccalaureum in Theologia.* 1606 (STC 6882)

(This is another treatise of Dillingham, 'tanquam antidotum, contra Pontificiorum venenatam doctrinam de poenitentia', following on his *Disputatio Brevis* of 1602 and his *Tractatus Brevis* of 1603, also against Bellarmine's *Controversies*.)

756. *Quaestiones duae De Sacris alienis non adeundis, Ad usum praximque Angliae breviter explicatae: Quarum prima est, An liceat Catholicis Anglicanis, rebus sic se habentibus, & Magistratu publico sub gravissimis poenis id exigente, Protestantium Ecclesias, vel preces adire. Secunda, Utrum si non precibus, at concionibus saltem haereticis, ad easdem vitandas poenas, licite possint interesse, easque audire. In utraque Quaestione pars negativa multis argumentis firmissimis asseritur: Ei in Secunda, Scripto etiam cuidam Anonymo in contrarium edito respondetur.* 1607

(The authorship is attributed to Robert Persons. He first prints the MS of his anonymous Catholic adversary, and then gives his answer, as follows:

Casus De Adeundis Haereticorum Ecclesiis in Anglia.

Responsum breve ad Scriptum Quoddam Incerti Authoris Pro audiendis Haereticorum concionibus in Anglia divulgatum.

Persons' *Brief discours* of 1580 on this question (his first printed book) had been republished in 1599 and 1601.)

757. *Nicolai Fitzherberti De Antiquitate & Continuatione Catholicae Religionis in Anglia. & De Alani Cardinalis Vita Libellus. Ad Sanctissimum D. N. Paulum Quintum Pontificem Maximum.* 1608.

(The first part of this book, 'De Antiquitate Catholicae religionis in Anglia', might seem to have contributed to the subsequent controversy on this subject in England; but Fitzherbert was living and writing in Rome, where he published this work, which had little impact on the controversies back home. The second part is entitled 'Vita Alani'. With it is bound the same author's *Oxoniensis in Anglia Academiae Descriptio*, dated 1602.)

758. *And. Willet Theologi Angli, De Gratia generi humano in primo Parente collata, De Lapsu Adami, et Peccato originali, De Praedestinatione, et De Gratia et Libero Arbitrio. Disputationes Theologicae, Bellarmino oppositae, ex IV Tomo Synopseos Papismi Anglice conscriptae, in linguam Latinam conversae, a M. Iona Volmaro.* 1609

(This translation of part of Willet's *Synopsis Papismi* — in its third enlarged edition of 1600 (STC 25698) — mainly against Bellarmine, was published in Holland, no doubt with a view to supporting the Calvinist cause against the Arminians.)

759. *A Defence of the Iudgment of the Reformed churches. That a man may lawfullie not onelie put awaie his wife for her adulterie, but also marrie another. Wherein both Robert Bellarmin the Iesuites Latin treatise, and*

an English pamphlet of a nameless author mainteyning the contrarie are
confuted by Iohn Raynolds. A taste of Bellarmins dealing in
controversies of Religion: how he depraveth Scriptures, misalleagthe
fathers, and abuseth reasons to the perverting of the truth of God, and
poisoning of his Churche with errour. 1609 (STC 20607)

(This is perhaps the first printed defence of divorce in English,
preceding Milton's treatise by thirty-five years; and it was published
after the author's death in 1607. While ostensibly attacking the
arguments of Bellarmine, this *Defence* was probably occasioned by the
anonymous English pamphlet, which may have been the MS of Edmund
Bunny's *Of Divorce for Adulterie*, which was published with the
author's name in 1610.)

760. *Censura Librorum Apocryphorum Veteris Testamenti, adversum
Pontificios, imprimis Robertum Bellarminum; Qua tum divina et
canonica Sacrae Scripturae autoritas asseritur solidissime: tum variae
Quaestiones & Controversiae, tam dogmaticae, quam historicae,
imprimis quae est de Duratione Monarchiae Persicae, & de 70. Hebdom.
Danielis expediuntur accuratissime; praelectionibus ducentis et
quinquaginta posthumis in Academia Oxoniensi tractata a Johanne
Rainoldo Anglo, Academiae Oxoniensis Professore Theologo, & in II
Tomos digesta.* 1611

(A massive work in two volumes, published posthumously in Germany,
presenting Reynolds' Oxford lectures against the Papists, and especially
Robert Bellarmine -- with reference to the authority of Scripture,
which was no longer a controversial issue in the Jacobean Age.)

761. *D.Guilielmi Whitakeri, Sacrae Theologiae in Academia Cantabrigiensi
olim Regii Professoris Responsio ad Guilielmi Rainoldi Refutationem, In
qua variae Controversiae accurate explicantur. Henrico Jacksono,
Oxoniense, Interprete.* 1612

(This is the Latin translation, by Henry Jackson, of one of Whitaker's
rare books in English, his *Answere* to John Reynold's brother, William
Reynolds, who had attacked his criticism of the Rheims *New
Testament* in *A Refutation of Sundry Reprehensions* (1583). Whitaker
was forced, against his usual practice, to publish his reply in English in
1585, since his critic had written in that language. This Latin
translation was published by the same German house as 760. The
relevance of these two works to the English scene may have been not so
much controversial as exegetical, in view of the recent publication of
the Authorized Version of the Bible in 1611.)

762. *Consilium Quorundam Episcoporum Bononiae congregatorum quod de
ratione stabiliendae Romanae Ecclesiae Iulio 3. Pont.Max. datum est.*

Quo Artes et astutiae Romanensium et Arcana Imperii Papalis non pauca propalantur. Ex Bibliotheca W. Crashauii, in Theolog.Bacchal et verbi div. ap. Tem. Lond. Praedic. 1613

(The short title on the page headings is: 'Consilium de Stabilienda Rom. Eccle.' This is a typical work of William Crashaw, who had antiquarian interests similar to Thomas James, though he was more of an amateur, and who contributed to the Protestant side in the controversies of his time by producing hidden bits of evidence to cast discredit on the Papists. Most of his publications fit in somewhere or other; but this work seems to have no appropriate place in a wider context, except in the author's own line of strategy.)

763. *Tessaradelphos, Or The foure Brothers. The qualities of whom are contayned in this old Riddle. Foure bretheren were bred at once/ Without flesh, bloud, or bones./ One with a beard, but two had none/ The fourth had but half one. Collected and translated, By Thomas Harrab.* 1616   (STC 12797, AR 379, ERL 172)

(This is a somewhat lone attack on Protestantism, which is divided into its four principal sects allowed in Europe: Lutheranism, Calvinism, Anabaptism, and Anglicanism. At the same time, mention is made of 'other petite Sects lurking in corners, as Brownists, Anabaptists, Family of love, and Traskites'. The conclusion for Catholic readers is: Better remain in the Catholic Church.)

764. *A Mittimus to the Iubile at Rome: or The Rates of the Popes Custome-House. Sent To the Pope, as a New-yeeres-gift from England, this Yeere of Iubile, 1625. And faithfully published out of the old Latine Copie, with Observations upon the Romish Text. By William Crashaw, Batchelor of Divinity, and Pastor at White Chappell.* 1625   (STC 6023)

(Yet another contribution from William Crashaw, out of his well-stocked library, for the purpose of informing his Protestant (and, if possible, Papist) readers of scandalous affairs in the Church of Rome. He opens his book with 'An Advertisement to helpe his Understanding in the reading of this strange Booke', which he presents as not unknown about 1550 — when he cites the critical comments of a Sorbonne doctor, Claudius Espencaeus — till it was expurgated by the Index. It consists simply of a list of serious transgressions against the law of God and ecclesiastical law, with the fee required for a dispensation from them. But Crashaw glosses the list with his outraged comments. The work is divided into two parts, the second of which has a separate title-page and deals with laws 'for the most part Ecclesiasticall'.)

INDEX

(References are to bibliographical items in the text.)

a) AUTHORS

b) TITLES